Please return or renew this item by the last date shown. You may return items to any East Sussex Library. You may renew books by telephone or the internet.

East Sussex County Council

0345 60 80 195 for renewals
0345 60 80 196 for enquiries

**Library and Information Services
eastsussex.gov.uk/libraries**

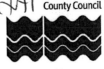

[and] rigorous investigation.'

—*Sunday Times*

'*Blood on the Page* is an In Cold Blood for our time — a brilliant and unflinching anatomy of a murder that is both brutal true crime and ...

... *urder Bag*

'A fine and fascinating read, bolstered by exemplary research and nuanced insights . . . Absorbing.'

Observer

'Harding's book *Hanns and Rudolf* was a marvel of investigative research. *Blood on the Page* is similarly diligent and thorough in its approach.'

Financial Times

'A real-life procedural.'

Guardian

'One of the most intriguing murder cases in British legal history . . . There are enough questions raised by Harding's meticulous research to suggest that reasonable doubt still hangs over the conviction.'

Jewish Chronicle

'Harding follows the twists and turns of the investigation in the best traditions of the true crime narrative . . . The research is meticulous and the account of the murder investigation, detailed, painstaking and fascinating.'

Evening Standard

'Absolutely gripping throughout and builds to a devastating conclusion. Just brilliant.'

Allan Little

'Reads like a fast-paced thriller.'

Ham & High

Blood on the Page

A Murder, a Secret Trial, a Search for the Truth

Thomas Harding

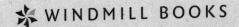 WINDMILL BOOKS

1 3 5 7 9 10 8 6 4 2

Windmill Books
20 Vauxhall Bridge Road
London SW1V 2SA

Windmill Books is part of the Penguin Random House group of companies
whose addresses can be found at global.penguinrandomhouse.com.

Penguin
Random House
UK

Copyright © Thomas Harding 2018

Thomas Harding has asserted his right to be identified as the
author of this Work in accordance with the Copyright,
Designs and Patents Act 1988.

First published by William Heinemann in 2018
First published in paperback by Windmill Books in 2018

www.penguin.co.uk

A CIP catalogue record for this book is available from the British Library.

ISBN 9780099510925

Plate sections designed by Dinah Drazin

Typeset in 10.8/14 pt Bembo Book MT Std by Jouve (UK), Milton Keynes
Printed and bound in Great Britain by Clays Ltd, Elcograf S.p.A.

MIX
Paper from
responsible sources
FSC
www.fsc.org   FSC® C018179

Penguin Random House is committed to a
sustainable future for our business, our readers
and our planet. This book is made from Forest
Stewardship Council® certified paper.

For James

CONTENTS

List of Illustrations	xi
Maps	xiv
Cast of Characters	xix
Author's Note	xxiii
Prologue	I

Part I: The Crime

I.	The Discovery	9
2.	Allan Chappelow	28
3.	The Murder	55
4.	The Victim's Family	67
5.	The Investigation	79
6.	The Pathologist	89
7.	The Chase	99

Part II: The Suspect

8.	Wang Yam	109
9.	The Evidence	123
10.	Arrival	141
11.	Extradition	153
12.	The Funeral	173

CONTENTS

Part III: The Prosecution

13. The Arrest   179
14. *In Camera*   193
15. The Trial   207
16. The Verdict   223
17. Prison   241
18. The Court of Last Resort   261
19. Alone   272
20. The Decision   280

Epilogue   296
Postscript   301
Notes   307
Acknowledgements   333
Bibliography   335

LIST OF ILLUSTRATIONS

Section 1:

Front door of 9 Downshire Hill, June 2006 (Rex Features)
Manuscripts blocking doorway, June 2006 (evidence/Met Police)
Allan Chappelow's missing-person photograph, June 2006
    (Rex Features)
Kitchen at 9 Downshire Hill, June 2006 (Rex Features)
Allan Chappelow's bed at crime scene, June 2006
    (evidence/Met Police)
Allan Chappelow's shoes under manuscripts, 2006
    (evidence/Met Police)
Exterior of 9 Downshire Hill, June 2006 (Rex Features)
Ground floor sketch of 9 Downshire Hill (evidence/Met Police)
Entomologists at 9 Downshire Hill, June 2006 (Rex Features)
Allan Chappelow's shirt, June 2006 (evidence/Met Police)
Living room at 9 Downshire Hill, June 2006 (Rex Features)
Back room at 9 Downshire Hill, June 2006 (Rex Features)
Courtroom sketch of Wang Yam, January 2008 (artist Julia
    Quenzler)

Wang Yam's Curry Paradise receipt (author photo)

Justice Sir Duncan Brian Walter Ouseley (Topfoto)

Pete Lansdown, former Senior Investigating Officer, Metropolitan
  Police (Cayman Islands police department)

Section 2:

Illustration of 9 Downshire Hill from *Old Homes in England* by
  Archibald Chappelow, 1953 (Harrison & Sons)

9 Downshire Hill front hall, 1920s (Burgh House)

Allan Chappelow in the Hall School cricket team, 1930
  (The Hall School)

Allan's mother Karen in front of 9 Downshire Hill, 1952
  (Merete Karlsbourg)

Allan, his father Archibald and aunt Lise, 9 Downshire Hill, 1952
  (Merete Karlsbourg)

'The Chucker-Out' photograph of George Bernard Shaw by Allan
  Chappelow, July 1950 (Allan Chappelow family/National
  Portrait Gallery)

Downshire Hill with Allan Chappelow's motorcycle in street, 1967
  (Historic England)

Allan Chappelow in leather jacket, 1980s (Allan Chappelow
  family)

Allan Chappelow and Patty Ainsworth in Austin Texas, April 2006
  (Steve Derrick)

Wang Yam student ID, 1980s (author photo)

Ren Bishi, Wang Yam's 'grandfather', circa 1950 (public domain)

Wang Yam's 'father', 'grandmother' and 'aunt', 1987
  (Helen Praeger Young)

Wang Yam and Li Jia's wedding, 1991 (author photo)

Wang Yam's certificate of naturalisation, 1992 (author photo)

Wang Yam's UK immigration photo, 1992 (author photo)

Wang Yam on CCTV at Tesco Express, June 2006 (evidence/Met Police)

Wang Yam's daughter Angela, self-portrait, 2008 (author photo)

Wang Yam and Dong Hui cut wedding cake, Belmarsh prison, 2008 (Wang Yam)

Wang Yam's flat at 13c Denning Road, 2017 (author photo)

Wang Yam, prison cell, 2017 (art Wang Yam/author photo)

Wang Yam, prison self-portrait, 2017 (art Wang Yam/author photo)

'Spanking bench' at West Heath, 2017 (author photo)

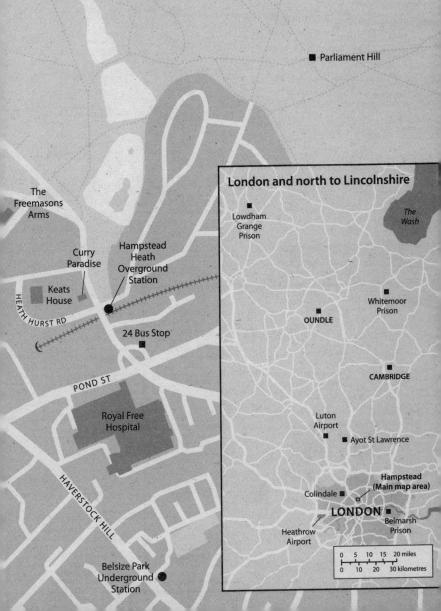

HAMPSTEAD

HEATH

■ Parliament Hill

The Freemasons Arms

Curry Paradise

Hampstead Heath Overground Station

Keats House

HEATH HURST RD

24 Bus Stop

POND ST

Royal Free Hospital

HAVERSTOCK HILL

Belsize Park Underground Station

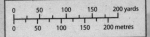

0   50   100   150   200 yards
0   50   100   150   200 metres

London and north to Lincolnshire

■ Lowdham Grange Prison

The Wash

■ Whitemoor Prison

■ OUNDLE

■ CAMBRIDGE

■ Luton Airport

■ Ayot St Lawrence

■ Colindale

Hampstead (Main map area)

LONDON ■

■ Belmarsh Prison

Heathrow Airport

0   5   10   15   20 miles
0   10   20   30 kilometres

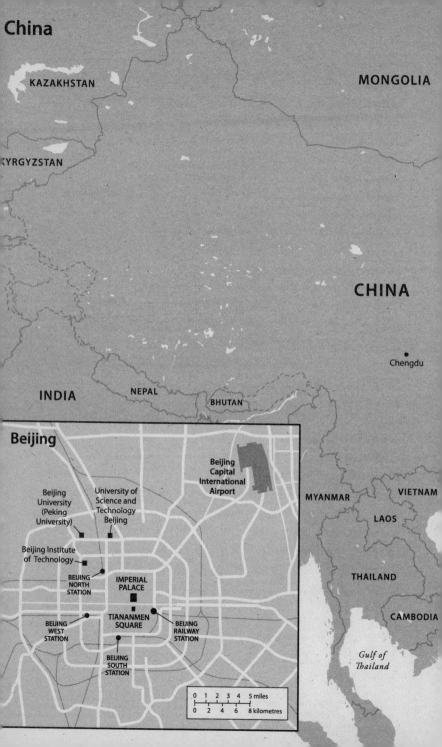

China

KAZAKHSTAN

KYRGYZSTAN

MONGOLIA

CHINA

Chengdu

INDIA

NEPAL

BHUTAN

MYANMAR

VIETNAM

LAOS

THAILAND

CAMBODIA

Gulf of Thailand

Beijing

Beijing
University
(Peking
University)

University of
Science and
Technology
Beijing

Beijing Institute
of Technology

BEIJING
NORTH
STATION

IMPERIAL
PALACE

Beijing
Capital
International
Airport

BEIJING
WEST
STATION

TIANANMEN
SQUARE

BEIJING
RAILWAY
STATION

BEIJING
SOUTH
STATION

0 1 2 3 4 5 miles
0   2   4   6   8 kilometres

RUSSIA

Beijing

NORTH
KOREA

*Sea of
Japan*

SOUTH
KOREA

JAPAN

*Yellow
Sea*

Xi'an

Shanghai

*East
China Sea*

RYUKYU
ISLANDS

Quangzhou

TAIWAN

Hong Kong

Macau

Philippine Sea

HAINAN

*South
China Sea*

PHILIPPINES

| 0 | 100 | 200 | 300 | 400 | 500 miles |

| 0 | 200 | 400 | 600 | 800 kilometres |

CAST OF CHARACTERS

Allan Chappelow
Paul Chappelow (brother)
Karen Chappelow (mother)
Archibald Chappelow (father)
George Chappelow (grandfather)
Torben Permin (first cousin's son)
Merete Karlsborg (first cousin's daughter)
Patty Ainsworth (distant cousin)
James Chappelow (distant cousin
Michael Chappelow (distant cousin)

Wang Yam★ (born Ren Hong)
Ren Bishi (grandfather)
Ren Yuanyuan (father)
Zhang Xiulan (mother)
Ren Jining (half-brother)
Zhu Xiaoping (first cousin)
Li Jia (first wife)
Dong Hui (second wife)

Angela (daughter)
Brian (son)
* According to Wang Yam

Allan Chappelow's Neighbours and Friends
Lady Listowel
Steve and Jane Ainger
Peter Tausig
Nigel Steward
John and Peggy Sparrow
Thomas Carr (handyman)

Police
Pete Lansdown (Senior Investigating Officer)
Peter Devlin (officer day-to-day in charge of case)
Gerry Pickering (police detective/family liaison)
Rob Burrows (police constable)

Lawyers
Geoffrey Robertson (Wang Yam's barrister)
Kirsty Brimelow (Wang Yam's barrister)
James Mullion (Wang Yam's solicitor)
Peter Wilcock (Wang Yam's barrister)
Edward Preston (Wang Yam's solicitor)
Mark Ellison (barrister for prosecution)
Mr Justice Ouseley (judge at Old Bailey)

Journalists
Duncan Campbell (*Guardian*)
Richard Norton-Taylor (*Guardian*)
Dan Carrier (*Camden New Journal*)

AUTHOR'S NOTE

Wang Yam vs Regina was the first murder trial in modern British legal history to be held *in camera*, excluding the press and public from the process. This followed a government request that parts of the trial be heard in secret for reasons of national security and/or for the protection of the identity of a witness.

Following this request, an order was made on 15 January 2008 under section 11 of the Contempt of Court Act 1981 imposing wide-ranging reporting restrictions on the trial. It stated that journalists can not reveal evidence, submissions, judicial decisions or other matters heard or dealt with *in camera*, nor can they speculate as to why parts of the trial were heard behind closed doors. Equally no report about the *in camera* trial – whether it be in an article, interview, letter, testimony or other document – can be quoted or republished for fear of being in contempt of the order, even if such reports are already in the public domain. This means that there is a necessary lacuna at the heart of the book.

Wang Yam vs Regina was one of the strangest and most complicated murder trials in recent legal history. After months of research, and interviews with all the pivotal figures, I believe that the fact that some of the evidence was heard behind closed doors did make justice hard to deliver but, and this is crucial, I do not believe that the evidence itself had any impact on the trial's outcome. The secret material is not, and never was, the key to unlocking the case.

What follows then is the story in full, or as close to full as possible. It is also, as far as I can tell it, the truth.

泥人怕雨,谎言怕理
As a clay figure fears rain, a lie fears truth

Chinese proverb

PROLOGUE

There was no return address on the white envelope that arrived through my letterbox on 18 December 2015. From the postmark, I saw that it had been sent from Peterborough, England, two days earlier. Inside was a card, its cover featuring a blue hummingbird hovering next to a white honeysuckle. Opening the card, I read the child-like writing:

> Dear Mr Harding
> Thank you speak with James!
> I ask Inside Justice send you my related legal papers and ask my cousin give you a call. I hope you can come meet me one day!
> Merry Christmas & Happy New Year.
> With best regards,
>
> WANG YAM

The man who signed the card, Wang Yam, was serving a life sentence in Whitemoor Prison for murder. A decade earlier, his case had attracted considerable media attention – both for the shocking nature of the crime, but also because it was held *in camera*: closed, carefully controlled, secret.

'James' was Wang Yam's lawyer, James Mullion. Inside Justice was a non-profit group that provided legal assistance to prisoners. The card itself was a surprise – my wife was not thrilled to be receiving post from a convicted murderer.

At some point in May 2006, an 86-year-old man named Allan Chappelow was bludgeoned to death in his home in Hampstead, north-west London. He was discovered more than four weeks later, buried under five feet of paper, curled up in a foetal position, partially burned and covered in wax. In September 2006, Wang Yam, a Chinese dissident, was arrested in Switzerland. He was extradited to Britain and convicted of Allan Chappelow's murder. Ten years later, he was still protesting his innocence.

The police were certain that they had the right man, yet no forensic evidence was found linking the defendant to the crime scene. A pathologist described the killing as particularly brutal, but the prosecutors were unable to prove that the accused had a history of violence. The police said that after murdering Allan Chappelow, Wang Yam had repeatedly stolen post from his house in an attempt to assume his identity, but credit cards, PIN numbers and a passport were found untouched and in plain sight on the victim's bed. The more I read about the case, the more confusing it became.

Allan Chappelow was my neighbour and Hampstead was my first home. In the 1970s, I delivered newspapers through its brass letter-boxes, bought sweets from the Post Office, walked on Hampstead Heath with my family. It was on the Heath that I learned to ride my bike one summer – my father said he would pay me £1 if I could do it – and where I went sledging whenever it snowed.

Despite being so close to the metropolis, there was always a strong sense of community in Hampstead. For the Queen's silver jubilee, we ate lunch at a long line of cloth-covered trestle tables arranged up and down our road. At the Keats Grove Library, kind old ladies read stories to me and other local children. And though we were Jewish, we joined our neighbours for Midnight Mass at the elegant church across the street most Christmases. On Halloween, my friends and I rang our neighbours' bells, and when they did not answer, or they failed to hand over treats, we pushed lit firecrackers through their doors. Later, in my teenager years, I loitered outside Hampstead Tube station with my friends and our first girlfriends, unashamed of our displays of public affection.

Hampstead was not only the backdrop to my childhood, it was the stage upon which it took place. I knew the trees on the Heath and the names of the most generous shopkeepers (who gave me lollipops if I waited quietly while my parents shopped). I knew where to have the heels of our shoes replaced, our watches mended, our pictures framed. I knew which shop baked the best bread, sold the best flowers, made the best hot chocolate. It was, is, a physical knowledge. It's a place I thought I knew well.

The murder of Allan Chappelow is a tragic and shocking story – and one that is, for what appears to be an open-and-shut case, uncomfortably complicated. Indeed, as I began to research it further, a senior barrister warned me that I was heading into 'murky, murky waters'. He was right.

A crime of this significance reduces its perpetrator and victim to familiar tropes – an elderly man beaten to death, a killer on the run. But there was so much more to it than that. I wanted to find out not only about Allan Chappelow's death, but also his life. How does a man come to live by himself in a derelict house in one of the smartest streets in London? And I also wanted to know about the man blamed for his death. How is innocence proved? What drives someone to murder? In a court of law, two stories are put forward, a jury is asked to decide which they believe and one version wins out. Life, however, is very rarely that neat.

I also realised that this story offered a rare chance to understand how a modern murder investigation works. In an age of constant connectivity, cheap international travel, DNA testing, blood scatter analysis and forensic phonetics, tracking a criminal and then building a solid case that will persuade a jury requires dedicated methodical investigative work, and long tedious hours spent collecting, documenting and then sifting through evidence; a far cry from the 'Eureka' moments featured on television police procedurals. But the more I tried to connect the police's dots, the less clear the picture became.

And so I looked beyond the investigation. I tried to establish who these men really were. To accurately chronicle the lives of others is never an easy task; 'objectivity' is corrupted by the subjective lens of the author and the sources he or she relies upon. My effort, however, was made harder still because the crime took place within a shadowy world inhabited by conmen, eccentrics and fantasists, where nothing was quite as it seemed. I tracked down witnesses and experts never interviewed by the police, who shed new light on the case. One question led to another, one piece of evidence led to ten more, and so new and competing narratives began to emerge.

As my research continued, larger questions loomed. Why was the trial of Wang Yam held in closed court? Is it possible to hold a fair trial in secret? In this time of growing terrorist and criminal threats, are individuals and press freedoms being sacrificed on the altar of national security?

More than this, there was something about these two lives, both

Wang Yam's and Allan Chappelow's, that intrigued me. Perhaps through their stories, I could hope to better understand what it is like to live on the fringes of society, what takes place behind closed doors, what can happen when no one is watching.

Blood on the Page is a work of non-fiction. I have tried to be transparent in my process and to articulate the ambiguities of the case. Where possible, I have allowed the story's main characters to speak for themselves, uninterrupted, relying on their version of events. I have also noted where doubts have emerged about the veracity of their claims, where I have struggled to unearth the truth, or if I have been prevented from disclosing certain facts.

Obtaining the police's point of view proved difficult, with those officers still active in the Metropolitan Police declining to share their memories. Luckily, the two investigators in charge of the case had both recently retired and were willing to speak to me. Their recollections proved invaluable. To further understand the police's case, I read through thousands of pages of evidence and reviewed witness statements, expert testimony, forensic reports, bank records, travel documents, letters, photographs and email correspondence.

To explain Wang Yam's role in this tale, I relied primarily on his memory. During thirty hours of telephone interviews, conducted from his prison cell, I asked him probing questions about his life, frequently going back over the same material to double-check the details. Where I could, I attempted to verify his recollections by speaking with family members or former associates.

For Allan Chappelow's biography, I was dependent on his own words, in various books and letters; his photographs, shot over half a century; along with the testimony of his relatives, friends and neighbours. I also knew Allan Chappelow myself. For eighteen years,

I lived four doors away from him. That is to say, I knew him as a child knows the peculiar old man who lives up the street, the neighbour who occasionally said hello as he passed by, though I don't think he'd have recognised me and certainly wouldn't have known my name. Nevertheless, it was because I knew him that I never forgot that at its heart this was a deeply sad tale, about the killing of a frail old man, whose friends and family still mourn his loss. A tragic story with long-lasting consequences.

So when I received the Christmas card from Wang Yam, I was faced with a decision: look away or try and seek out the truth. I wrote back. I wanted to know why the trial was held in secret. I wanted to know who killed my neighbour.

PART I

THE CRIME

'*Imagination, of course, can open any door — turn the key and let terror walk right in.*'

Truman Capote, *In Cold Blood*

I

THE DISCOVERY

On a clear day it is possible to see the whole of London from the top of Parliament Hill. The south edge of Hampstead Heath stretches down to a running track at Gospel Oak, before giving way to the family houses of Kentish Town and the tower blocks of Camden. The arched roof of the international railway station at St Pancras comes next, and beyond lie the capital's many iconic buildings: St Paul's Cathedral, the BT Tower, the Gherkin and the Shard. Then the London Eye and the Houses of Parliament, marking the route of the River Thames, and, still further, mounting the horizon, one can spot the chalk downs that hug the city's southern rim nearly 30 miles away.

In summer, Parliament Hill, with its near constant breeze, is a popular place to fly a kite, have a picnic, or just sit on one of the many wooden benches and take in the view. Heading westwards down the slope away from the city panorama, a narrow paved path leads through a tunnel of oak, maple and beech trees, before crossing between two ponds, one inhabited by swans and ducks, the other for the men and women brave enough to take its cool waters. Further on, the path widens into a flat scrubby area. Twice a year for the Easter and summer bank holidays, this space is filled with

Ferris wheels, haunted houses, merry-go-rounds and bumper car rides. It is here that Hampstead Heath, London's largest park, with its 320 hectares of grasslands, woods and waterways, finally comes to an end, and the streets of Hampstead begin.

For centuries a village outside of London, Hampstead was untroubled by the intrigues and passions of England's capital. Later, it attracted patients with pulmonary disorders, its altitude providing a refuge from the city centre's polluted streets. Next came the poets and the artists, the novelists and the actors, creating Hampstead's bohemian culture and colourful reputation. By the end of the twentieth century, given its proximity to central London – it is only a thirty-minute bus or train ride to Soho or Covent Garden – and with its beautiful houses, boutique shops and elegant cafés, Hampstead was colonised by corporate lawyers and top-flight bankers, international celebrities, oligarchs, media moguls and art dealers.

But Hampstead is also said to have a dark side. At night, when the shops are shuttered and the streets empty, when the blue light of television screens flicker through the curtained windows, a tension descends. Residents know not to approach Hampstead Heath after sundown. The police declared parts of the Heath 'no go areas' following a string of violent robberies. Delinquents, thieves and perverts were believed to roam the woods, prowling for lone walkers, women, children. The stuff of gothic novels.

When the sun is out, however, it's a different world. On the south-west edge of the Heath, drinkers congregate on the large front terrace of the Freemasons Arms, a sprawling inn located at the foot of Downshire Hill, one of London's most expensive streets. Moving up Downshire Hill towards Hampstead High Street, walkers pass a handful of eighteenth- and nineteenth-century brick homes, each in fine repair, with wrought-iron gates and tidy front gardens. Further along, on the corner of Keats Grove – a narrow, steeply descending lane where the poet John Keats once lived – is St John's, a cream-coloured church with a black and gold clock and bell tower. Opposite the church, on the right side of Downshire Hill, stands a row of elegant white-washed Regency properties set back approximately 50 metres from the pavement's edge.

A little further on, on the left side, squats an ultra-modern cube-shaped house made entirely of glass panes and thin blue steel beams, then a large Victorian red-bricked block of flats. Finally, dominating the top of the road, on the corners of Downshire Hill and Hampstead High Street, is a three-storey police station. Now empty, it had for more than a century stood sentinel, providing protection to the residents and shopkeepers of Hampstead.

At 11.55 a.m. on 12 June 2006, two police constables, Mike Cole and Sam Azouelos, were driving down Hampstead High Street when they received a request from dispatch on the Mobile Data Terminal. Cole was at the wheel of the white Ford Fiesta. They were to make their way immediately to 9 Downshire Hill in Hampstead. The message then provided the following background information:

HSBC customer ALAN [sic] CHAPPELOW (86 years old) has had unusual transactions made on his bank account, which may be fraudulent. The HSBC fraud department have tried to contact him but they have been unable to do so. When they rang his number an oriental man answered the phone pretending to be MR CHAPPELOW. The caller requests police check on the welfare of MR CHAPPELOW and if they manage to make contact with him, can he be asked to ring the informant asap.

Ten minutes after receiving the request, Cole and Azouelos arrived at Downshire Hill. Number 9 stood almost exactly half way down the road on the left-hand side, a hundred metres from St John's Church. Pulling up in front of the house, Cole and Azouelos saw two other uniformed police officers waiting for them: Chantal Thomas and Ben Roberts. Already 22 degrees centigrade, it was unusually warm for this time of year. The forecasters predicted that the temperature would climb to 24 degrees by mid-afternoon; there might even be thunderstorms later in the day. Leaving their jackets inside the car, Cole and Azouelos locked the doors and walked towards their colleagues.

The house could not be seen from the road. The view was barred by a crumbling stucco wall overgrown by a sprawling oak tree, rhododendron bushes which had gone wild and two ivy-strewn columns upon which hung a pair of wrought-iron gates. One of the columns stood straight, perhaps supported by the oak tree; the other leaned over at an acute angle, its curved crown boasting the words 'Manor House' in bottle-blue capitals. Someone had cared enough to rip the ivy stems away to reveal the house's name, but not enough to repaint its peeling letters.

The gate was ajar. The four police officers walked up a buckled concrete pathway, past an old Norton motorcycle shrouded by a moss-covered tarpaulin, towards the front door. In its prime, the house must have been extraordinarily handsome: a three-storey cream-coloured building with two ornate balconies, arched windows and a flat roof. Now it was dilapidated. Giant ivy climbed up its façade, extending skywards in the shape of an upturned pitch-fork, partially covering the windows.

PC Azouelos, leading the unit, knocked firmly on one side of the tall, blue double-fronted doors, but there was no answer. The doors were locked and there didn't appear to be any signs of forced entry. Looking to see if there was another way into the building, Azouelos walked around the property, peering into the ground-floor windows, each of which was barred by blue steel rods. To the right of the house was a narrow passage blocked by a brick wall.

Azouelos pulled himself up on to the wall between numbers 9 and 10, walked carefully along the narrow ledge, and then jumped back into the alley on the other side. Now in the back garden, so over-grown by trees, bushes and shrubs that it was hard to tell where one plant began and another ended, he found that the home's rear windows were also locked and barred by steel rods.

Returning to the front of the property, Azouelos spoke to his colleagues. After a brief discussion, they decided to enter the building by force. The heavy front doors were eight feet high, with small glass windows cut in at eye-level. Azouelos pulled his black baton from the holster on his belt and smashed one of the panes. He then reached in and tried to open the lock from the inside but there was a board attached to the back of the door preventing him from releasing the catch. Taking a step back, the police officer kicked hard at the lock and the door swung open.

Inside, the front hallway reached back into darkness. It was fifteen feet long and entirely filled with rubbish. The floor was covered with old newspapers, plastic bags, bottles, fragments of wood and rubble. Loose electricity cables hung from the ceiling. At the far end of the hallway was a large white door, also locked. Azouelos tried kicking it open too, but this time, even though he used considerable force, it would not budge.

Once again, the police officers discussed their predicament. Worried that something may have happened to the elderly occupant – perhaps he had fallen and couldn't make it to the phone, or he was locked in a room – they agreed that entry was necessary, and for this they would need better tools. While their colleagues remained at the house, Azouelos and Cole now drove to their home police station in West Hampstead and, having secured authorisation from their supervising officer Detective Sergeant Nick Giles, returned to Downshire Hill shortly after 1 p.m. This time they were armed with a bright red tubular steel battering ram a little over half a metre in length that they called the 'enforcer'. Back at the house, and with his partner standing behind him, PC Cole grabbed the handles of the enforcer with his gloved hands and swung it at the door. Nothing happened. It took five or six attempts before the lock finally gave and they were able to push their way through.

'It was immediately apparent how untidy and cluttered the house was,' Azouelos later wrote in his official police report. 'There was dust everywhere and bits of paper, books and junk piled up high in every room. It looked as though the owner had never thrown anything away.' Stepping further into the house he noted a certain odour. 'I have smelt death on previous occasions, and I can only describe the smell as being sickly and sweet. The house did not smell like this, but more like what I believed to be urine from some sort of animal. There was so much rubbish and junk in [it], and it was so poorly looked after, I thought that the smell could be attributed to anything.'

In one room he found a tartan shopping trolley containing empty boxes of Mr Kipling Bakewell tarts. To the left of the staircase was a large living room that faced the street. It was too dark to see inside. Towards the back of the house, overlooking the garden, was a smaller room, piled chest-high with books, papers, metal shelves, and other detritus. Given the amount of rubbish, he decided not to enter.

Returning outside, he placed a call on the radio asking for a third unit to assist. He and Cole continued with their search. They looked downstairs in the basement, a dark cavernous room filled high with junk, bundles of yellowed papers, piles of books and broken furniture. They explored the kitchen, which housed a small wooden table, two chairs and a fridge that didn't look like it had been used in years. They looked in another large room on the ground floor – perhaps at one time a dining room, it too was crammed with broken furniture, piles of papers and bags of rubble, as if someone had stopped mid-way through a renovation project. The air was heavy with dust and the place was damp and dark; none of the lights worked.

Azouelos walked upstairs, noticing what appeared to be buckets of urine on the steps. On the next floor he found a bathroom, its tub overflowing with books, magazines and plastic bottles. The toilet was stuffed with paper. In a bedroom, he looked under the blankets and beneath the bed, opening a cupboard and pushing around bundles of clothes. Nothing. He then entered another room where a bed was covered with old clothes and a blue sleeping bag. He assumed this was Chappelow's bedroom. On a small shelf next to the bed was an old radio cassette player. Another shelf contained some books and diaries. The room was hot and sweaty, which made the search uncomfortable. On the bedside table was a bottle filled with a brown liquid. Azouelos guessed that it too was urine. Various documents littered the floor. Amongst these was a *Daily Mail* newspaper dated 6 May 2006.

More officers arrived at the house, bringing powerful torches to make the search easier. Despite extensive efforts, however, they were unable to find traces of the owner. One of the investigators later recalled how 'every surface and area was covered in dust and everything had a grey look to it'. She approached the stairs but was worried that they were too unsafe to climb. One room was piled so high with papers and other rubbish that she could not see in. 'The house', she wrote, 'had the appearance of a derelict property which was not inhabitable.'

Two hours after he and Azouelos had first entered the house, Mike Cole called Detective Sergeant Nick Giles and provided him with an update. If a body was found it would be Giles's responsibility to secure the site and then inform the homicide squad, who would in turn dispatch a crime scene investigation team. But a body had not yet been found. Giles told Cole to look for evidence that might point to Allan Chappelow's whereabouts. A short while later, Cole found papers documenting a flight to the USA, leaving on 26 March and returning on 1 May, six weeks before the search. They also found a cheque book, a Sainsbury's credit card, a British passport (all in Chappelow's name) and an article about the history of the American avocado plant.

Finally, at around 5 p.m., they ended the search. Cole called a local carpenter to 'board up' the broken front doors, and a few minutes later a young man arrived. He screwed two hooks above and below the lock of the white door at the back of the hallway, before adding two padlocks to secure the site. The blue double doors at the front of the house were pulled shut but left unlocked. Back at the West Hampstead police station Giles told Cole to file a 'comprehensive low risk' missing person report on the Metropolitan Police's Merlin database.

A few hours later, at 10 p.m., Mike Cole called the neighbour, Lady Listowel, who lived at 10 Downshire Hill. She reported that Chappelow had indeed returned from holiday at the start of May, but that she had not seen him for a few weeks. He would have told her if he was going away again. Before finishing his shift, Cole made a copy of the photograph in Chappelow's passport and asked the night sergeant to drop it off at the missing persons unit.

What had happened to Allan Chappelow? Cole wondered. Perhaps, despite his neighbour's assertion, he had gone away again on holiday, or maybe he was staying with friends. Either way, HSBC needed to be informed that so far they had been unable to find their elderly client.

Allan Gordon Chappelow was born in Copenhagen, Denmark, on 20 August 1919. His father, Archibald Cecil Chappelow, was a 37-year-old English decorator and upholsterer, who was at that time teaching a course on antique restoration at Copenhagen University. Keen to avoid military service at the outbreak of the First World

War, he had moved to Denmark, which remained neutral throughout the hostilities.

Allan's 39-year-old mother Karen grew up in the small town of Hillerød, just north of Copenhagen. She and Archibald had met three years earlier at the university and had married soon after. Karen spent her days managing the family's home and looking after the children, particularly Allan's older brother Paul who had cerebral palsy. In a letter to an American cousin, Archibald wrote that Paul 'had the misfortune to be injured at birth and is a cripple. His hands are affected somewhat and his speech jerky and his walk somewhat haphazard. He is, however, nice looking, cheerful and healthy and is a great reader and a book grubber.'

Soon after Allan's birth, and within six months of the war's end, the family returned to London, moving in with Archibald's father, George Chappelow, who lived in a small house in Hampstead. It was a little cramped, but the family was happy to be reunited. Archibald then joined his father's firm: George Chappelow & Son, which had been established before the war. According to the company's letterhead, they were 'Building and decorative contractors, General House and Property Upholders'. Based at 27a Charles Street, off Berkeley Square in Mayfair, their clients included the theatres, galleries, restaurants and clubs of London's West End. Allan's father and grandfather loved working together, and when not in the office, they played lawn tennis and billiards, or took their wives to the theatre.

A few years later, and with help from George, Archibald, Karen and their two sons were able to move into the large house at 9 Downshire Hill in Hampstead. They were glad to finally have their own space. Built in 1823, their new house was in fine condition, both inside and out. Up until the end of the nineteenth century the property had been home to the lord of the manor of Belsize (from *bel assis*, meaning 'well situated'), and was therefore called

Manor House. The property contained both front and back gardens filled with a mixture of trees and shrubs, and the face of the house sported two elegant iron balconies. Inside, there was an L-shaped double drawing room, with long French windows leading outside, and a wood-panelled staircase that the Chappelows agreed would be well-suited as a picture gallery. 'It is well-nigh a perfect example of late Regency,' Archibald later wrote in his book *Old Homes of England*. 'It might be a small country house set amidst natural wood surroundings', he noted, but 'it is only 2 miles from Oxford Street' in central London.

Allan's parents were political progressives who supported radical reform. As members of the Fabian Society, which had been founded in 1884, they believed in a transition towards socialism, particularly a more equal distribution of assets. Growing up, Allan was repeatedly told stories about his pioneering relatives. His great-great-grandfather, Joseph Stevens, for instance, was a preacher and an advocate for social change, campaigning for an improvement in factory conditions. In 1838, Stevens had been arrested and charged with 'attending an unlawful meeting' and was sentenced to eighteen months in prison. He emerged, however, with his reputation intact and was well regarded by his peers. Allan's second cousin was Grace Chappelow, one of the leading members of the women's suffrage movement. She had been arrested on numerous occasions, had participated in prison hunger strikes and had suffered the humiliation and pain of being force-fed by the authorities. And then there was his uncle Eric Chappelow, Archibald's brother, a poet who had been a conscientious objector during World War One. Arrested and charged with cowardice and treason, he was one of 6,000 'conchies' to be imprisoned by the British during the Great War, causing a national outcry and calls for reform. Despite the family's protests, Eric had spent four months in prison. Later, the government admitted that it had been wrong to imprison Eric and the other conscientious objectors.

In a letter to a cousin in the USA, Archibald talked about his personal values and described the family's character:

Personally I never <u>did</u> believe in War and never shall be able to. I often wonder if it might not be nice to bring my family over to some place where the sun shines and live a simple open life, avoiding newspapers and not worrying about money except just to live. I think the Chappelows manage to get a good deal out of life, although few of them seem to make money, or keep it when they do! I believe the history of our family is very interesting; we have done quite good things in our time and always been an outspoken, fearless people. We are 'honourable' too, for I do not know of any member of the family having gone bankrupt.

In addition to stories about his heroic relatives, the young Allan was also told about the tragedies that had befallen the family. One tale in particular was often repeated by his grandfather George, leaving the boy with a profound sense of the importance of personal security.

Edward Rayner Chappelow, Allan's great-uncle, had been fond of adventure. He joined the merchant navy and sailed the seas, he fought against the 'kaffirs' in South Africa and loaded guano onto boats in Peru. In the spring of 1885, Edward arrived in California ready to settle down. He abstained from drink, purchased his own nursery and began cultivating the land. One day Eric went to a small community in east Los Angeles to collect a $2,000 debt that he was owed. As it was late, he was unable to deposit the money in a bank. On his way home he was attacked by a gang of youths who stabbed him to death, dragging his body to a small wooden shed which was then set on fire with paraffin. Edward was just twenty-seven years old.

★

No matter his family's colourful history, Allan's childhood was typical for someone brought up in middle-class Hampstead. In September 1927, he started at The Hall, a private elementary school fifteen minutes' walk away from Downshire Hill. Known for its high academic achievement, as well as its pink blazers, cap and tie, it was here that he was taught Shakespeare, learned to read Latin, and how to purchase tasty sweets at the tuck shop.

According to headmaster Gerard Wathen's private notes, after a 'baddish' first term, Allan was 'much improved', 'intelligent' and 'good with his hands'. Another entry reported that the pupil was 'not at all hopeless' and 'in some ways unusually clever'. Wathen recorded that Allan's father was an 'artist-architect', his mother was a 'Dane', and his brother 'daft'. The headmaster also recorded that in February 1930 Allan was 'caned' by a Ms Bolton. The infraction's cause was not, however, given.

Like many other institutions of the day, corporal punishment was employed at The Hall. Indeed, in the 1932 edition of the school magazine, a student composed the following playful alphabetised verse:

> R is for Rudeness (no not Mr Rotherham). It's what the staff say when the boys come to bother 'em.
> S is for Sita, best-seller it seems, for some humourist said, 'Go to him for ice-creams.'
> T's for Thrashing, a penalty rare. You go to the study, the Principal's there.

Sport also featured prominently in Allan's youth. While he didn't play tennis with his father and grandfather, Allan was encouraged to participate in team sports. In his last year at The Hall, he was the wicket-keeper for the school's cricket team, and his efforts for the rugby team warranted a headmaster comment in the 1933 school magazine. 'Chappelow (forward) needs more energy', wrote Wathen. 'He is more useful in mud than on dry turf, when greater speed is necessary.'

In his free time, Allan fed the ducks at the ponds on Hampstead Heath and climbed Parliament Hill to catch the view over London. He collected bread from the Rumbolds bakery in South End Green and accompanied his mother while she purchased fruit and vegetables at the market on Hampstead High Street. While he didn't attend St John's Church across the road, or any other congregation for that matter – his family were strictly atheist – he enjoyed the holidays: standing on the roof of 9 Downshire Hill to watch the Guy Fawkes fireworks, taking part in Easter egg hunts in the back garden, and enjoying Christmas lunches with his family in the formal dining room.

Even at a young age Allan was an avid reader, made easier when an optician prescribed a pair of thick-glassed spectacles that corrected his long-sightedness. He spent hours in his small bedroom, poring through the popular books of the day, such as *Swallows and Amazons*, *Emil and the Detectives* and *The Railway Children*. In pride of place next to his bed was a small wooden bookshelf in which he arranged his favourite titles.

Most of all, Allan loved stamp collecting, for, like his mother Karen, he was an ardent philatelist. Whenever a letter arrived at the house, he pleaded that he be given the envelope. If successful, he used a gently boiling kettle to carefully steam off the stamp, before setting it aside to dry and then adding it to one of his albums, according to its colour, value and type. He particularly liked the foreign stamps, which featured heads of states, exotic animals and strange-looking plants. Sitting on his bed he idled away the hours leafing through the albums, thinking of distant lands, which he hoped one day to visit.

★

The second day of searching 9 Downshire Hill began at 3 p.m. on Tuesday 13 June 2006. Mike Cole had spoken again to his supervisor, Detective Sergeant Nick Giles, who said that Allan Chappelow's bank had reported another attempted use of his credit card. With suspicions rising that a serious crime had been committed, the police decided to return to the property as soon as possible.

As his partner, Sam Azouelos, was now on leave, Mike Cole drove with Police Constable Terry Seward to Kentish Town police station, 2 miles from Hampstead, where he picked up the keys and continued on to 9 Downshire Hill. DS Nick Giles was waiting for them outside the gate. Cole opened the front door and provided a brief tour of the ruined property. Their plan was to make a more thorough search of the premises.

'On entering the house,' Seward later wrote in a report, 'I could smell dust and the smell of something rotting.' The house was cool, despite the heat outside. Seward put on a pair of disposable gloves and headed up to the first floor. Half way up the stairs he noticed a swarm of bluebottle flies buzzing near a window. 'The rotting smell was at its worst here,' he wrote.

Seeing a ladder upstairs, DS Giles climbed into the attic, opened a trapdoor and stepped onto the flat roof. He walked around for a few minutes, but there was no trace of the elderly man. He looked over the edge to where Chappelow may have fallen, but all he could see in the garden below were trees and bushes. He saw Seward in front of the house and called down to him to check the garden, but nothing was found.

While the search continued inside the house, other police officers collected statements from the local residents. The neighbours told the police officers that they had seen little of Allan Chappelow in recent years. They had come to view him as an eccentric and recluse. When one of the neighbours had asked if they could visit him at

THE DISCOVERY

home, Chappelow had politely declined. It was assumed that he was embarrassed about the state of his house.

Lady Listowel, who lived at number 10, repeated that she hadn't seen her neighbour since his return from America at the beginning of May. A slight but elegant woman in her seventies, she and her husband William Hare, 5th Earl of Listowel, had moved into their large Regency house in 1987. She knew Allan quite well, she said, and kept an eye on his home whenever he was away. When people on the street mocked Allan for being a recluse or for not taking care of his property, Lady Pamela defended him. 'He is a very dear boy,' she would say. She rather liked his overgrown garden and the wildlife it attracted, and she appreciated his colourful character. She found him to be intelligent, charming and outgoing and she was never bothered by the condition of his house. Some people might not like to live like that, most people in fact, but Allan had lived there since he was a teenager; it made him comfortable, and so who was she to judge?

Peter Tausig, who lived at number 11, said he too hadn't seen Allan for a while. Sixty-six years old and now retired from his job as a banker, Tausig said that he often bumped into his elderly neighbour on the street, typically when Allan was on his way to read the newspaper at the library in Keats Grove. Tausig believed that he was one of the few people on the street who was close to Allan. Two or three years earlier, Allan had told him that his post was no longer being delivered. Tausig offered to help. After learning the problem was Allan's overgrown garden, he arranged for some of the trees and bushes to be cut back. From then on, Allan occasionally popped in for tea at Tausig's house. He would not talk about himself; instead he spoke about politics, particularly his loathing for George Bush and Tony Blair and their 'unwarranted' invasion of Iraq.

Four months earlier, Allan had told Tausig that he was planning

23

to visit Texas. 'He seemed excited,' Tausig remembered. 'He said that he was onto something new, something big, that his next book on George Bernard Shaw would be his *magnum opus*.'

Meanwhile, inside 9 Downshire Hill, Cole looked for any correspondence or useful information that he may have missed the day before. He spent a few hours leafing through bank statements, letters, magazines and diaries, but nothing useful could be found. Cole asked DS Giles what he should do with the travel documents and passport that he had removed the previous day. His boss told him to put them back where he had found them.

After another look around the property, Cole and the other policemen left the premises. The doors were locked once again and the keys were returned to Kentish Town station before dinnertime.

By the morning of Wednesday 14 June, two days after Cole's first visit to the house, DS Nick Giles decided to take command of the search. He had been in touch with Allan Chappelow's distant relatives – Michael Chappelow, an art dealer, and James Chappelow, a teacher from Hemel Hempstead – who both said it was extremely unlikely that the old man would be anywhere but in his house. The detective sergeant was becoming increasingly concerned that something untoward had happened. After two days of searching, it was still not clear whether Allan Chappelow was or was not in 9 Downshire Hill. Half of the rooms were so filled with debris that they had been unable to conduct a comprehensive investigation. The best way to be entirely sure would be to empty every room. This would take weeks, however, as a specialised search team would have to carry out the work with each item having to be photographed and catalogued prior to being moved. In the meantime, there was one other option: the dog unit.

Around 3 p.m., DS Giles returned to the property where he met Paul Vardon and Scott Stepney, each of whom was accompanied by a black-and-tan German Shepherd. Stepney and his dog went upstairs whilst Vardon took his dog, Lacey, around the ground floor. The hallways, stairs and the room on the left proved of little interest to Lacey, but as soon as she approached the room to the right, which was piled high with papers, she let out a specific low bark and started digging at the papers with her paws. Vardon told Giles that it was reasonable to conclude that there was some sort of decomposing flesh in the room. It could be anything from rotting food to a dead animal, but Vardon said that most likely it was a corpse. The only way to check was by carefully removing the debris. Satisfied that they were at last making progress, DS Giles once again locked the front entranceway, and then cordoned off the entire property with blue and white tape.

At 4 p.m., and now back on the pavement in front of the house, it was time for DS Giles to pass the case up the chain of command. He called his boss and told him that they had found something, and although he couldn't yet be certain, he thought it highly likely that it was the body of Allan Chappelow. He now recommended that a crime scene investigator be sent out to the property before it was further disturbed.

This was now a matter for north-west London's homicide unit, and the officer on call, Pete Lansdown.

CASE NOTE

Decided to try and keep track of my research: who I talk to, what they say, any interesting threads.

First step, need to speak with officer who ran the investigation: Pete Lansdown. Found his number on the internet after a few hours of searching, and called. He was surprised I'd tracked him down and suggested I'd make a good investigator. We met in a small quiet office at the Metropolitan Police's Peel Centre in Colindale, north London. His sister who also worked for the Met brought us tea and biscuits. He said that he shouldn't be seeing me as the correct paperwork hadn't yet been signed, but that he had told those in charge that he'd been unable to contact me to cancel the meeting (they would send a contract in the next few days). Told me that Chappelow's death was very sad, a terrible way for an elderly man to die. Suggested I also speak with Peter Devlin, the detective who managed the case day-to-day. Devlin was retired, Lansdown said, and now lived in Ireland, but he didn't have the address. He explained to me how a homicide investigation was conducted, and what he saw as the secret to establishing a successful case. He said that there are four key 'building blocks': evidence, witnesses, crime scene and 'victimology' (the victim's social circle). From this it is possible to establish method, motive and opportunity: why a crime happened at a particular time, in a particular place and in a particular way. As I stood up to leave, Lansdown said that the murder of Allan Chappelow was 'one of the best whodunits I've ever seen'.

Have been trying to get a copy of transcripts from Allan Chappelow's murder trial. Only available, I have been told, if I pay thousands of pounds to DTI Global who hold the exclusive transcription contract for trials at the Old Bailey. This in contrast to USA where transcripts are freely available to read at any courthouse. Received an email from DTI Global: 'We have now performed the search at the Courts', they said, 'and unfortunately due to the age of the case, the tapes are no longer available.' Adding that: 'We will be unable to assist you with your request for the transcript.' Very surprised they have lost the records, especially for a case that is only ten years old and still being appealed. Frustrated that I cannot read or hear what the witnesses and lawyers said in open court.

Wrote to Wang Yam who is being held in Whitemoor Prison in Cambridgeshire. Haven't heard anything back yet.

2

ALLAN CHAPPELOW

In September 1933, at the age of fourteen, Allan Chappelow was dispatched to Oundle boarding school, a two-hour drive north of London and 15 miles south-west of Peterborough. Allan's elder brother Paul remained at home because of his cerebral palsy.

Located in and around the medieval town of Oundle and situated on the banks of the River Nene, the school comprised cloistered accommodation and classrooms, an array of cricket, football and rugby playing fields, a gothic stone hall built in 1908, and the imposing St Anthony's Chapel. It also owned the Elmington outdoor shooting range, which at 460 metres was one of the longest in the country. It was Oundle's reputation as a centre for engineering and scientific excellence, as well as its progressive teaching methods, that had attracted Allan's parents.

Upon arrival, Allan was assigned to New House under the housemaster Mr King, a kind, elderly man who treated his pupils with respect and compassion. Allan joined up for many of the school's activities. He took piano lessons and joined the photography club. In his spare time he wandered the school grounds taking pictures of trees, flowers and animals. Later, he toiled away in the school darkroom, soaking the paper in foul-smelling chemicals, improving his skills as a developer. Despite his family's non-military leanings, he was also obliged to participate in the Officer Training Corps.

In early December, Allan returned to London to spend Christmas with his family. It had been an uneventful first term, but it felt good to be in his own bed in Downshire Hill. Waking up the next morning he put on his glasses and reached for his favourite stamp album, the one featuring his overseas collection. It wasn't on the shelf where it had last been left. Surprised, and now a little more awake, he explored the rest of his bedroom. Under the bed, behind his books, in the chest of drawers. It was nowhere. Now upset, he joined his parents at the breakfast table and told them that his most valuable stamps were missing. After further searches, his parents concluded that one of the family's servants must be at fault. Later that day, despite protestations of innocence, they sacked the servant. The precious album was never found, however, and Allan remained miserable.

Karen strove to console her son. 'You can start again,' she encouraged him kindly. It was an opportunity, she said, to redefine the type of stamps he wanted to collect. Over the course of that holiday, they worked together to track down new and even rarer samples, asking relatives to hang onto their stamps and trawling through local flea markets. When he returned to school the next term, Allan spent many of his breaks with his friends in the schoolyard comparing and swapping stamps. He was keen on finding unusual letters and postcards, particularly those from overseas. It would take some time to rebuild his collection, but he was on his way.

Allan enjoyed his studies and became known for both intelligence and hard work. At the end of his first year, for instance, he was awarded a French prize on Speech Day (he could also speak passable Italian, Danish and German). The following year, in December 1934, he took part in a student-led symposium called the Junior Scientific

Conversazione where he stood in front of the entire school and presented a map of cable and wireless stations of the world. He also teamed up with three other pupils and explained how a hollow vessel – such as a boat or a skull – can collapse if the 'outside force is great enough'. A pamphlet was published about the event, the first time that Allan's name appeared in print. On its cover, the seventeenth-century mathematician John Newton was quoted as saying, 'I cannot tell whether anything be better learned than that which is learned in Play.' In his final year at school, Allan felt sufficiently confident in his photography to submit one of his pictures to a local newspaper and was delighted when they published it along with his name.

Upon graduation in July 1938, however, all dreams of a career in journalism were put aside when his father said he needed to get a job with a dependable income. Wanting to prove that he could make it on his own, Allan started an apprenticeship with a bank in central London just before his nineteenth birthday. His brother Paul meanwhile had found a job selling tobacco and cigarettes at a local shop in Hampstead. Archibald and Karen were pleased to have their two adult sons living at home.

Pete Lansdown considered himself a local boy. He had grown up in 'The Coombe', a tall tower block in King's Cross with a fine view over Regent's Park and London beyond, the son of a secretary and a gunner in the Royal Tank Regiment. Lansdown was what they called 'a lifer'. He had joined the Met aged eighteen, learning the ropes as a uniform in London's West End, before quickly climbing the career ladder. Lansdown's first murder inquiry had been in Chinatown: a gambling den had burned down, killing several people. Three years later he became an accredited detective, and was sent to

Harlesden in Brent, where he joined a team that focused on the violent gangs that then dominated north-west London.

In 1990, Lansdown had been posted to the Regional Crime Squad, which dealt with organised and major crime, and then in 2000 he was appointed senior investigating officer or SIO for north-west London's Murder Investigation Team 3. Since starting as an SIO, he had been in charge of more than fifty murder cases, only one of which, he was proud to say, remained unsolved. In fact, the Metropolitan Police had one of the highest success records in the world, with a clearance rate (charged and/or prosecuted) of 75 per cent, compared to 64 per cent for the FBI. According to the UN Office of Drugs and Crime, at the time of Allan's murder, London had one of the lowest capital city murder rates in the world, with only 1.8 murders per 100,000 compared to 5.6 murders in New York, 4.8 in Mexico City, 4.6 in Moscow, and 4.4 in Amsterdam. In 2006, there were 172 murders committed in London, of which eleven took place in Camden, the borough that includes Hampstead.

Just over six feet tall with a bald head, broad shoulders and the thighs of a rugby player, Lansdown was not the kind of man with whom one would want to get into a fight. Yet his pinstriped suit, white starched shirt, stylish tie, rimless glasses and well-polished brogues suggested a more refined side. The only hints of sentiment were his Falklands War cufflinks. He had the manner of an instructor, sharing his knowledge with others, using technical words and phrases that he then had to explain. At home he studied murder cases from around the world and read books on the latest investigative techniques. But he had other interests too: in his spare time he took care of his fleet of antique cars, his prized possession being a 1978 MGB convertible, painted in racing green with shiny chrome wheels. As a young police officer his colleagues had called him 'Lips', for his physically large mouth. This nickname had stuck, even as he became a senior officer. Perhaps because of his propensity to talk.

It was close to 4 p.m. on 14 June 2006 when Pete Lansdown received the call from DS Giles telling him that a body may have been found at 9 Downshire Hill. At the time, Lansdown was sitting at his uncluttered desk on the second floor of the Metropolitan Police's Peel Centre in Colindale, 4 miles north of the crime scene. As one of six senior murder investigating officers in north-west London, it was his turn to take charge of any new case. In theory, he had been told, if he didn't have the available resources he didn't have to take on a new 'job'. But five years into his position as head of one of the Met's murder investigation teams, Lansdown had learned that he was always busy – as were his colleagues – and rejecting a job would just make things harder for someone else. At any one time he had fifteen active murder investigations on the go, along with another fifteen that they were readying for trial. Every six weeks he was on call, and it was then that he worked at least sixty hours a week, twenty more than was required by contract. As always, he accepted the new job.

'The media likes to think of the murder investigator as a lone operator, with a bad past,' Lansdown commented. 'In fact, solving a murder is a matter of teamwork.' He listed some of the professions involved: forensic experts, crime scene managers, intelligence officers and pathologists. 'Having said that,' he added, 'it's also a question of character, leadership, drive.'

Lansdown had twenty investigators working for him, supported by eight civilian staff. One of his first decisions was how to categorise the murder inquiry. This depended on what he called its 'solvability'. If it was 'level C', an easily solvable case, he would only assign six or seven of his officers. A 'level B' case would oblige him to use all twenty of his investigators, at least for the first few days. The top level, A or A+, required him to contact Scotland Yard and ask for help. A few of the highest-level murder inquiries involved as many as 400 police officers. He instinctively felt this would be a B or B+.

Lansdown's first step was to dispatch a Homicide Assessment Team (HAT) to Hampstead. Thirty minutes later a crime scene manager named Steve Smale arrived at 9 Downshire Hill. It would be Smale's job to photograph the entire property, and to ensure that the place was preserved as best as it could for the forensics teams that might come later.

Once the house had been photographed, Steve Smale and Nick Giles began clearing debris from 'Room Six', as the room had become known where Lacey the dog had barked. At the top of the heap were large bundles of paper, A3 in size, folded in sheaves six inches tall. On each page was the book's title, *Shaw – The Chucker-Out*, and the author's name, 'Allan Chappelow'. These, they discovered, were the manuscripts of a book which the home-owner had written in 1969. They were all from the same work, a biography of the playwright George Bernard Shaw.

The investigators' progress was painfully slow. Before each bundle was moved, they had to search for human contact – footprints, fingerprints, traces of blood, fibres – and take another series of photographs. Five hours later, and only three-quarters of the way through the pile, the team had still not found what had excited Lacey. At 10 p.m., Nick Giles called it a day and left the investigators to continue the search. If they found anything, he told them, they should call Lansdown immediately. Outside it was growing dark as Giles climbed into his car. It was a relief to be in the open air, which was cooler and less fetid than inside. The street was almost deserted as he drove up Downshire Hill and headed back to the police station. It was late on a Wednesday evening; most people were home watching the World Cup.

Half an hour later, and with more of the manuscripts now relocated, Steve Smale saw something protruding from the pile. After a few more items were removed, Smale recognised it as a human leg clothed in a shoe and a sock. He called Pete Lansdown, who was still at the office: they had found what they had spent the last three days looking for.

Each morning during the summer of 1938, Allan read the newspapers on his way to work at the bank in central London. He saw that the tensions between Germany and Britain were growing more intense and like most of the population he was anxious. The papers also reported that Adolf Hitler was rapidly rebuilding the German army and air force in clear contravention of the 1919 Treaty of Versailles. Then in September 1938, Prime Minister Neville Chamberlain travelled to Munich to attend a peace conference with Adolf Hitler. On his return to Heston Aerodrome to the west of London, Chamberlain declared that he had secured 'peace for our time'.

Many in the British establishment were unconvinced by the Munich Agreement, and over the course of that winter and into the New Year there was increased talk of another war with Germany. While mandatory military service had been rescinded after the First World War, a limited form of conscription was re-introduced on 27 April 1939 in response to Germany's rearmament programme and rising belligerence. From this point forward, single men aged between twenty and twenty-two were now called up for service. Though of an age that would trigger enlistment, Allan's brother Paul was provided with a medical exemption and continued to work at the local tobacconist. When Allan turned twenty in August 1939, however, he had no such excuse. A few days later, a letter arrived through the door at 9 Downshire Hill instructing him to report for duty.

He was now faced with a choice: would he enrol at the local army office as had been requested, or would he be inspired by his forebears and take a political stand, objecting to military service? This decision was made acute when, on 1 September, Hitler's tanks invaded Poland. Two days later Britain was at war with Germany.

Allan was conflicted. In addition to the influence of his family and their radical friends, perhaps Allan's greatest inspiration was the writer, orator and playwright, George Bernard Shaw. Though only twenty years old, Allan had read most of Shaw's plays, including *Saint Joan*, *Pygmalion* and *Man and Superman*, along with many of his speeches. Although Shaw's objections to the First World War ran counter to the prevailing public mood, they had inspired Allan. Now, with the start of another major war, Shaw had once again declared his opposition to military conflict, though this time he seemed to have more sympathy for the German and Italian governments than his own. Most of all, Allan was inspired by Shaw's argument that the working classes from different nations should stick together, and not fight the wars of the rich and powerful. After discussing the matter for days with his parents he made his decision.

So it was that on 9 March 1940, Allan set off for the tribunal. He took a bus alone from Downshire Hill to St Pancras and there waited on a bench outside the courtroom. When it was his turn, he walked forward and was interrogated by a panel, comprising a lawyer, a trade union member and a layperson. None belonged to the military. When asked why he refused to serve, Allan declared, 'I am a conscientious objector.' He stated that he disapproved of war of any type, as a matter of principle based on moral, rather than religious grounds.

Allan was one of 60,000 men and 1,000 women who applied to be exempted from the British armed services during the Second World War. In an effort to avoid the scandal of the previous war, the government attempted to delineate between the various applicants. Close to 3,000 were approved for 'unconditional exception', a further 18,000 were rejected as not being 'genuine'; 3,000 were imprisoned (mostly pending appeal), and the remainder were assigned civilian work. Allan fell into this last category. He was told that he must leave the bank and begin work for the War Agricultural Executive Committee. In early June, therefore, he started working as a labourer on an estate outside of Southampton. A few months later, he was moved to another farm near Winchester. To his surprise, he preferred this work to the clerical tasks he had been given at the bank. He liked being outdoors, the comradeship with the other farm workers, being close to the land.

Allan's father, however, was scathing of the government's policy. In a letter to an American cousin, written on 14 May 1940, Archibald wrote: 'In what way the country will benefit from my son quitting his job at the bank, where he is useful, to do land work of which he knows nothing, and will therefore be useless is beyond my comprehension! It is a form of spite, the government says you may have a conscience but it marks its disapproval by putting you into something or other by way of penalty. How small and petty it all is!'

Allan's father went on to describe how the war was affecting his business and how it threatened their house on Downshire Hill.

Many of us are worried by loss of income – in my case complete total loss. Yes, I think my uncle and father are well out of it – I am going down to ruin myself, and would not mind being out of it too, were it not for my dependents. Owing to my difficult position I shall have to sell my pretty Regency house in Hampstead. It was my heart's delight.

While his father worried about saving the family home, his son's troubles with the law were not over. In early April 1941, Allan was wandering through the Winchester streets when he noticed a building that had suffered extensive damage from a recent air raid. Saddened by the scene, he began taking pictures until a police sergeant, who happened to be walking by, rushed up and placed him under arrest.

At the local police station, Allan was charged under the Control of Photography Order 1939. According to the arresting sergeant, Allan had been caught 'red-handed' taking an unauthorised photograph of a bombed-out building. Three weeks later, on 28 April 1941, Allan was summoned to appear before a magistrate in Winchester. He was represented by a lawyer, a Mr A. D. N. Nabarro, who said that his 22-year-old client was 'an expert photographer and always carried his camera with him'. As soon as the offence was pointed out, his lawyer continued, Allan did all he could to make amends. In his summing up, the magistrate, Mr F. O. Langley, addressed the defendant: 'He objects to taking part in the war, but he goes around and takes a photograph of war damage. It seems inconsistent to me.' The story was covered across the country, perhaps as a cautionary tale. The *Hartlepool Northern Daily*, for instance, noted that Allan was fined the not-inconsiderable sum of £20 plus £5 costs.

Twice chastened by the law, Allan decided to keep his head down, and for the remainder of the war managed to keep out of trouble. On weekends he was able to leave the farm, to visit his brother and parents in London, and in the summer he was given a few weeks off. It was during one of these breaks, in July 1942, that Allan stayed for a fortnight at the Fabian Society summer school at Frensham Heights, 25 miles east of Winchester. There he met the leading socialist thinkers Sidney and Beatrice Webb, who allowed him to take a series of photographs. Allan cherished his first celebrity portraits almost as much as he had prized his first stamp collection.

In October 1943, Allan was told that he had been assigned a new job back in London. He was now to work as a spotter for the Civil Defence. Each evening he set off from 9 Downshire Hill, dressed in a khaki uniform, carrying his white helmet stamped with a 'W' for air raid warden, and took a bus to Marble Arch. There he spent his nights standing on the roof of the Cumberland Hotel overlooking Hyde Park and central London, looking out for incoming German planes and rockets. If spotted, he and his colleagues sounded the siren, warning the local residents to move immediately to the closest air raid shelter.

During the day, and once caught up on sleep, Allan found that he had time on his hands, so he enrolled at Birkbeck College in central London. For two years he attended classes on ethics and philosophy, particularly impressing one of his lecturers, Ruth Saw. 'He has genuine philosophical interest and much ability,' wrote Saw. 'Besides an interest in his fellow creatures and their problems of conduct, Mr Chappelow has a strong desire to be of use to them.'

This was Allan's life – studying moral theory during the days while looking out for missiles at night – when on 8 May 1945 the war finally came to an end on Victory in Europe Day. With the outbreak of peace, he wondered what he should do next.

At 8 a.m. on 15 June 2006, Pete Lansdown convened a meeting at the Hampstead police station, less than 200 metres up the road from 9 Downshire Hill. While the homicide unit's offices in Colindale would serve as the investigation base, Lansdown had decided it was more efficient if today's meeting took place near the crime scene. It was already warm outside and only likely to get warmer; everyone was in short sleeves. Gathered around him were all those already involved: the attending police officers, the crime scene managers, the missing persons officers and the HAT personnel. Those more junior would work alongside their more experienced colleagues, a mentor system of sorts, so that they could develop their skills and techniques.

The purpose of this gathering – or 'hot meeting' – was to assemble all the facts currently known and to agree a plan of action for the next twenty-four to forty-eight hours. For it was during this period, which Lansdown called the 'Golden Hours', that they were most likely to make swift progress. This was the time when a perpetrator was typically most vulnerable, most likely to make mistakes, which would make it easier to catch them. In addition, the Golden Hours were also likely to generate the best forensic results.

Lansdown began by informing his colleagues that the investigation would be known from this point forward as Operation Barnesdale (such names were generated randomly by the operations room in Colindale as soon as the murder was registered, and had no specific meaning). Since they had first been made aware of the case the evening before, his investigators had found scant trace of Allan Chappelow. He rarely used his mobile phone and he did not have a landline or internet access. Neither did he appear to have a social media presence or a prior criminal record. In addition, apart from the trip to the USA, his neighbours knew next to nothing about his recent activities.

To make matters trickier, Lansdown continued, beyond Michael and James Chappelow, distant cousins who were seldom if ever in touch, Chappelow appeared to have no immediate family. The team's family liaison officer, Gerry Pickering, added that the victim was unmarried, had no children, no living parents, brothers or sisters, and few if any friends. He was, according to many, a recluse. This, Lansdown told his team, would make things difficult for what he called 'victimology'. Without friends or family, it would be much harder to understand the man, his habits, his relationships, his drives, all of which might help them establish a motive as well as a culprit. Everyone in the room knew that over 80 per cent of murderers were linked to their victims. This lack of intelligence could prove a severe hindrance.

The forensic examination would also be challenging, Lansdown continued. The body, once it was fully uncovered, was likely to be severely decomposed given that a significant time had elapsed since death. None of this was made easy by the house's condition. Even to get to Chappelow would require considerable effort. They could not start where he lay. The POLSA team, or police search advisors, would have to begin where they assumed the murderer had entered the property, at the front gate, removing the vegetation and debris as they progressed, and make their way slowly to the body. Though this part of the crime scene had already seen the greatest disturbance from the investigators, they wouldn't want to miss any clues. It would take days.

In their favour, they had four pieces of significant evidence. Lansdown passed around a report he had been given the previous evening from Peter Moutre, a constable at Hampstead police station. Moutre had written that just six weeks earlier, shortly after 5 p.m. on 2 May, Allan Chappelow had visited the police station and stated to the officer on duty: 'I have had mail stolen.' After giving his name, age and address, Chappelow said that he had been away for five weeks but his neighbour, Pamela Listowel, had been pushing large items of post through his letterbox. Returning home the day before, he had found that his front door had been forced open. The hallway was empty of post.

Lansdown then handed out a second report from another colleague from the Hampstead police station, Teresa Weston, who was a crime prevention officer. In her statement, Weston wrote that, on 4 May, she had walked down to 9 Downshire Hill, knocked loudly on the door, but received no reply. She had left a letter informing Allan Chappelow that if he required a crime prevention visit, he should contact her. There was no further contact with the victim.

It had been a third piece of evidence, Lansdown said, that had triggered the welfare visit on 12 June by Cole and Azouelos. This was the call from HSBC requesting that the police check on Mr Chappelow. HSBC had reported that someone had tried to deposit cheques made out to Allan Chappelow into their account, and that Mr Chappelow had not responded to the bank's requests to contact them.

The final piece of evidence concerned the victim's mobile phone. Despite three days of searching, Allan Chappelow's handset had not been found. Given the appalling state of 9 Downshire Hill, Lansdown conceded, it might yet turn up, but he thought it unlikely. Instead, he believed that it had been stolen. From an old bill found in his bedroom, they had learned Allan's mobile phone number and that his service provider was Orange. After a quick call to Orange they had been told that his was a black Nokia handset and that his SIM card had been used numerous times in the previous few weeks. That was all that they were prepared to say at this point. A full breakdown of the calls, when and to whom they had been made, could only be provided upon receipt of an official request, which would have to be made through the Metropolitan Police Telecommunications Intelligence Unit (MPS TIU) at Scotland Yard.

To understand the crime, Lansdown now told his colleagues, they had to develop a narrative. Why did this murder happen at this place and at this time? From the information available at the hot meeting, it appeared to Lansdown that there were two possible theories. Perhaps the victim had befriended a conman, who he had allowed to enter the house, and an altercation had taken place, resulting in Mr Chappelow's murder. The more likely answer, he said, was a bungled burglary: a fraudster had been breaking into the front hallway at 9 Downshire Hill and opening Chappelow's mail. While Chappelow had been in the USA, the thief had stolen various cheques. Caught in the act by the occupant upon his return, a struggle had ensued. The thief had then pushed the elderly gentleman back into Room Six – a matter of only a few steps – and killed him. For now, this would be the operating theory.

Closing the meeting, Lansdown pronounced the chain of command. As senior investigating officer, he would be in charge of overall strategy and deciding which lines of inquiry to pursue. As it was a complex case he would rely on his best officers. Lansdown's deputy would be Bill Jephson, a swarthy Scot who specialised in telephone investigations. Sometimes his abrupt manner rubbed his colleagues up the wrong way, especially when he pulled rank and told them what to do, but Jephson worked tirelessly and had earned respect for being the first to arrive and last to leave the office. The case officer would be Peter Devlin, a Glaswegian homicide investigator with whom Lansdown had worked for years. Devlin was particularly knowledgeable about financial investigations, which the SIO suspected would be key to this case. Jephson and particularly Devlin would be in charge of the day-to-day investigation.

Lansdown now delegated the tasks. One team was to go door-to-door collecting witness statements. They were to find out all they could about Allan Chappelow: who were his associates, what was he like, what did he do? A second team of Scene of Crime Officers (or SOCOs) was to continue the forensic examination of the house, cataloguing the items found, photographing the evidence and, by noon that day, fully uncovering the body. A final team should gather telephone and banking information, and from this hopefully track down Allan Chappelow's last known activities. Maybe, given that someone appeared to have stolen the victim's telephone and mail, they might even get a lead on the killer himself.

Leaving the hot meeting, Detective Sergeant Peter Devlin walked down the street to take a look at 9 Downshire Hill for himself. According to protocol, he made sure that he didn't go inside the property, for it would be his responsibility to arrest the culprit – whenever that might be – and he wanted to avoid any possible cross-contamination between himself and the murder scene.

His first impression of the case was that it would be a 'sticker', that the investigation might take a while because the house's poor condition would complicate the forensics team's efforts. 'When a new job comes up you hope it's going to be a good one,' he said. 'I thought to myself that this one is going to be interesting.' Most murders involve a family member, friend or acquaintance, making them relatively simple to solve. A suspect is identified within the first twenty-four hours, and then evidence is collected to support the inquiry. This investigation, instead, would be more of a challenge, which pleased Devlin. Even better, he liked the location. They would be spending the next few months in Hampstead where he knew the geography and the people. As a bonus, it also had great cafés. 'I was as excited as you got after thirty years in the business.'

Peter Devlin was born in 1953, a long way from the leafy streets of Hampstead Village. With his parents and two younger siblings, he grew up in a tenement building in Glasgow's Pollokshaws district. 'It was a slum,' he remembered, 'with an outside toilet and a view of the fire station.' His father was a rubbish collector, a 'hard man with a reputation for being honest', and his mother worked as a cleaner in a private home. She was a short, stout woman with a good sense of humour. Despite theirs being a Romeo and Juliet marriage – he came from a family of devout Catholics, she belonged to the Protestant Orange Order – the household was full of love; a safe and warm place to come home to.

In 1970, Devlin left school and started work as a bank clerk. Three years later, bored with office life, he joined the police and was stationed at Glasgow's busy Oxford Street branch as a uniformed officer. At the age of twenty-four, he married Denise, a Yorkshire-born girl who also lived in Glasgow, and shortly afterwards suggested that they head south, though neither of them had ever been to London. 'Let's do it,' she said bravely, 'let's go.' A few months later, Devlin joined the Metropolitan Police, starting again on the bottom rung of the career ladder. 'I was a believer in the Celtic imperative that the first born moves on,' he said. 'I was looking for adventure.'

Over the next two decades his hunger for adventure propelled him to jobs with ever increasing excitement. He moved from tracking down pickpockets and petty thieves to infiltrating drug dealers and investigating police officers with links to organised crime. Gradually, he changed from being the novice Scotsman into the hard-boiled London detective sergeant who was surprised by little. In 2000, still hankering for adventure, he had joined Pete Lansdown's north London homicide investigation team.

Having visited the crime scene at 9 Downshire Hill, Devlin now returned to his office in Colindale. There he put in a request that a pathologist be allocated to examine the body and establish the cause of death. Unlike his colleagues, many of whom found a way of being home so that they could watch the England v Trinidad World Cup match at 4 p.m., Devlin remained at his desk through the afternoon and late into the night, reading through the preliminary forensic and other investigative reports piled high on his desk.

Near the top of the heap was a statement collected earlier that day from Nicholas Sullman, a postman who worked at the Hampstead sorting office. Sullman reported that he was responsible for delivering mail to the residents of Downshire Hill and over the years had become familiar with the elderly eccentric who lived at number 9. 'The garden is a mess,' the postman had told one of Devlin's colleagues. 'For some time I was unsure whether anyone lived there.'

Five to six weeks earlier, perhaps Friday 5 or 12 May, Sullman had arrived at 9 Downshire Hill around 10.30 a.m. and found the front door blocked by fallen branches. Unable to push the homeowner's mail through the letterbox, he had returned to the sorting office before continuing on his rounds. About forty-five minutes later, he was approached by a man on Heath Hurst Road, about 400 metres away from Allan Chappelow's house. The man 'asked me if I had delivered the mail to 9 Downshire Hill'. When Sullman said that he'd been unable to because the door was blocked, the man asked if he still had the mail and Sullman replied that the letters were now at the sorting office. The man then 'told me that he was the uncle of the man' who lived at 9 Downshire Hill and that 'he would get the path cleared'. The next day the branches were gone, the postman said, pointing out that 'it would have taken quite a lot of work to get this done'.

When asked for a description of the person who had stopped him on Heath Hurst Road, Sullman said he was a 'Chinese man. A bit shorter than me. I'm five feet eight inches. He was about fifty years old. He had an English accent, although after speaking to another resident today, she jogged my memory and his accent may have been American.' He added that the man was 'of average build, perhaps a bit stocky' and that 'I remember he may have had a bag over his shoulder, beige clothing, perhaps cord trousers. He was a bit scruffy. His hair was black with a fringe and collar-length.'

Finishing the statement, Devlin wondered whether he had just read the first description of the man who murdered Allan Chappelow. Sometime around one or two in the morning, he said goodbye to the night sergeant on duty in Colindale, climbed into his car and drove home. It would all start again at 9 a.m. the next day and he needed to be fresh.

With the war's end, Allan wanted more than ever to become a photo-journalist. His brief time at the bank had put him off office work. Yet he still understood his father's warning, that it would be hard to make a living taking pictures. The solution, Allan concluded, was to first obtain a degree.

In the autumn of 1945, he applied to study at university. His school grades had been excellent and Allan was hoping his interest in photography might give him an edge over the other students. He worried, though, that his years as a conscientious objector might cast a shadow over his application. He was surprised, therefore, when he received an invitation for an interview at Trinity, the largest college at Cambridge University, and even more bewildered when he was accepted to study Moral Sciences, as part of their two-year degree programme. Despite his anxieties, the university appeared to be giving him a second chance.

Allan spent the summer of 1946 helping his parents around the house and preparing for Cambridge. In his spare time he pursued his photography, taking portraits of family members and anyone he was able to persuade to sit for him. On 13 August, for instance, he managed to take a photograph of the 79-year-old author H. G. Wells. The picture was taken at Wells's home at 13 Hanover Terrace in central London, and captured the celebrated author looking serenely off camera. Allan was happy with the head-and-shoulders image; it would make another useful calling card for other potential subjects.

A few weeks later, in early September, the 27-year-old Allan Chappelow said goodbye to his parents and brother, and set off for university. He mounted his Norton motorcycle, parked in the front garden of 9 Downshire Hill, and with his few belongings packed into two black leather side panniers, he rode through the suburbs of north London, up the A1, and across the flat lands of Cambridgeshire.

He loved his new home immediately. The large courtyards and Great Gate through which he walked each morning. The oak-panelled dining room where the food was plentiful and free, and the Wren Library, whose quiet made for calm, productive study. Most of all, he enjoyed the River Cam that flowed behind the college, and upon whose grassy banks he could read, take photographs of the pink, yellow and blue wildflowers, or better yet, set off in a punt.

Allan flourished in Cambridge, working hard and receiving reasonable grades from his tutors. He lived for one year in college, and one year on 22 Portugal Street, where he shared lodgings with

Prince Dimitri Obolensky, a 28-year-old lecturer in Slavonic studies. They soon became friends, with Obolensky telling his new roommate how after the 1917 revolution the British navy helped his family flee Russia, together with the Tsar's grandson, and Allan recounting stories of his radical ancestors and their run-ins with the establishment.

In 1947, and then again in 1948, Allan was awarded the Trinity College Hooper Prize for declamation, speaking first about the author H. G. Wells, and then on James Keir Hardie, the first Labour Member of Parliament. He also gained second place in an English essay competition. And while he made few friends – Allan wasn't very good at small talk and didn't enjoy parties – he didn't make enemies either. Most of his time was spent in the library, by the river, or in his room.

In the summer of 1948, Allan graduated with a third-class degree. His low final grade was a surprise to both the candidate and his tutors, the former believing that illness had reduced his score, the latter believing 'width of interests may have handicapped his course work' but that he was capable of achieving a class II degree. In a memo, Allan's tutor R. M. Rattenbury wrote, 'There is no doubt that he is an intelligent man,' and 'he has shown promise of good work.'

Though his grades were far from excellent, Allan felt at home in the academic world and enjoyed the freedom it allowed. The following spring, therefore, he applied to the London School of Economics to study social psychology and nineteenth-century social history. He proposed that the subject of his thesis would be his radical relative, the preacher Joseph Stevens, with a particular focus on the reform movement of the mid-nineteenth century.

During a long interview on 20 May 1949 with Professor Beale of the London School of Economics, Allan explained that his third-class grade did not 'represent his real ability' and offered a number of testimonials to certify that he could do better. 'He is terribly keen to be accepted straight away,' Beale wrote in his notes. 'I doubt very much whether we should accept him this term,' adding that 'he talks mercilessly, has a very high opinion of himself.' Despite Beale's reservations, on 16 June, the dean of postgraduate students wrote a letter to Allan accepting him for the following term.

In his funding application written in July 1949 to the Ministry of Education, Allan wrote, 'My family relationship with Joseph Stevens (he was my great-great-Grandfather) gives me access to original documents and other evidence not otherwise available.' His ultimate aim, he concluded, was to 'establish myself in an Academic career; i.e. in social psychology (a field in which there seems to be considerable scarcity)' or alternatively 'some other practical work within the general field of Social Science'. By return of post, Allan heard that he had been awarded two years' funding by the government.

Living with his parents reduced Allan's expenses and enabled him to pursue his photojournalism. It was hard work. Lacking a track record, he was unable to sell a story before he had written it. Instead, he had to write 'on spec', assuming the costs of travel himself and running the risk that an editor would reject his work, which happened more often than not.

Allan's big break came in the spring of 1950. One sunny morning in late March, he decided to try and interview his hero George Bernard Shaw. First, he typed a letter to Shaw and enclosed copies of photographs he had taken of Wells and the Webbs. He then rode his motorbike forty-five minutes north of London to the picturesque village of Ayot St Lawrence, where Shaw lived. By this time the great writer was in his tenth decade and sequestered at his home 'Shaw's Corner'. Arriving at the house at 12.15 p.m., Allan walked through the wrought-iron gate and up to the front door and, after knocking loudly, was greeted by a man who introduced himself as Dr Loewenstein. After hearing of Allan's mission, Loewenstein declined the proffered package and said, 'It would do no good, we receive so many letters by post. You will only be losing your prints for no purpose.'

Disappointed, Allan remounted his bike and headed back to London. A few minutes into the ride he decided that he shouldn't take 'no' for an answer and returned to Shaw's Corner. This time he was met by a middle-aged lady. 'Yes-s-s, what do you want?' she asked, sternly. Allan explained that he wanted to leave his letter and photographs, which the woman grudgingly took, saying, 'I will see that he gets it. Mr Shaw is a very busy man.' And then the door closed again.

Six days later, an envelope arrived for Allan at 9 Downshire Hill. To his surprise it was from George Bernard Shaw. The letter had been typed on light blue paper, the few typos corrected by hand. 'An old skeleton at 93½ is all that is left of me,' Shaw wrote. 'Better leave well alone. In any case, I have warned off all visitors until the hours are longer, as I am never free until 4 p.m., by which time the lanes here are dark, the way hard to find, and the fogs dangerous at all times.'

Driven by the impetuousness of youth, Allan wrote back the same day. 'Why describe yourself as an old skeleton? Shame on you! Pshaw! Why, you're SUPERMAN! Put the skeleton back in the cupboard and carry on as the living proof of your own Life Force theory.' This time there was no reply.

One Sunday morning three months later, Allan was showing his photographs at the open-air exhibition next to Whitestone Pond in Hampstead, one of the highest spots in London with far-reaching views over the city. 'It was one of those particularly glorious summer days,' he later wrote, 'when the beaming sun, the blue sky, the singing birds, and the green foliage rustling in a gentle breeze, make it almost impossible for anyone to feel other than benevolent towards life and his fellows.' Acting on a sudden impulse, he decided to ride out to Ayot St Lawrence one more time. As always, he had his camera with him, though half of the roll of film was already exposed. Eager to get going, rather than return home for more film, he mounted his bike and set off.

An hour later, he was standing at the front door of Shaw's Corner. Again, it was answered by the grey-haired housekeeper, who this time introduced herself as Mrs Laden. She seemed pleased to see him, saying that his photographs of the Webbs had sat out on the table for some days, but regretted that Mr Shaw would not be available for a meeting as he had experienced some recent medical troubles. He would be going out for his early evening walk at 4.30 p.m., but should not be disturbed.

Despite the bad news, Allan remained on the front steps talking with Mrs Laden and enjoying the good weather. Then, at 4.30 p.m. exactly, they heard the sound of footsteps inside. 'That's him,' said Mrs Laden, 'preparing for his walk.' Allan was thrilled; he could at least tell people that he had heard the 'giant moving around his lair'.

Mrs Laden walked inside and returned a few minutes later. 'Oh, Mr Chappelow,' she said, 'Mr Shaw will be pleased to see you in the drawing room. Will you come this way?' Astonished, Allan followed the housekeeper into the house 'as if in a dream'. He was led into the living room. On the mantelpiece stood a small sculpture of Shakespeare; next to it was a golden Oscar statuette for *My Fair Lady*, the film adaptation of *Pygmalion*. On the wall opposite was a picture of Shaw's wife, and in the bay window a bust of Shaw himself. Overcome with emotion, Allan now worried what he would say to Shaw, and perhaps worse, what ferocious words Shaw might say to him. 'My heart pounded like a sledge hammer,' Allan later wrote. Then the door slowly swung open and Shaw walked into the room.

I was literally speechless with the wonder and fascination of it. What an eternity there can be in a brief moment of chronological time! So intense was my interest in seeing in reality what had right up till a few minutes ago seemed hardly even the remotest possibility, that for several moments I could only look at him. Bernard Shaw for his part also just stood there, motionless, with one hand on the doorknob, and another holding a stick, and returning my gaze with a most quizzical, half-amused expression. At last he broke the silence. When he began to speak and chuckle he became the most charming and delightful person I have ever met. In a beautiful rich, mellow and resonant Irish voice he said, 'As you see, there's not much left to me.'

Before long, the pair were sitting across from each other in deep conversation. Shaw said that he recognised Allan's surname, and they worked out that Shaw's mother had taught music to Allan's cousin, the suffragette Grace Chappelow. Then Shaw asked what camera Allan used, and Allan passed over his Zeiss Contax for the playwright to examine. Soon they were discussing the pros and cons of various makes and models. A few minutes later, Shaw invited Allan 'to take as many photographs as you like'. So, over the next hour, Shaw generously walked Allan around the house and gardens, striking poses when asked. In all, Allan managed to take six high-quality portraits. With the elderly writer tiring, and Allan out of film and keen not to outstay his welcome, he said goodbye, shaking hands with the great man three times.

The next day, Allan developed the film. When he had finished he was pleased with the results. All six pictures had come out sharp and well framed. Tom Todd, a publishing friend of his father's, came to tea the following Sunday and told him that the pictures were good enough to be printed in the newspapers. Allan worried that Shaw had only allowed him to take the photographs as he was a supporter of the Fabian Society, and that he wouldn't give him permission to print them. 'Rubbish,' said Todd. 'I think he would be disappointed if you didn't publish.'

The following day Allan again rode out to Ayot St Lawrence. Along the way his motorcycle had a puncture and after fixing it, he didn't arrive until after 7 p.m. At the front door Mrs Laden said it was probably too late to see Shaw but, after checking, Allan was invited in for a brief visit. A few minutes later, the two men were standing next to each other in the drawing room looking at Allan's photographs. Shaw seemed pleased, especially of one image with him standing in the porch, leaning on his stick and looking defiant. The author chuckled, 'This is alive – this ought to be published. Call it – "The Chucker-Out"!'

Allan's interview with Bernard Shaw appeared in the following week's edition of the *Daily Mail*. He had a large 20 x 16-inch print made of 'The Chucker-out' and had it delivered to Shaw's Corner. On Sunday 10 September 1950, six weeks after celebrating his ninety-fourth birthday, Shaw went into the garden to prune some bushes. He slipped and whistled loudly for help. He was rushed to hospital and diagnosed with a fractured leg. After surgery, Shaw spent twenty-four days in hospital before returning home for what would be his last few weeks of life. His housekeeper set up a bedroom on the ground floor of his house. Opposite him on the wall was the portrait by Allan Chappelow. When friends visited, Shaw said that it was his favourite picture.

CASE NOTE

_____

Received an email from the daughter of one of Allan's neighbours. 'We were all very fond of Mr Chappelow who was a lovely, gentle man.' She then said that he was extremely private and that he would have been upset to have his life (and death) made public. I am hoping that I will have better luck with the other neighbours.

Have been unable to find a Peter Devlin in Ireland, at least one who used to work for the Met. So I called the Police Pension Scheme. The helpful lady on the phone confirmed that Devlin was retired but actually lived in England. If I wrote a letter, she promised to forward it to him.

I called Wang Yam's lawyer James Mullion. Explained that I was researching the case and was in need of information. He said he could only speak with me and give access to the defence files if his client gave permission. He also told me that the letter I had sent to Wang Yam in jail had been confiscated by the prison governor.

At the Holborn Library, I trawled through the Camden New Journal *clippings archive. In their first article on the Allan Chappelow murder, they* reported that the police were 'following a line of inquiry that Mr Chappelow was killed by thieves who broke into his house and stole his identity, skimming his account of thousands of pounds'. Another article outlined Wang Yam's basic story: that though he was a 'bit player used by a gang of fraudsters' he had nothing to do with the killing. I need to find a way to speak to him.

3

THE MURDER

_____

Early on 16 June, a call came into the newsroom of the *Camden New Journal*. The caller said that there was significant police activity outside of number 9 Downshire Hill, and perhaps they might want to take a look.

Hampstead was Dan Carrier's beat, so he was given the tip. The 32-year-old was known locally for his tenacity and his integrity. He had first worked for the *Journal* aged twelve, delivering papers at 1p per copy. In his twenties Carrier joined the paper as a cub reporter, and never left. Owned by its staff, and based in a terraced house opposite Sainsbury's in Camden Town, the *Journal* was one of Britain's last remaining truly independent weeklies. Turnover was low, morale was high, the walls needed painting and the toilet was in need of repair.

Dan Carrier had first heard of Allan Chappelow five years earlier when English Heritage had added 9 Downshire Hill to their list of 'at risk' properties. Standing outside the dilapidated house back in 2001, a number of questions had popped into his head. Who owned it? Why was nobody looking after the house? Was there someone living there with a broken heart who had let it go to ruin, Miss Havisham-style? He thought that it had a 'touch of the Boo Radleys' about it.

Knocking on the blue double-doors he'd waited. Then it opened and there was Allan Chappelow, looking dishevelled and not a little cantankerous. 'What do you fucking want?' the homeowner had asked. When Carrier began asking questions about the house, Chappelow said 'no, go away, go away' and shut the door in his face. Over the next few years, the journalist had tried to speak to Chappelow five or six times. Each time he'd been rudely rebuffed.

Now, driving over to Hampstead, Carrier felt frustrated he'd been unable to get to the bottom of the story. It was only when he arrived at the house that he was told that Allan Chappelow had been murdered. 'I was fairly upset and shocked,' Carrier recalled. 'I had a sense of ownership over Allan. I was kind of upset I hadn't been able to get to know more about this strange bloke, what the old boy was really about.' The journalist watched as a stream of white-suited crime scene officers went in and out of the house. A yellow skip had been positioned next to the curb and every so often a handful of rubble, furniture or other junk was deposited.

Carrier chatted with a few neighbours and took some photographs, but it was hard to understand what was going on. He tried starting a conversation with some of the policemen milling about, but nobody was willing to speak with him. It appeared that the higher-ups had instructed them not to talk to the press.

In the Metropolitan Police, overall responsibility for media relations lay with the director of media and communications. It was the director's job to provide transparency to the public, while allowing police officers to get on with their investigations and safeguarding the Met's reputation. According to tradition, direct contact with local and national media was left to the senior investigating officer. In this case, of course, the SIO was Pete Lansdown.

In Lansdown's view, there was always a balance between

protecting the family's privacy and using the press to help develop leads. Media coverage could bring the case to the public's attention and might inspire witnesses to come forward. If they were lucky, a story might provoke the suspect into making a rash move. Lansdown, however, was well aware that journalists could also cause problems. They could speak to witnesses before his team made contact, they might disclose details that he would prefer kept secret and, most irritating of all, they could question how the investigation was run.

Back at the *Camden New Journal*, Dan Carrier started work on his article. Murders were rare in Camden, but not unheard of. The journalist was therefore familiar with the various stages of a homicide inquiry. A number of stories would come out of this, he hoped, so he would call his contacts in the police for an update in the next few days. For now, however, he focused on what he knew. Featuring quotes from a few of the local residents, a short biography of the victim, and a photograph of the police activity at Downshire Hill, his piece would focus on the crime's local angle.

The first national outlet to cover the murder was the *Daily Mail*. It was a story too good to miss, involving an elderly reclusive writer, a brutal murder, identity theft and an exclusive location. On the morning of 16 June, they published a story under the headline, 'AUTHOR IS FOUND MURDERED IN HIS £2.5M HOME DAYS AFTER IDENTITY THIEVES RAIDED HIS BANK ACCOUNT.' In an article that filled page 5, the *Mail* quoted a 'police source' – presumably Pete Lansdown – saying that the Met were working under the assumption that the victim disturbed a burglary and was killed. They carried an aerial photograph of 9 Downshire Hill along with Allan Chappelow's 'Chucker-out' photograph of George Bernard Shaw. They also quoted a neighbour who did not want to be named who called the victim 'one of life's eccentrics' and said that he was a 'multimillionaire', a reference to the value of 9 Downshire Hill.

On 19 June the *Guardian* offered a second possible narrative. 'Mr Chappelow was not known to have enemies,' they reported. 'One theory is that an intruder beat and tortured Mr Chappelow to get his bank details from him, before battering him to death.' The article added that Pete Lansdown 'refused to speculate on a motive'. All he was prepared to say on the record was that they had used dental records to confirm that the identity of the victim was indeed Allan Chappelow.

At 2 p.m. on the afternoon of 16 June 2006, the pathologist Dr Robert Chapman arrived at 9 Downshire Hill to look at Allan Chappelow's body before it was transported to a morgue. Considered one of the best in the business, Chapman had performed thousands of post-mortems, including those for Princess Diana, Dodi Fayed, and the victims of the London Underground bombings in 2005.

Over the previous eighteen hours, the debris covering Chappelow had been carefully removed, revealing a fully clothed man lying in a foetal position, face down, with his hips and knees flexed. He was wearing a dull blue sweater, blue trousers to which were attached a pair of braces, and brown leather shoes. His head was turned slightly to the left and rested on the laminate flooring. His arms were bent beneath him.

As with all those who had entered the house after it had been declared a crime scene, Chapman was wearing personal protective equipment, or PPE, an all-in-one white jumpsuit that covered him from head to ankle. He also wore a face mask, latex gloves to cover his hands and plastic booties to cover his shoes. According to Locard's Principle, named after the French forensic expert Edmond Locard, a perpetrator of a crime will bring something into the crime scene and leave with something from it. This was why the outfit was obligatory, to prevent any contamination of the crime scene, which might make it harder to track the murderer.

Now leaning forward for a closer inspection, Chapman checked for a pulse and was unsurprised to find the victim unresponsive given that the body was so decomposed. The body felt icy cold. When he touched the jaw, arms and legs they were stiff and hard to move. The head and hair were black with what looked like dried blood, and the skull appeared to be fractured, as if struck repeatedly by a blunt instrument. The pathologist also noted that a trail of blood had sprayed upon the objects gathered near the head and was careful to avoid disturbing this trace evidence. He then covered each of Chappelow's hands and the head with a paper bag to preserve their condition for later examination. Some pathologists took a body temperature at this time by placing a thermometer in the rectum, but Chapman preferred to leave this procedure till the autopsy proper.

This, he felt, would do for now. The key task at this stage had been to observe the victim *in situ*, to see where the person had died, whether he was injured, how he had been concealed and whether the body had been moved after he had been killed. Most of all, he had been careful to avoid doing damage to the body. Any further investigation would have to wait for the clinical conditions of the mortuary.

Once the pathologist had indicated that his initial exam was complete, the entomologist Samantha Pickles stepped forward to collect samples from the body. With metal tweezers in her gloved hands, she carefully removed clumps of blowfly egg masses from the victim's clothes, along with a number of puparia (which hold the pupa) around his neck and right elbow, and adult blowflies from his head area. She placed these samples into plastic beakers that contained ethanol solutions, added labels and then stored them in a cool bag for later examination. Signalling that she was done, she left the room.

Now, with the pathologist looking on, two crime scene officers gently enclosed Allan Chappelow's body in a black plastic pouch and then lifted him onto a stretcher. As he was carried to the ambulance outside, the other crime scene investigators stopped what they were doing, pausing out of respect. Once the body was strapped down and the doors closed, the ambulance set off up Downshire Hill. It would be a twenty-minute drive through light afternoon traffic to reach the mortuary in St Pancras.

In September 1951, Allan returned for an additional year at the London School of Economics. 'Mr Chappelow finds it difficult to finance his research,' wrote one tutor, 'and so his work is difficult to report on.' Another wrote, 'Have only seen him once and I am doubtful whether he will ever complete his thesis.'

Allan received no financial support from his parents, and though he was still living at home, his government grant was insufficient to cover his costs. In July 1952, Allan wrote to LSE's administration. 'I have been very seriously handicapped', he said, 'by the necessity of working at a job to earn enough to buy even essential books and meet various incidental living expenses.' Blaming the government's refusal to extend his grant, Allan stated that he would not be registering for the next year's classes.

In contrast to his academic carrer, Allan's journalism career began to blossom. In the five years following his George Bernard Shaw scoop, he wrote at least nine feature-length articles for the *Daily Mail*. His work was also carried in the *Contemporary Review* and the *Illustrated London News*. He interviewed the writer Somerset Maugham, the artist Augustus John and the philosopher Bertrand Russell. Allan's subjects tended to be elderly men, typically artists, politicians and philosophers, who ruminated about their life's work and their potential legacy. In October 1952, for instance, Allan interviewed the 85-year-old artist and recluse Sir Frank Brangwyn. 'Sir Frank vented his views on art and life, giving a display of vocal fireworks comparable to nothing in my previous experience,' Allan wrote. 'The vitality of the man, in his eighty-sixth year, was simply amazing.'

In the summer of 1954, a year after the death of Joseph Stalin, Allan joined a group of twenty-six students on a tour of Russia. According to Allan, this was the first time a group of ordinary tourists had visited Russia since 1939. The trip was organised by the Travel Department of the National Union of Students and cost £95 per head. The group was non-political in nature and was part of an exchange in which an equivalent group of Russian students toured around Britain. Allan hoped that this trip might also provide enough material for him to write a book, an ambition he had harboured since childhood. Before he left London, therefore, he approached a number of publishers, finally winning interest from George G. Harrap & Co., who also published Winston Churchill's memoirs and the popular illustrated children's book *The Cave Boy of the Stone Age*.

Ever since sharing lodgings in Cambridge with Prince Obolensky, Allan had wanted to visit Russia. 'I was intensely curious at the possibility of seeing something at first hand of the Soviet Union,' he later wrote. 'What was Russia really like? How did Russians live? I had only the haziest notion. For example, somehow I just couldn't imagine a Russian in a bathing-costume, enjoying himself at the seaside.' Instead, Allan had a vague mental image of a 'stern, inhuman and difficult people who always, or nearly always said "no".'

The party of British students travelled around Russia by train and bus, visiting museums and other cultural centres. In addition to Moscow and Leningrad, they toured Stalingrad and the resort town of Sochi. After a month, they returned to England, exhausted but satisfied by their trip. Allan then sat down and wrote an account of his travels, a manuscript he titled *Russian Holiday*. It contained various unremarkable anecdotes from his adventures behind the Iron Curtain, colour pictures that Allan had taken of everyday life on the Russian streets, along with an introduction by the MP and Nobel Peace Prize winner Sir Norman Angell. In his conclusion, Allan somewhat naively reported that 'we were always quite free to wander around' and our hosts never 'tried to force their opinions on us or made any attempt to influence us in any way in our impressions'. He added that he 'never saw a single unhappy, miserable or wretched child' and that 'the people look reasonably happy and contented (often smiling) and healthy'. Allan finished his book with the following passage:

> Ignorance is the very negation of civilisation. Ignorance breeds fear. Fear breeds hate. Hate breeds hysteria. And hysteria can lead to war. Another war could be utterly disastrous for the whole of mankind. The simple realisation that the average Russian (or the average Englishman) is an amiable, good-natured human being with much the same basic needs as the man in the street of any other nation, plus a belief in the mutability of human institutions and the natural evolution of the human spirit, are the first steps towards a more peaceful world.

In the spring of 1955, *Russian Holiday* was released, receiving favourable reviews in the press. It turned out that writing was an occupation to which Allan was well suited. Intellectually curious yet preferring his own company, hard-working and diligent, he was prepared to invest the long hours it takes to succeed as a writer.

Hoping to repeat the success of *Russian Holiday*, Allan travelled to Albania with the Albanian Society of Britain in August 1957. He again claimed that this was the first British group to enter this communist country since the war's end. During his trip, he befriended shoe-shine boys, custom officials and shopkeepers. And he wandered into a restricted town, where he was greeted with friendly curiosity by the locals (his group's arrival had been announced in that day's newspaper) before being arrested and briefly detained by the Albanian police.

Returning home, he wrote a long feature about his adventures for the *Daily Mail*. 'Albania is a medley of colour and sound against a background of wild but often beautiful mountains, blue skies and tropical heat,' he wrote. 'Constantly I found it almost impossible to believe I was in Europe and not India or Afghanistan.' Aged thirty-five, Allan appeared to have found his calling.

CASE NOTE

Heard back from retired police investigator Peter Devlin. 'I will gladly help you so far as I can,' he said, 'bearing in mind the Official Secrets Act and possible court orders.' We met at the Pain Quotidien restaurant next to the Nelson Mandela statue on London's South Bank. Was noisy but didn't mind as Devlin shared much interesting information on the investigation. He said that he never believed Wang Yam's story and that they had never been able to track down his alleged associates. 'There's no meat on those bones,' he said. He added that Wang Yam's lawyers had played games with them, not releasing their client's statement until Christmas Eve, just before the start of the trial. He thought that Wang Yam's long-term objective had been to gain control over 9 Downshire Hill. I am struck by how speculative this theory is – how can a property be transferred without a seller to agree or sign the necessary paperwork? And if Wang Yam had succeeded, surely someone would have noticed?

Met Wang Yam's lawyer James Mullion at his offices near Buckingham Palace. Said that his client had given permission for me to see his defence files but I was only allowed to see the documents relating to open court hearings. Mullion was candid that there may have been mistakes made in the defence trial strategy. Wang Yam was 'stubborn', he said, and refused to admit to any of the charges, despite the evidence that he had handled stolen goods being 'quite compelling'. He added that 'in my personal view, he would have been acquitted [of murder] if he had pleaded to dishonesty' in the first trial. I spent rest of afternoon looking through the defence files. They included witness statements, pathologist reports, crime scene images (including sketches of 9 Downshire Hill where body found) and a CV produced by Wang Yam. One of the police statements was taken from Jane Ainger, Allan Chappelow's next-door neighbour, who said that she had seen him at start of June 2006, less than two weeks before the police found the body. But Ainger's statement contradicts the police view that Chappelow's body lay in the house for weeks before being discovered. I need to find entomologists report and speak to Ainger. They can't both be right.

I spoke with Tony Hillier – lived at 36 Downshire Hill until 2013, former chair of the Heath & Hampstead Society. Gave an overview of local residents' attitudes. Allan Chappelow was regarded as a 'friendly eccentric' by the people on the street, Hillier said, and the reaction to his murder was one of 'shock and horror'. He added that there had been a 'fair amount of contact' between Chappelow and Steven Ainger, at number 8. 'There was a bit of tension there, I think.' It had something to do with planning issues. In contrast, the neighbour on the other side, Lady Listowel at number 10, was 'well disposed' towards Allan and 'kept an eye on him'. The other person who 'took a charitable interest in him' was Peter Tausig at number 11. Tausig made 'a point of getting to know him and protecting him, he took on that role, definitely, so I think the rest of the street thought there is a small army of people' who would take care of him.

Had tea and biscuits with Peter Tausig. He said he'd advised Allan to install a water meter to reduce costs and that he'd been 'extremely grateful'. After this, Allan 'started relying on me for things', including help with the Aingers next door whom Allan said 'were persecuting him' and 'making his life a misery'. Allan said that his house was 'the' house on the street, that he wanted to preserve it for history. At one point, Peter Tausig asked to see its interesting *features, but the old man 'said no', that it was in 'too bad a state'. Tausig only visited 9 Downshire Hill after Allan's death. He was shocked at its dilapidated condition. Beginning to understand the neighbours' dilemma: on the one hand they wished to help their vulnerable neighbour, on the other they wanted to respect his desire for privacy and independence. Were they too cautious?*

Hoping to find out more about Allan's trip to Albania, I contacted the Anglo Albanian Society. Pat Swire, the society's secretary, replied saying that in the 1950s there were two British–Albanian societies: the anti-communist Anglo-Albanian Association, with a mixed membership of British people interested in Albania and members of the Albanian diaspora in England; and the Albanian Society of Britain, which was more mono-British and pro-Communist. Allan was a member of the latter. Upon his return from Albania, Allan attended Albanian Society meetings 'but hardly spoke to people.' After the collapse of the Soviet Union, the two British–Albania groups merged but Allan continued to pay his dues. 'Our records show he certainly paid an annual subscription in November 2005,' Pat wrote, 'so he was a member when he died.' She offered to place an advert in their e-newsletter to see if any members remembered Allan.

Received a letter from prison governor saying my request to visit Wang Yam had been denied. According to the government's policy (PSI 37/2010), prisoners can be visited by journalists only under 'exceptional circumstances'. The only exception (according to PSI 37/2010) is if the journalist is able to persuade the Ministry of Justice that the face-to-face interview is in the public interest, such as a miscarriage of justice. I don't understand why I am being denied access, as Wang Yam says that he has suffered a miscarriage of justice. Maybe I just need to try harder.

4

THE VICTIM'S FAMILY

Late in 1958, Allan made contact with the publisher Charles Skilton. In addition to Luxor Press, which released titles such as *Lesbian Love Old and New*, *Phallic Worship: A History of Sex and Sex Rites*, and *Fanny Hill: Memoirs of a Woman of Pleasure*, Skilton also produced books of a less pornographic nature under his own name, including the highly successful Billy Bunter series.

Despite more than thirty biographies having been written about George Bernard Shaw since his death in 1950, Allan was able to persuade Skilton that there was room in the market for one more. Over the next two years, Allan conducted a series of interviews with the residents of Ayot St Lawrence – the postman, shopkeeper, chemist and various neighbours of Shaw's – a group of voices he called a 'symposium'. He believed that there were two sides to Shaw: there was the great 'GBS' figure familiar to the public, and the other, 'the human being – hidden by his mask or façade – whom I found to be virtually the opposite: sensitive and diffident almost to the point of shyness'. Allan's new book would be a celebration of the latter.

Allan spent the winter of 1960/1961 correcting the proofs for the book, which he was calling *Shaw the Villager and Human Being*.

Then, on 19 February 1961, Allan's mother Karen died. She was seventy-nine years old. The doctors said it was old age. Allan, who was forty-one at the time, was deeply distressed by his mother's death. He had always been closer to her than to his father, and whenever they had argued, it had been Karen who had calmed the situation. At the start of *Shaw the Villager*, which was published later that spring, he wrote: 'This book is dedicated to my mother. In memory of her never-failing sympathy and encouragement in all things, at all times.'

Unlike *Russian Holiday*, however, Allan's new book was not well received by the press. One critic who called himself the 'Literary Lounger' described it as 'interesting' but 'confused'. Another said that Allan's comments 'have the tone of an over-anxious host trying to keep the conversation going'. The most painful review was carried in the *Daily Mail*, which Allan considered to be 'his paper'. Under the headline 'GBS on rubbish and vice versa', the unnamed reviewer called *Shaw the Villager* an 'elephantine 344-page compilation', a 'jungle of trivia' and containing 'fatuities' from Shaw's barber such as: 'I was surprised at the interest Mr Shaw showed in everything, especially the electric clippers. He loved 'em. He was not a bit old-fashioned.'

In a 'Note to the reader' at the back of *Shaw the Villager*, Allan promised a second volume, which he said would be entitled *Shaw – 'The Chucker-Out'*. Responding to both the literary criticism and the loss of his mother, Allan threw himself even harder into his work.

Following Karen's death, and in contrast to Allan's withdrawal, Archibald Chappelow now went out more. He particularly enjoyed attending the Players' Theatre, a rowdy and somewhat lewd music hall in Covent Garden. During one of these visits Archibald met the theatre's manager Peggy March, an attractive and fun-loving woman twenty-five years his junior. Peggy shared Archibald's positive outlook on life, and they soon started going out together. Before long, he was buying her jewellery and had rented a flat for her in the West End. None of this particularly pleased Allan, who felt that his father was being disloyal to his mother and overgenerous with his limited funds. His father's business had never fully recovered after the war and Allan would have preferred that if money was to be spent, it should be invested in the house, which was in urgent need of repairs.

In the early autumn of 1965, with the weather turning unseasonably cool and damp, Allan's older brother Paul caught pneumonia. Despite his disability, Paul had progressed from selling cigarettes at a local shop to becoming book-keeper for a tobacco merchant based on Charles street in Central London. People with his moderate level of cerebral palsy usually lived close to the general population's life expectancy. It therefore came as a severe shock when Paul's condition worsened and, on 7 October 1965, he died in his bed in Downshire Hill. He was only forty-nine years old. In the space of four years, Allan had lost both his mother and brother.

His depression worsened with the publication in 1969 of *Shaw – 'The Chucker-Out'*. This book, which was a series of excerpted passages from Shaw's writing and speeches and contained an introduction by Vera Brittain, was universally panned. Stanley Weintraub for instance, a renowned Shaw critic writing in the *New York Times*, described the book as 'valuable not for Chappelow's editorial interpositions but in spite of them'.

The following summer, the mood in the house was lightened somewhat by the arrival of Torben Permin, Karen's 25-year-old great-nephew. Flying in from Copenhagen, Denmark, Torben's plan was to spend a week in London attending a language course to improve his English skills. The house was in a terrible mess; there had been few repairs done to it in years. Torben slept on a sofa on the first floor, the walls and furniture covered with dust. Every available space was filled with antiques and pictures in various stages of renovation. The bathroom was filthy, the tub green and black with algae and mould. For breakfast, Archibald cooked fried bacon and eggs for Torben on a small stove in the cramped cellar.

During his stay in London, Torben accompanied Allan's father and his girlfriend Peggy when they went out to the theatre, cinema and restaurants. Allan refused to join them, instead staying in his bedroom. If Allan and his father saw each other on the stairs or near the bathroom, Torben observed, they might say 'hello' or 'good morning', but that was the extent of their interaction. He was told that the only time that father and son sat at the same table was for Christmas lunch.

Letters written to family members were one of the few ways that Allan interacted with the outside world, and provide a rare insight into his state of mind at this time. On 17 December 1973, for instance, he wrote to his cousin Margaret Ainsworth in Austin, Texas:

> As regards any contribution I can make to the family tree, the fact is that a) I do not know a great deal about it and b) although I am interested and would like to do some research on it, I am too desperately busy on a second edition of my book *Shaw – The Chucker-Out* to have a minute to spare – and genealogical research – as I expect you have discovered – can be a very difficult and time-consuming affair.

Allan no longer wrote for the *Daily Mail* and stopped selling his photographs to other newspapers. He spent long hours in his room reading and re-reading the letters, speeches and manuscripts of George Bernard Shaw. When asked, he told his friends that he was working on his next book about the great writer. The truth was that there was little to show for his efforts.

In September 1976, Allan's father Archie died in his bed at home. He had just turned ninety-four. Allan arranged for his father's body to be removed from the house and for it to be cremated. He chose not to intern his father's ashes in the grave shared by his mother and brother at the cemetery in Highgate. Nor did he organise a memorial service, to the surprise of his British, Danish and American cousins.

Front door of 9 Downshire Hill, June 2006

Manuscripts blocking
doorway, June 2006

Allan Chappelow's missing-person
photograph handed out by police,
June 2006

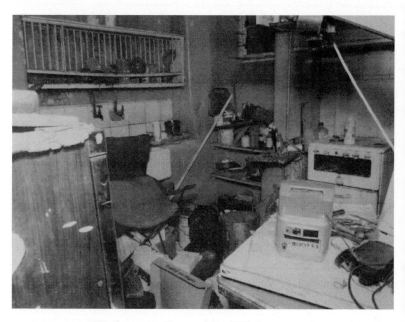

Kitchen at 9 Downshire Hill, June 2006

Allan Chappelow's bed
at crime scene, June 2006

Allan Chappelow's body with two shoes
under manuscripts, 2006

Exterior of 9 Downshire Hill, June 2006

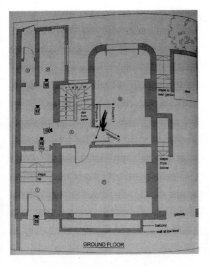

Ground floor sketch of
9 Downshire Hill

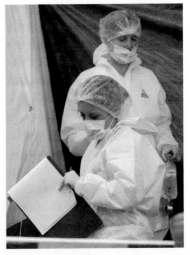

Entomologists at 9 Downshire
Hill, June 2006

Allan Chappelow's shirt, June 2006

Living room at 9 Downshire Hill,
June 2006

Back room at 9 Downshire Hill, June 2006

Courtroom sketch of Wang Yam,
January 2008

Wang Yam's Curry Paradise
receipt, evidence submitted
in court

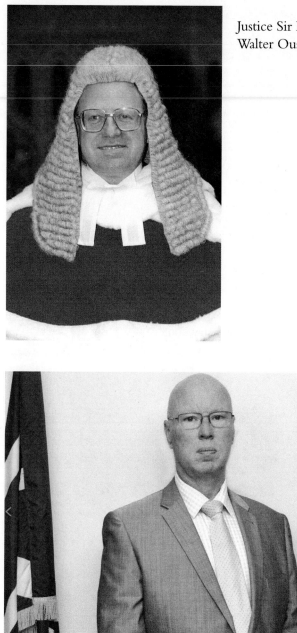

Justice Sir Duncan Brian Walter Ouseley

Pete Lansdown, former Senior Investigating Officer, Metropolitan Police

Soon after his father's death, Allan decided it was time to purchase a new motorbike. He parked his old Norton in the front garden, covered it with a tarpaulin and went shopping. There was really only one choice for him, the Vincent HRD 1000, also known as the 'Black Shadow', a terrifyingly fast bike that boomed as it flashed past. One day, when riding down the street, he was stopped by a policeman and cautioned for not wearing protective clothing. Allan purchased a soft leather pre-war helmet, and from then on was seen with it on his head whenever he rode through the Hampstead streets, an old grey gaberdine Mackintosh coat tied by a rope around his waist, flapping behind him in the wind.

It was around this time that Allan met John Sparrow, who lived nearby in Dartmouth Park with his wife Peggy. John and Allan had both decided to earn a little extra cash by working for the post office during the Christmas rush. After a week's basic training, they found themselves sitting next to each other, sorting mail into small wooden racks according to postal code. 'He was a friendly guy,' remembered John Sparrow. 'He was never short of words, he could talk about anything.' After two weeks, the temporary work finished but their friendship continued.

Perhaps because his father had just died, Allan talked openly about their relationship, describing him as a 'brute', who treated his wife and son cruelly and who was 'extremely unpleasant' to those around him. A man who 'mooched around' and 'never greeted people'. His father never fixed up the house, Allan said, because he didn't want to change its original state. The plumbing, therefore, was primitive, with many of the water pipes running along the outside of the house, with the result that they often froze. From this conversation, and others, it appeared to John Sparrow that it was 'quite possible', even 'likely', that Archibald had beaten his sons and wife.

Yet Allan was also slippery with the truth. He told his new friend that he hadn't seen action during the war because he was obliged to look after his disabled brother. He also said that he had talked his way into Cambridge because he did not have the necessary entry qualifications. In addition, he told Sparrow that he'd had romances with numerous girls and that he would soon get married. Given Allan's body odour and his habit of wearing dirty clothes, not to mention the run-down condition of his house, Sparrow didn't believe any of these stories. He believed them to be 'fantasies'.

John Sparrow was one of the few, if not only, friends that Allan invited to the house, and this happened just once. Upon entering 9 Downshire Hill, Sparrow noted that an enormous amount of old and valuable furniture was stored in the downstairs rooms. On the upper floors, there were columns of books and writing papers. 'He was quite secretive,' said Sparrow. 'There was a mystery about the house.'

If Chappelow was to meet with friends, it was always on his terms. He would mount his motorcycle and 'make the rounds', as he called it, dropping off Christmas presents or stopping in for a drink. Without a home telephone it was hard for people to reach him to make appointments and he was constant in denying entry to his house.

Despite criticising his father for the very same thing, Allan also refused to invest in the house. He did not have the funds to restore the property to its former glory, and rather than updating the electrics, plumbing and heating systems, which he felt would alter the house's historic fabric, he chose to do nothing. So it was that the building started to crumble around him. The garden became overgrown, the paint on the walls cracked and peeled. Inside, the stacks of papers, ancient books, half-restored paintings and old furniture grew into piles, then unmanageable heaps, until finally there was no more available floor space and it became impossible to pass through many of the rooms. The plumbing ceased to work; the cold-water tank fell through the attic floor and was not repaired. The kitchen stove became yet another surface upon which to store belongings.

Hampstead Village had also changed since the time of Allan's youth. During the 1960s and 1970s, its reputation had grown as a desirable place to live and, given its proximity to central London and its attractive mix of Regency, Georgian and Victorian houses, as well as the benefits of living next to the Heath, house prices soared. Larger homes were split and separated into flats, allowing landlords to gather higher rents. Equally, the traditional shopkeepers were forced out by prohibitive leases and rising council taxes. Hegner's the art supply shop, Morris the pharmacist, Rumbold's the baker and Ruby's the garage closed down and were replaced by fashion boutiques, tapas bars, designer cook shops and new blocks of flats. A similar fate faced the family-owned delicatessen, jeweller and coffee shop, which were superceded by chain stores and fancy restaurants. Finally in 1980, McDonald's purchased a property on Hampstead High Street. This was perhaps one step too far for the local residents, who set up a campaign to prevent the burger chain from obtaining planning permission, a dispute that would rumble on for more than a decade.

Given the increase in market values, it would have been easy, sensible even, for Allan to move to a smaller, more manageable property. Indeed, a week didn't go by when an envelope wasn't pushed through his door asking if he was interested in selling. But Allan, like his father, was deeply committed to keeping the house. To Allan, 9 Downshire Hill was far more than a Regency building in a desirable location. He felt comfortable here, he knew its every nook and corner. It reminded him of his mother and brother. Many might not enjoy living in the increasingly squalid conditions, but Allan didn't mind it at all. He would do anything to protect the property. It was his home.

*

Throughout the morning of 16 June 2006, the designated family liaison officer Gerald Pickering tried to establish contact with Allan Chappelow's relatives. He had spoken with two of the victim's English cousins, Michael and James Chappelow, but this was a dead end. The cousins were distant, barely knowing Allan Chappelow, and unable to provide contacts for other family members. James Chappelow admitted that he had never even met his cousin; the one time he attempted to pay a visit to 9 Downshire Hill, his knock went unanswered. Equally, Michael had not seen Allan Chappelow for years, and had no useful intelligence to share.

Pickering, however, had one family lead. It was during their first search of 9 Downshire Hill that the police had found a letter from Allan's American cousin, Patty Ainsworth. It was dated 4 March 2006, a few weeks before his plane trip to the USA.

Through Interpol, the international police network, Pickering made contact with the Attorney General's office in Austin, Texas. A few days later, two members of the AG's office arrived at Patty's small clapboard house in Delwood, a quiet neighbourhood in the south-east of the city. When there was no reply, they walked around the side of the house and found Patty unloading groceries from her car. Showing their IDs, they asked her to confirm her name and then told her, without warning, that her cousin Allan Chappelow had been found dead at his house in London.

'How did he die?' she asked just as the men were turning to leave. 'He was murdered,' they said, and asked her to get in touch with Gerry Pickering from the Metropolitan Police in London. He wanted to know the last time she had heard from Allan following his return to England. A few hours later, Pickering received an email from Patty Ainsworth. 'Detective Pickering,' she wrote. 'The letter that I received from Allan was written on May 4 and postmarked May 6. He talks about his trip to Austin. If you need a copy of this letter, just let me know and I can mail or fax it to you.' A few hours later,

Pickering replied that the letter was important as it would prove when Allan was still alive. He would indeed like to see it, he said, but suggested she send a copy so that the original did not get lost in the post.

Pickering received another email from Patty Ainsworth the following day; this time she attached a copy of Allan's 4 May letter. 'I have been in touch with Michael Chappelow,' she wrote, 'and we were wondering if you have by chance found a will in Allan's papers.' Pickering replied the same day, explaining that he had had the letter examined by the post office and they had said that it was posted between 6.30 p.m. on Friday 5 May and midday on Saturday 6 May. 'So you can keep hold of the letter as it is now an exhibit in the case. We are still trying to trace Allan's last movements.'

With regard to her cousin's will, Pickering said that they had been unable to find a copy in 9 Downshire Hill and that they would be checking with the victim's banks to see if he had a solicitor. 'At present the house will be handed over to the local council later this week as we have not been able to trace any next of kin. Meaning siblings, brothers, sisters or first cousins.' The message was clear: she and Michael Chappelow were unlikely to benefit from Allan Chappelow's substantial inheritance.

It didn't take much longer for Pickering to track down Allan Chappelow's Danish cousins. While looking through his 1994 diary, which the crime scene managers had collected from 9 Downshire Hill, Pickering spotted a Christmas card list. On top of this was the name 'Merete'. He also discovered a business card with the same name, and decided to make contact.

By telephone, Merete Karlsborg confirmed that she was the daughter of Allan's first cousin – her grandfather Aage Permin was Karen's brother – making her the closest living relative he'd found to date. Merete then introduced the British detective to three cousins with equally close ties to Allan, one of whom was Torben Permin.

Given that Torben spoke excellent English and had visited Allan in London, he was nominated to be the family's main point of contact for the British police officers.

When Torben asked about funeral arrangements for his cousin, Pickering said that it would be up to the family to decide, though they would have to wait until the investigating officers were prepared to release the body. Pickering said he would be back in touch as soon as he had an update.

CASE NOTE

———————

Called probate office in London. Allan Chappelow died intestate, i.e. without a will. According to the 2006 court decision, his nearest relative or relatives inherited 9 Downshire Hill and other assets (worth over £4 million at time of his death). The court record referred to the lawyer who managed the probate and also the name of one of Allan's relatives: Torben Permin. Called lawyer who said that Torben Permin lived in Copenhagen, but recalled no other details. I was only able to find one 'Torben Permin' on the internet, so sent him a message.

Had tea with a friend of a friend who is a senior QC. I asked him to explain the basics of how a criminal case proceeds through the court system in the UK. We also talked about the near impossibility for a journalist to access prisoners and difficulty obtaining court transcripts (compared to USA). The QC said, 'I am not a fan of open justice.' Added that the UK system worked well with barristers at its centre to make sure it runs efficiently and smoothly.

Anxious about the secret trial, my publisher has decided to make use of outside legal counsel. I have been asked to summarise the research that I have collated and detail my sources. As a journalist I need to protect my sources but also want to make process as smooth as possible. Told publisher that outside counsel cannot share material with anyone else.

Following the advert placed in the Albanian Society newsletter, I heard that Allan had visited Albania for a second time in September 1993. Antonia Young, who also went on this trip, recalled Allan saying that he had been a 'teacher' and that she never 'got to bottom of his background.' She added that 'He didn't seem to have original ideas' and that he merely repeated what others had said. Antonia put me in touch with Steve Cook (Oregon USA), the organiser of the 1993 trip. By email, Steve wrote, 'I suppose we are talking about the same guy, but it is difficult for me to believe that the Allan I knew was a famous writer. He was one of the oddest people that I've ever met, seemed to be in a fog the entire ten days that we trekked through the Albanian Alps.' Cook added that, 'I was saddened to hear that he had been murdered. My wife did some Google searching and we read about the whole affair, and with shock.'

Was watching television when the telephone rang. My wife said 'don't take it', but the number on my phone looked unfamiliar so I picked it up. 'Hi, it's Wang Yam,' said the voice on the other end of the line. 'Do you know who I am?' We spoke for over an hour. He said that he had just been moved from Whitemoor Prison (Category A) to Lowdham Grange (Category B) where they were allowed to make calls. He was calling on a pre-paid wireless handset from his prison cell. We agreed to talk again the following night at 5 p.m.

5

THE INVESTIGATION

In the summer of 1993, the now 73-year-old Allan Chappelow saw an advert in *Outside* magazine. An American adventurer called Steve Cook was organising a ten-day trek through the Albanian Alps and was looking for people to join. With the communist regime having fallen only two years earlier, and with his 1950s trip to Albania still fresh in his mind, Allan submitted a letter of application.

Two months later, Allan flew to Tirana, Albania's capital, from where he took a bus to the ancient city of Shkoder in the country's mountainous northwest. There he met Steve Cook and three other Americans. Cook was surprised to find that Allan – or 'Mr Allan' as he quickly became known by the porters – appeared totally unprepared. He was wearing blue mechanic's overalls and a pair of thin shoes. He hadn't paid any attention to the notices Cook had sent about rugged trekking or the need for stout boots. Concerned for the safety of the elderly Englishman, Cook asked if Allan was ready to go. 'I'll be fine,' Allan insisted.

They set off on foot the next morning: to Bajram Curri, up the Valbona River and then starting at 200m above sea level, up and over the Valbona Pass, a climb of 1700m. As they pushed forward, the cragged treeless peaks of the 'Accursed Mountains' towered above them. Cook later recalled that 'Mr. Allan crapped out just a little way up the pass. So we enlisted some Albanians with a mountain pony, piled Mr. Allan onto a pack saddle with rope stirrups and away we went.' The path had been used for centuries by the locals but had not yet been made safe for tourists. As such it had some perilous sections, with narrow sharp drops of over a hundred metres over the side. 'Mr. Allan' however, 'was oblivious, hanging on with one hand and taking random photos with the other.' Finally the going became too treacherous even for the intrepid Londoner. The Albanian wranglers instructed Allan to dismount and hold onto the pony's tail. He was then dragged up the remainder of the steep slope.

Having rested a while, the group walked down the other side of the mountain and spent the night at the small village of Theth. The next day they trekked to Selce in the north, but again Allan found it difficult to manage, so the group returned to Theth for another night. Over the following days they rode in the back of ancient Chinese trucks along hazardous roads to Shkodra, Tamara and Vermosh, where they explored a little before returning to Theth. Again, Cook remembered Allan as being relaxed about these 'dangerous' excursions.

At one point Allan pointed to one of the group's members and asked Cook 'who is that person?' It was Cook's wife Marash who had been with them for eight days. Another of the American participants said that he had taken a look at Allan's journal, and it was filled with 'nonsensical scribbles and gibberish'. Allan told the group that he was from Oxford, and implied that he had been a professor. Later, he said that he worked as a postman. Throughout this trip Allan 'never seemed to have any idea what was going on,' Cook said 'or where we were, even though I patiently repeated things over and over.' Cook also noted that Allan wore the same overalls every day and that he never took a shower.

After ten days, which included a lot of riding in the back of old trucks and not much actual trekking, the group returned to Shkodra. They said their goodbyes, and Allan returned to Tirana from where he flew home. Over the next few months, Allan repeatedly wrote to Cook asking questions about the trip, along the lines of 'On this day where were we?' and 'What did we do on this day?' That Christmas, Allan sent Cook a card with a naked lady standing inside a red phone box in London. Besides the festive greeting, the message was lost: the writing inside was almost indecipherable.

Two years after Allan's return from Albania, a new couple moved into number 8, next door to Allan Chappelow: Steve and Jane Ainger. Within a short time, the Aingers proposed building an extension that would abut his property. The result, Allan now told his other neighbours Peter Tausig and Lady Listowel, would be to transform his house from a detached property into one that was semi-detached, thus ruining its historic and architectural splendour. How could this be the 'Manor House', he asked, if it was connected to another building?

Throughout the late 1990s and into the new millennium, Allan engaged in a constant war of words with the Aingers. In January 1998, for instance, he submitted a four-page objection to the council in response to his neighbours' planning application. 'I have lived here for the past sixty-four years,' he wrote, 'and throughout the years we have never had the slightest problem with the previous occupiers at no. 8. Both were authors, like myself, and thus members of a category particularly respecting and needing peace and quiet, and absence of noise and other distractions which might interfere with their work.' He then added, 'In Wordsworth's words, "Recollection is tranquility".'

As he moved through his seventies, Allan Chappelow became more solitary; a hoarder and an eccentric. For more than twenty years he had lived alone, and the condition of 9 Downshire Hill ever worsened. He was now rarely seen on his motorcycle, although sometimes he fiddled with it in his garden. Once a day he visited the public library on Keats Grove, a five-minute walk from his house, where he read the *Daily Mail*, before returning home. Typically, that was the entirety of his social interaction.

In early 2001, Allan Chappelow befriended Thomas Carr, a 56-year-old carpenter who lived with his wife in a small flat in Highgate, a twenty-minute bus ride from Downshire Hill. From time to time, Chappelow asked Carr to help him with house repairs. The handyman was the only person granted permission to enter 9 Downshire Hill.

Carr helped around the house, for instance removing sections of wood panelling from the basement. He was never asked to fix the broken bathrooms, however, or the holes in the roof. Indeed, to prevent water from entering his house, Chappelow climbed onto the roof himself and covered various sections with large sheets of black plastic.

'The only time that I knew Mr Chappelow to be in his garden', Carr later said, 'was when he was either going out or coming home. He had little regard for his furniture. A lot of the rooms were full of junk to the point where you could hardly open the doors.' Chappelow never used the back door, he added, and he couldn't have done so without moving the furniture stacked against it. 'The house and its contents', he said, 'were in a bad state of neglect.'

Carr also told the police that Room Six, where Chappelow's body was later found, was quite well organised. It was here that his employer stored his manuscripts, stacked neatly on metal shelves arranged against the wall.

DS Devlin spent the rest of the day on 16 June 2006 focusing on what had happened to the victim's money. Following a series of phone calls to credit card companies, bank managers and telephone operators, reams of statements, emails, faxes and other correspondence started arriving at Operation Barnesdale's headquarters in Colindale.

Allan Chappelow had four bank accounts: RBS, HSBC, ING and Alliance & Leicester. He also had a Sainsbury's credit card that was paid off automatically by direct debit from his HSBC account. These bank accounts held less than £1,000 between them, the exception being the ING account, which boasted a little over £52,000. The elderly writer also held a stock portfolio, including over 40,000 shares in the entertainment company Rank. These shares occasionally produced dividends that were sent to him by mail.

Given the alert raised by HSBC, Devlin was interested to see if Allan had suffered any other fraudulent activity. In talks with the victim's banks, Devlin discovered that on 26 May 2006, an application had been made to create an online account for Allan's RBS account and an activation code was sent automatically to 9 Downshire Hill. This was suspicious given that the victim was not known to use the internet. Six days later, on 1 June at 12.22 p.m., the RBS online activation code was used from a computer (which was traced to the Internet Lounge in Charing Cross Road) to generate a password and PIN number. Shortly afterwards, these were used to view Allan Chappelow's online RBS account, including a check of his direct debits and bill payments.

Later that day, at 2.26 p.m., a call was made to ING Direct from a cell tower near Langham Place, a twenty-minute walk from Charing Cross Road. The caller said he wanted to withdraw money but had forgotten his PIN number. When he was unable to answer the security questions this account was blocked and a new PIN number was sent to Chappelow's home address.

Four days later, just before noon on 5 June, Allan's ING Direct account was accessed from a computer located at Crystal Amusements

Ltd, a cyber café on Charing Cross Road, by someone using the new PIN number. After this person failed to enter the memorable date, a call was made to ING and, having correctly provided the PIN, the caller was allowed to change the memorable date to one of their choosing. A few minutes later, the ING online account was successfully accessed via the internet, and £20,000 was transferred to Allan's RBS account. Two days later, shortly after 4 p.m. on 7 June, Allan's RBS account was accessed from the Qaran internet café on Pratt Street. An online mandate was set up and £10,000 was transferred to an account called 'Money TT reference Jenny'.

Then, on 13 June, halfway through the second day's search, the PIN number for Allan's Sainsbury's card was changed at an ATM outside of Tesco in Kentish Town, and soon after, £20 was withdrawn at Abbey National a little down the road. That night, Allan Chappelow's credit card was used again, this time at the Curry Paradise Indian restaurant in South End Green, less than a ten-minute walk from 9 Downshire Hill.

It was just after lunch on 16 June – three days after this last transaction and a day after the homicide investigation had been officially launched – that Detective Sergeant Peter Devlin first called the Sainsbury's credit card fraud unit. Normally, Devlin would have been unable to obtain information from a financial institution without a Production Order, a five-page official request that required time and effort to put together and might take weeks to process. Yet that evening, given the seriousness of the case, the clerk on the other end of the line was eager to help. It was during this phone call that Devlin learned about the recent use of Allan Chappelow's card at Curry Paradise.

Having updated Pete Lansdown on the news and received approval to interview the restaurant staff, Devlin jumped into his car and, together with Police Constable Stewart O'Brien, made his way towards the Curry Paradise in Hampstead. For the first time since the investigation had started, Peter Devlin felt that he was on the trail of Allan Chappelow's killer.

A little after 4 p.m. on Friday 16 June 2006, Peter Devlin and Stewart O'Brien pulled up outside the Curry Paradise, an Indian restaurant sandwiched between the Hampstead branch of the independent bookseller Daunt Books and an estate agent's office, and less than a hundred metres from Hampstead Heath train station.

Inside, the police officers met the manager of Curry Paradise, Ali Shahid, and his head waiter Rafique Uddin. The Paradise, as it was known locally, was a sophisticated venue. With its modern oak and glass finishing, halogen lights and bare brick walls, the interior evoked the atmosphere of a Californian bistro more than a tandoori shack. While O'Brien spoke to the waiter by the bar counter, Devlin sat with the owner in the tabled area. Shahid confirmed that on 13 June an oriental-looking couple had eaten dinner at the restaurant. When they were finished the man had asked for the bill, saying that they were in a rush as they were late for an appointment to view a house. The customer's credit card was rejected by the machine, however, so he had then telephoned the bank. He had called himself 'Allan', recalled Shahid. The bank had refused to unblock the card so the customer, who had no cash with him, had left his phone with the restaurant manager as a deposit, and promised to come back in a few minutes to pay the bill.

An hour later the female customer returned, and paid the bill partly with her credit card and partly in cash. She left a £2 tip. Shahid listed the male customer's features: he was in his forties, he thought, approximately five feet ten inches tall, spoke English but with a strong Asian accent, with short grey receding hair at the front and a day or two's growth of stubble. This was a fairly close match to the postman Sullman's description of the man near Downshire Hill. Shahid also provided a profile of the woman: about five feet three inches tall, also spoke with an accent. Her hair was black and tied in a ponytail. He was positive he could ID the man, Shahid said, if he saw him again.

Devlin glanced up and saw his colleague walking towards him looking excited. 'He used a silver flip-phone,' O'Brien said, 'to call the bank. He used his phone.' Devlin, however, didn't understand his colleague's point. The bank would have only spoken to the fraudster, O'Brien explained, if they thought they were talking to Allan Chappelow. They would have identified their customer through his SIM card. But the restaurant waiter remembered that the phone that the customer had used was a silver flip-phone, which didn't match the description of Allan Chappelow's handset. This meant that Allan's SIM card had been used inside the fraudster's phone. Scotland Yard's Crime Intelligence Unit (CIU) might be able to find the fraudster's home address through the flip-phone's unique IMEI number.

Devlin immediately called Bill Jephson and asked him to make an emergency request to Scotland Yard. With luck, they could use the data captured during the phone call to the credit card company and supply a street address for the handset's owner. The problem, Devlin realised, was that it was now late on a Friday afternoon. It was unlikely, therefore, that anyone at CIU would get to this until Monday morning. Devlin just hoped that by the time they heard back the fraudster would still be living at his address.

CASE NOTE

Wang Yam called at 5 p.m exactly. He asked for my landline number as it was cheaper to call. I gave it to him, thinking it would make it more likely we would speak. I should have first checked with my wife and daughter. I asked him about how he spent his days and he said that he liked music class best. He then sang me a song that he had written. He also said that he wasn't sleeping well (his cellmate snores). We agreed that the phone call was probably being monitored by the prison authorities. He spoke at length about his childhood and his time growing up in China. I questioned him about the crime. 'Did you kill Allan Chappelow?' I asked. 'No,' he said (calmly), 'I am innocent.' He admitted receiving the victim's stolen cheques and credit cards from a Chinese gang, but said that he had never met Allan Chappelow or been to his house. He then raised an interesting question: Why, if as the police claimed the mail fraudster returned to 9 Downshire Hill _after_ he knew that Allan Chappelow was dead, would he not have searched the house and removed the passport, address book, credit cards and PIN numbers lying in plain view on the old man's bed? This seems a reasonable point.

Allan's Danish cousin Torben Permin responded. He works as an engineer for a telephone company and lives in one of Copenhagen's suburbs. Wary at first, *he offered to help when I explained that I wanted to know more about Allan's life. Torben said that his cousin and goddaughter Merete had received a larger share of Allan's inheritance as she was an only child (Torben's share was split with his brother and sister). Though this followed the rules set down by the British courts the disparity had caused bad feelings in the family and he had not spoken to Merete for years. He added that they might have some of Allan's old letters and photos. If he found them he would let me know.*

Also received a letter from the Metropolitan Police's Events Sponsorship & Copyright Manager saying that he would be happy to provide police officers to be interviewed for my book, but that he would charge me £775.15 for this service. He stated that prior to publication I would have to 'obtain the prior written consent' of the Metropolitan Police and of the interviewee. Effectively this means they want editorial control over what I'm writing, I'm obviously not happy with that. Need to find a way to talk to officers involved with the case without getting permission of higher-ups.

6

THE PATHOLOGIST

Despite the impression given to his neighbours, family members and journalists that he was a retiring recluse, Allan Chappelow had the appetite for at least one more international trip. On 18 February 2006, three months before he was murdered, he wrote to his cousin Patty Ainsworth in Austin, Texas and told her that he was planning to visit.

In his letter, Allan explained that the *Daily Mail* had been trying to support the ailing travel industry by offering free return tickets to the USA. Over the winter, he had collected the necessary twenty-five coupons and he was now in a position to travel at half the normal cost. He would be flying from London to Boston on 26 March 2006, where he would spend three days researching at the Boston College library, and then he would fly on to Austin on 29 March to conduct research at Texas University's Harry Ransom Center, keepers of the Shaw archive and one of the largest collections of literary and cultural artifacts in the world. 'I have been thinking about accepting your mother's invitation (of thirty years ago!),' he wrote, 'but somehow it has not become a reality till now, and I naturally want to make the most of my great opportunity.' Would Patty like to see him?

Allan arrived in Austin-Bergstrom International Airport on Wednesday 29 March 2006. He was excited to make contact with his American family and to carry out research at the University of Texas. Equidistant from Houston and Dallas, Austin was the state's capital and home to a little over 700,000 people. Located on the banks of the Colorado River and only a short drive from fertile hills and canyons, Austin was one of the nation's fastest developing conurbations, newcomers attracted to its diverse landscape and cultural dynamism. Over the previous decade, it had become famous for its alternative rock scene and the South by Southwest film festival, the small city becoming known for being a liberal island in a sea of conservativeness. As with the rest of Texas, spring temperatures could soar in Austin. Indeed, when Allan stepped off the plane, it was 26 degrees celcius outside. The papers said that by the week's end it would top 37 degrees.

From the airport, Allan took a taxi to the International Hostel on Lakeshore Drive in the city's western suburbs. There he was shown a dormitory with four white metal bunk-beds. Thankfully for the 86-year-old, a bottom bunk was free. A rough grey blanket, a sheet and a thin pillow lay folded on the mattress. He was also given a towel and, in return for a $5 deposit, a locker where he could store his suitcase. After a fitful night's sleep in the airless room, he ate from the breakfast buffet laid out in the dining area next to the hostel entrance: Cheerios, white bread, peanut butter, jam, an urn filled with weak but hot coffee. There was also a large stainless steel bowl from which residents were encouraged to grab an apple or banana. 'Eat Healthy', declared a poster. The blackboard hanging on the wall told him about the day's cultural offerings: a yoga class at noon, a mid-afternoon workshop on transgender politics, and a sunset walk along the beach.

The lady at the front desk said that the best way to get into town was by the number 7 bus, and sold him a day pass. After a ten-minute walk up a busy road, cane in hand and bag over his shoulder,

Allan waited fifteen minutes for the bus. Though early, it was already brutally hot outside and his clothes were sweat-soaked by the time he was seated. Rumbling along East Riverside Drive's potholed six-lane highway, past car mechanics, payday lenders and cantinas, the bus stopped every two hundred metres, picking up Hispanic workers on their way to the morning shift. After ten minutes the bus turned sharply right, crossing the Colorado River at the narrow South 1st Street bridge. They were now in downtown. Then up the numbered streets, past coffee bars and entrances to glass-faced towers – Austin had far fewer high-rise buildings than many other American cities – stopping near the steps of Texas's white-domed Capitol, and onto the university campus.

After a forty-minute ride, Allan disembarked, and walked another ten minutes along the dusty Martin Luther King Jr Boulevard, his limp more pronounced after the exertion. Finally, he arrived at the Harry Ransom Center, the central library and archive for the University of Texas. Entering the cube-shaped concrete building, he took the elevator to the second floor and explained to the receptionist that he was here to research the author and playwright George Bernard Shaw.

'I remember him well,' the research librarian, Richard Workman, reported; 'he was a colourful character.' Richard had shown Allan how to use the computer system to request documents from the archive. Each day he sat in the same wooden chair, near the research librarian's main station, and leafed through the files he had requested from the repository. 'He was a little curt,' said Richard. 'Even though he came here every day for a month he did not engage with the staff.' Such behaviour was unusual, he pointed out. Working from 9 a.m., when the library opened, to 5 p.m., when it closed, he was able to go through each and every item in their George Bernard Shaw collection.

Sitting in this quiet library 5,000 miles from England, Allan came across an exchange of letters between himself and Shaw which had been written more than half a century earlier. There were two parts to the correspondence; Shaw's brief hand-corrected response declaring himself too old and frail for visits, and Allan's typed second letter in which he asked if Shaw remembered his great-great-grandfather Joseph Stevens. Allan was thrilled by this discovery. Over the next few days, he continued to review the files. Of particular interest to him was Shaw's later years. In his spidery handwriting he made a note of the documents that he wished to photocopy.

One evening, Allan asked the guard at the library's front entrance if he could place a telephone call to a cousin who happened to live in Austin. Apologising, the guard explained that he didn't have access to a phone, and suggested that Allan find someone who was still working in one of the administration offices. Upstairs on the third floor, Allan found librarian Tom Best still at his desk. Explaining that he needed help, Allan handed over a letter from his cousin with the words 'hope you'll visit us someday in Texas', along with a telephone number. Tom agreed to help but found that the telephone number didn't work. Noting the age of the man standing in front of him and knowing that public transport didn't run to the suburbs, Tom offered to drive Allan to his cousin's house in his old pick-up truck. 'It would be a lark,' Tom recalled thinking.

No one was home when they arrived at the small white clapboard-sided house in the Delwood neighbourhood. Tom knocked on a few nearby doors while Allan stood by the pick-up truck in the blazing sun. When nobody answered, Allan said he would wait at the house but, concerned about the high temperature, Tom offered to drive him back to the hostel, suggesting they leave a note for Allan's cousin on her door.

As they drove along I-35 in the heavy traffic, they chatted. 'My old truck was low on fuel and threatening to overheat,' Tom remembered. It was noisy, there was no air conditioning and Allan was hard of hearing, so they were yelling at each other. They mostly talked politics, both complaining about their leaders. Tom said something unflattering about George Bush and then Allan waved his arms indignantly. 'Blair is no socialist!' he huffed loudly. 'He's a capitalist, round and round!' An hour later, Tom dropped his new friend off at the hostel and, promising to stay in touch, headed back into the evening's congestion. 'I remember Mr C as old-fashioned in his manner,' Tom said, 'precise, methodical possibly, pleasantly exasperating.'

At 10.20 a.m. on Saturday 17 June 2006, Dr Robert Chapman commenced the autopsy of Allan Chappelow. The examination took place on the ground floor of St Pancras Hospital in north London, a two-storey red-brick building that was overdue for modernisation. It was a large mortuary filled with stainless steel gurneys, trays full of gleaming instruments and a polished concrete floor at whose centre lay a drain. Dressed in blue scrubs, blue hat, gloves and face mask, Chapman reported the basic information into a digital recorder. This included the date, start time and location of the autopsy, along with his name and those of the four members of Lansdown's team who were in the room.

Having taken extensive colour photographs of Allan Chappelow, including close-ups of his injuries, the pathologist started the external examination. He noted that the victim's blue sweater was covered by congealed wax and there was an extensive burnt area to the front of the garment. He also found that the red sweater and sleeveless vest underneath also bore burn marks and damage to the sleeves. Next to the skin he found a cream-coloured corset secured by Velcro which was worn to hold in the chest and stomach. In the pockets of the blue trousers he found a pen, a scrap of blank paper, a tape measure, a pen top and a plastic film container. The sweater had been tucked into the trousers with the braces on top. The trousers were undone and unzipped. Under the victim's head was a purplish blue rain jacket which had been contaminated with bodily fluids and was burnt on its outside.

The pathologist noted that the body was 1.69 metres (5 feet 6½ inches) in height. He was of slim build and, despite his age, had kept his brown hair. The body was heavily decomposed and the skin was discoloured. Maggot damage was widespread, he observed, and the skin was leathery and yellowy-brownish in colour, particularly around the hands and knees, due to dehydration or what the pathologist called 'mummification'. Chapman found that extensive injuries had been suffered to the head and neck area, including the jaw, facial bones and cheekbones. Critically, he found that there were 'very severe injuries' to the bones of the skull on both sides of the head, forehead, nose and upper jaw; there were fractures of the larynx 'indicative of pressure applied to the front of the neck by hand or as a result of a blow' (suggesting strangulation); as well as further fractures to the ribs 'resulting from blows to the upper part of the chest and lower part of the trunk'.

After approximately four hours, Chapman concluded his examination. In his report he stated that Allan Chappelow had suffered a minimum of five heavy blows which had resulted in multiple injuries to the skull. Given the extent of the wounds, it was more likely that he was struck with a heavy object such as a hammer or piece of wood than simply stamping or punching. The cause of death was given as 'head injury'.

The pathologist's report was typed up and emailed over to Lansdown, who picked up on the burn marks and the congealed wax. Maybe Chappelow had been using candles for illumination, as there was no power in the house, and some of the wax had spilled? Or perhaps the intruder had dripped wax onto the victim to force him to reveal his credit card PIN number?

There were still too many holes in the narrative to understand how and why Chappelow had died, Pete Lansdown realised. To crack the case, it was essential to unearth more of the victim's story. Why was this strange man living by himself in a ruin in the leafy environs of north-west London? Who was Allan Chappelow?

A few days after leaving the note on his cousin's door in Austin, Allan received a message from her at his hostel. The following night, Patty Ainsworth and her husband Steve collected Allan from the library and took him out for dinner at the Salt Lick barbecue, a family-run restaurant 6 miles outside of Austin. Over ribs, mashed potato and corn bread, Allan told Patty and Steve that he had lived in the same house for more than six decades and was 'proud of it'. They also talked about politics, and Allan said that he was 'fearful of the Chinese' and again criticised the policies of Tony Blair.

Allan told Patty that now that he was in the USA he wished to learn more about their family, particularly about William 'Avocado' Chappelow, his great-great-grandfather, who was one of the first to cultivate avocados in California. Could she put him in contact with one of their joint relatives? he asked. Later that week, Patty told Allan that she had spoken to the most direct Californian descendant but he was sadly unwilling to speak to Allan. Though disappointed, Allan appeared to quickly adjust, and told Patty that it would at least give him more time to research in the library.

Before leaving Austin, Allan handed the head librarian a list of documents that he wished to have copied. In all, there were 360 pages that would have to be shipped to his home in England. The woman at the desk said that this might take a few weeks and asked Allan for his credit card details.

On 29 April, a month after arriving in Austin, Texas, Allan flew to Boston where he spent another couple of days at the Boston College library. Two days later he flew overnight to London Heathrow, arriving at 7.30 a.m. on 1 May 2006.

CASE NOTE

————————

After repeated attempts, finally managed to speak with Steven Ainger who lives at number 8 Downshire Hill. Ainger said that Allan was 'an excellent neighbour, quiet, no problem, what more could you want?' When I asked again about Allan Chappelow, Ainger said that he didn't want to talk with me further because of Wang Yam's ongoing appeal. I probed why Wang Yam's legal affairs impacted his relationship with Chappelow, he didn't respond. Perhaps he doesn't want to speak ill of the dead?

I also had a telephone conversation with Nigel Steward who lives on Keats Grove, less than 100 metres from 9 Downshire Hill. He said that he had been 'very friendly' with Allan Chappelow, though he never really got beyond cordial greetings. 'The persona you get in public around here', he said, 'is not always what the person is like.' He said that around the time of Allan's murder he'd been chair of the Hampstead Safer Neighbourhood scheme and he had been made aware of numerous incidents of mail theft and stealing of rubbish bins. He estimated that this had happened at least six times in late 2006 and through 2007 (while Wang Yam was in custody). Each time he passed along the information to his contact at the Hampstead police station. 'The criminals came around in lorries,' he said, 'picked up people's bins before the rubbish men came, and took it to a warehouse in east London where it was sorted. Back then, estate agents and banks were much more relaxed about privacy, and there was a lot of identity fraud.' Despite the similarity and proximity to Allan's burglary, Steward said that no police officer had taken his statement during the murder investigation. Perhaps Allan Chappelow's murder was part of a wider spate of thefts, but had nothing to do with Wang Yam?

I called Lansdown and asked whether the possibility of other mail thieves in the area would undermine his theory that there were no other viable murder suspects. 'It could do', he said. 'It begins to nibble away, doesn't it?' I pushed. 'Yeah,', he replied, 'it has to, yes.' He added, 'But there was no intelligence information, there was nothing like that. Had there been other burglaries in the area? Have there been other attempts to do defraud in this manner? There was nothing like that.' He said that he was 'absolutely confident' that they had got the right man.

Turns out that there was a fire at 9 Downshire Hill less than a week after the property was declared a crime scene. In her official police statement (which I found deep in the defence files), Crime Scene Manager Francesca Spennewyn reported that 'On 15 [June] the Evidentiary Recovery Unit started their work and finished on 18. The POLSA team started their work on 18 (gdn clearance) searches carried out on 19th 20th 23rd (fire) and 29th . . . A fire occurred on the ground floor just outside of Room 6. The property needed to be made safe for the search to continue'. According to the Camden New Journal, up to a third of the ground floor was damaged. In a phone call, Peter Devlin confirmed that there was a fire and that it was caused by one of the investigator's halogen lamps falling over. He added that all the important evidence had already been removed from the house.

After a short conversation, Wang Yam passed me to his prison friend Jack Hemming (previously 'John Moody', he changed name in prison). Jack said they'd first met in Whitemoor five years earlier. Whitemoor was much tougher *than Lowdham Grange. When they were not playing table tennis (they played three times a week, Wang Yam was much better) or working (Jack taught art), they locked themselves in their cells to stay out of trouble. Jack was serving thirty years for murdering his Norwich girlfriend and her lover. He admitted killing them (though he doesn't remember stabbing them) but said it was a crime of passion and should have been a manslaughter charge. Jack said that he doesn't think Wang Yam could hurt anyone, 'but then again,' he added, 'I didn't think I could either.' Jack talked about Wang Yam's character. 'He is generous, very gentle and very caring.' In prison there is little physical contact, he said, but they often hugged. Sometimes they cried and reassured each other. 'If it wasn't for Wang Yam,' he said at the end of our conversation, 'I would be very lonely.'*

7

THE CHASE

As soon as he arrived in the office on the morning of Monday 19 June 2006, Peter Devlin contacted the bank that issued the credit card used by the female customer at the Curry Paradise. Having explained the nature of his inquiry, and promising to fax them a formal Production Order in due course, he asked for the customer's name and enquired whether there had been any recent purchases. Her name, said the credit card company's representative, was Dong Hui, and yes she had used the card. In fact, she had purchased a ticket from easyJet that very morning.

Devlin called easyJet, and quickly learned that Dong Hui had booked a flight from Luton Airport to Zurich in Switzerland. Her plane had just departed. Frustrated, Devlin updated Pete Lansdown, who suggested that he look through the airport's CCTV footage. Perhaps Dong Hui had been caught on one of their cameras?

Around 4 p.m. that afternoon, Devlin and Gerry Pickering were still in Luton Airport's security office looking through footage when Bill Jephson called. The report from Scotland Yard's CIU had finally arrived, said Jephson. The silver flip-phone used at Curry Paradise was registered to 13C Denning Road, London NW3 and belonged to a man called Wang Yam. Jephson told Devlin to get over to Denning Road as soon as possible.

Though a house search was a matter of some urgency, the detectives would still need a warrant. To obtain one at short notice and at this time of the day would require some skill. Luckily, from a previous case, Devlin knew of a friendly magistrate who lived in Hampstead.

The drive to the magistrate's house took Devlin and Pickering just over an hour. They pulled up outside a small, detached property on one of Hampstead's side streets. Devlin rang the bell and shortly afterwards the door was opened by an elderly woman who appeared ready to go out. Having apologised for disturbing her, Devlin explained the reason for his visit and why he believed a criminal activity had taken place. A few minutes later, the magistrate signed the ten-page Application for Search Warrant and wished him luck.

Denning Road was a quiet, narrow street that sat in the heart of Hampstead Village. At the top of the street ran Willoughby Road, stretching on the left to Hampstead High Street with its boutique shops, pavement cafés and Underground station, and to the right the Wells Tavern and beyond that Hampstead Heath. On either side of Denning Road stood a row of three-storey brown-brick buildings, each with steps leading up to a pretty white porch. Devlin realised that the phone-owner's flat was just around the corner from Allan Chappelow's house, a walk of less than five minutes.

The flat's landlady Anna Toma was waiting for them at the bottom of the white stone front steps. Next to her was a large pile of green rubbish bags and discarded furniture. These belonged to Wang Yam and his girlfriend Dong Hui, Toma told the police officers after they had made their introductions. Her tenants had moved out over the weekend, she added; Devlin had just missed them.

Having glanced at the search warrant, Toma then escorted the police officers through the front door, up the wide carpeted stairs and onto the first floor. There she unlocked a padlock and opened the white-painted door to flat C. Inside, the two-bedroom apartment had been cleaned out. A few loose pieces of paper were scattered across the beige floors. The bedroom shelves were empty, as were the kitchen cupboards. The fridge, washing machine and dryer remained in place. An HMV student card was lying on the living room table. A hairbrush and a toothbrush had been left in the bathroom. Disappointed, Devlin realised that there was not much more that he could do. He told the landlady to lock the door and then sealed it with blue and white tape. It was now a crime scene.

Next, he placed a call to Colindale and asked for a forensic expert to examine the premises. If they were lucky, there would be something to connect the flat to 9 Downshire Hill or Allan Chappelow. While they were waiting for the forensics expert to arrive, the police officers spoke to the building's residents.

In the basement flat, the detectives found Teresa Rona, a Spanish native who had lived in the building since November 2004. She told the police that a Chinese couple had moved into the first-floor apartment about a year ago. Sometimes these new neighbours argued so loudly that Teresa's husband had banged the ceiling with a broom. Teresa reported that over the weekend she'd seen two Chinese women loading an old white van that had been parked outside the house. The belongings included 'ugly' plastic laundry bags. She presumed that the Chinese man was helping with the moving, but she hadn't seen him. The last time that she had seen the two Chinese women was around 10 a.m. that morning.

Bev Wilson in the top flat said that she had bumped into her Chinese neighbour in the communal front hall a week earlier, on 12 June. She had been struck that his hair was greyer than it had been. It was so different that she wondered whether it was the same person. Bev also told the police that in September 2005, worried by media stories about identity theft, she had ordered a background check on the building's residents. When it arrived she saw that next to Wang Yam's name appeared the words 'fraud' and 'material falsehoods'. She kept the information to herself, but from that time she had been wary of her neighbour and made sure that she had been the first to pick up the mail in the morning.

Seven weeks earlier, on the morning of 1 May 2006, and after his overnight flight from the USA, Allan Chappelow arrived back at his home at 9 Downshire Hill. As he reached the front door he immediately realised that something was amiss. It looked to him as if someone had forced the lock. There was no post in the front hallway. He had been expecting a tax refund cheque from the Inland Revenue, and was worried that it had been stolen.

The following day, he reported the forced lock at Hampstead police station, but was unconvinced that they would take action. By 8 May, the cheque had still not arrived, so he called the Inland Revenue customer helpdesk. He started by explaining his problem:

> What I want to do is report that I've been away abroad and I came back and found that somebody, only quite recently over the bank holiday I think, has broken into my front porch and stolen amongst other things letters and if my tax computation has already been sent out, which I think was probably sent out in April, there might be . . . there should be a cheque attached to it for a repayment of tax. I'd like you to put a stop on that cheque and issue a duplicate.

The customer service representative first asked him to answer a couple of security questions and then confirmed that a cheque for £4,628.35 had indeed been sent on 2 May to his home address. When

Allan said that the cheque had either not arrived or it had been stolen, the representative replied that she could cancel it and have it reissued.

The telephone call went on for another six minutes while the caller gave his contact details and the representative again confirmed that a cheque had been issued on 2 May. 'What is it now?' asked Allan Chappelow. 'I don't even know what the date is; I'm so confused on my return. Is it the 4th or 5th today?' The representative told him it was 8 May and that it probably hadn't arrived yet. 'That's all I wanted to know,' said the elderly man, 'it's not so good they stole all the letters but nothing else apparently, anyway we'll leave it at that, I've done my duties.' Saying thank you, Allan Chappelow ended the call.

After speaking to the tenants of 13 Denning Road, Peter Devlin now collected a statement from the landlady, Anna Toma. She had first come across the Chinese couple in June 2005, she said, after they responded to an advert she had placed in the free newspaper *Loot*. Toma wanted to move to Italy to care for her elderly mother, and needed to rent out the flat for a short period.

At the flat she met a woman who called herself variously 'Vivien' and 'Dong Hui', along with a man whom she described as her boyfriend and who introduced himself as 'John Wang'. Later, she came to know him as Wang Yam. She remembered him saying that he was a bank manager who owned various companies and that his Hong Kong family was wealthy. Dong Hui's parents, he added, would be staying at the apartment for a few months later that year, which is why they needed two bedrooms.

While Wang Yam checked the flat, his girlfriend remained by the front door. Surprised, Toma asked Dong Hui why she didn't look around and she replied, 'He is the boss and he is going to pay.' A few minutes later, Wang Yam returned to the front hallway and said that they would take it. There was something about him that had made the landlady nervous. She didn't believe his story about his job or family background. She couldn't be picky, however, as she needed to rent the flat out as soon as possible. After discussing a few small details – they would split the costs of buying furniture, for instance, and he would pay on the 22nd of each month – they signed a lease. He then handed over a cheque for £2,000, including the first month's rent for £1,235 and a deposit for £675. That evening, on 22 June 2005, Wang Yam and Dong Hui moved into 13C Denning Road.

A week later, Anna Toma's bank informed her that Wang Yam's cheque had bounced. When she called him, he apologised and sent another cheque. This cheque also bounced. Finally, after she pushed him, he gave her some cash, but he never caught up on the rent. When she returned from Italy in September, she put the flat on the market to sell but when prospective buyers came by, Wang Yam either refused entry or showed them around the grubby flat in his underpants. Toma's estate agent told her that she would not show the house until she evicted the tenant.

Anna Toma said that each time she spoke to Wang Yam about the rent or the viewings he gave excuses. One time he said that he was divorcing his wife and she wouldn't give him access to his daughter. Another time he reported that his assets had been frozen by the court. 'He was very good at making me feel sorry for him,' she told the police officers, 'but he was wasting my time and ruining my life.' Fed up, Toma asked her lawyer to issue an eviction notice.

At a court hearing on 26 April 2006, the magistrate ordered that the bailiffs evict Wang Yam by the end of the first week of June. He also ordered that the tenant pay the outstanding rent owed to his landlady, which by now had accumulated to more than £3,000. Following a petition from Wang Yam, the eviction was postponed till 20 June.

The landlady then told the police that on the previous evening, Sunday 18 June (four days after Chappelow's body had been found), she had received a message from Teresa, her tenant in the ground-floor flat, to say that the people upstairs were moving out. Toma immediately drove over to Denning Road and knocked at the front door of flat C. It took a long time to answer, she said, but eventually the door opened. It was Dong Hui. Wang Yam was out, she told the landlady. Toma reported that Dong Hui had appeared 'evasive', 'shifty' and 'dodgy'.

When asked for a description of the couple, she said that Dong Hui was around twenty-nine years old, with quite pale skin and dark hair bobbed just above the chin. As to Wang Yam, she said that he 'looks unshaven at times, but not all the time. He doesn't wear glasses. With a really plump face. He is Chinese-looking.' She added that he often wore a beige jacket and carried a bag with long straps over his shoulder. 'The last time I saw him,' she added, 'his hair was light brown and grey.'

By now the blood expert had completed the examination of Wang Yam's flat. First she had set up a camera that would record the test. Then she had sprayed the floor evenly with Luminol, a chemical substance that glows blue for up to thirty seconds when it comes into contact with blood. The results, however, were negative. There was no trace of blood. The flat was also swept for fibres and other organic matter such as human hair. These would have to be tested in the lab.

Where did Wang Yam go, wondered Peter Devlin; how did he come to be living in this flat on Denning Road, and what was his background?

PART II

THE SUSPECT

'The liar's punishment is, not in the least that he is not believed, but that he cannot believe anyone else.'

George Bernard Shaw, *The Quintessence of Ibsenism*

8

WANG YAM

Xian is considered one of China's four great cities. Located 660 miles south-west of the capital Beijing, Xian was once the historic departure point for the Silk Road, a starting place for the transport of goods to Europe, making it a key cultural and economic crossroads.

By 1961, however, and in comparison to the major cities of Europe or North America, Xian remained largely undeveloped. Few private motor vehicles populated its streets; instead the city's residents moved around by bicycle, bus or foot. Photographs taken around this time reveal dusty roads filled with men, women and children similarly attired in Maoist matching trousers, jackets and caps; shops filled with basic goods, unbranded and muted in colour; a city of mostly low-rise buildings, interrupted by few traffic lights, telephone poles or electricity cables.

Wang Yam was born in Xian's main hospital on 27 April 1961. His birth name was Ren Hong – he would change it in his thirties – Ren being the family name. His 21-year-old father Ren Yuanyuan was a round-faced man with short black hair who was an officer in the People's Liberation Army. His mother Zhang Xiulan was twenty-two years old and studying to become a doctor. With a kind face and of medium stature, she wore her dark hair long, as was the tradition. Her parents were from Heilongjiang province in the country's far north-east near the Russian border. They had arrived in Xian during the early 1930s following Japan's invasion of northern China.

Wang Yam's grandfather was Ren Bishi, one of the country's most famous revolutionary heroes. Ren Bishi was a key military leader of the 1934–36 Long March and a close friend of Mao Zedong, founding father of the People's Republic of China. When Ren Bishi died in October 1950, his pall-bearers included Chairman Mao and Peng Zhen, the mayor of Beijing.

Just a decade before Wang Yam's birth, Chairman Mao had enacted the Marriage Law, raising the marriageable age to twenty for men and eighteen for women and forbidding arranged marriages and weddings unsanctioned by government. The slogan was: 'Men and women are equal, each person one share.' As a result, by the early 1960s, over 90 per cent of marriages had become officially registered. Wang Yam's parents, however, went unwed. Instead, Wang Yam was what was commonly known as a 'secret child', someone born out of wedlock, who, if made known, would have been an embarrassment to the family. Wang Yam's arrival was not recorded in the official Ren family history.

Though his parents were romantically involved, Wang Yam rarely saw his father as he was soon stationed with the army in another province. His earliest memory was picking up his father's pistol from its place in the bedroom. When he heard someone approaching, he became scared. He ran outside and threw the gun in a well. Though his father often wondered what had happened to his pistol, Wang Yam never confessed.

When he was four years old, Wang Yam and his mother moved

to the capital so that she could continue her studies. At that time, Beijing was in the middle of an extraordinary period of growth, having quadrupled in size from 2 to 8 million since the early 1950s. While the rest of the country had suffered poverty and starvation following the Great Leap Forward – in which the country's agriculture had been brutally and ineffectively collectivised – Beijing had fared considerably better. By the start of the 1960s, whole areas of the city had been torn down to make way for factories, blocks of flats and government offices. The capital had grown as the centre of China's higher education, with the merging of established universities and the relocation of others to Beijing.

Wang Yam and his mother now lived in a small, one-room block home, which contained a single bedroom and a kitchen. Following Mao's exhortation that women and men be treated equally in the workplace, Xiulan was expected to work as hard as her male counterparts, though she was paid less and received minimal childcare provisions. Wang Yam, therefore, saw little of his mother. Sometimes he accompanied her to the hospital, a practice frowned upon by the other staff, but more typically he was looked after by a neighbour.

In the summer of 1966, Wang Yam and his mother heard the noise of a crowd walking through the streets. They walked out to join them, and he was amazed by the adults jumping up and down, singing songs and shouting in unison. They called out 'Long live Chairman Mao!' and held his *Little Red Book* in the air. To the young child they appeared to be dancing. In fact, he was taking part in a rally supporting the Cultural Revolution – and the attempt to erase the 'Four Olds': old customs, old habits, old culture and old ideas.

With parents from near the Russian border, Xiulan was now suspected of maintaining Russian connections by the authorities. Did she support the revolution, they wondered, perhaps she was a foreign spy? While she had been a fervent participant in the rallies over the spring and summer, Xiulan now redoubled her efforts. She stayed out late at political meetings and was always seen with her Maoist uniform: khaki trousers and jacket, a khaki cap, a *Little Red Book* in her pocket and a Chairman Mao badge that she had purchased in the street. By November 1968, however, despite her revolutionary zeal, Xiulan was ordered to relocate to a remote part of southern China to begin work as a village doctor.

Wang Yam's mother was not alone. Over the next few years, more than 17 million young people and professionals would move out of the cities to rural areas. This was part of Mao's 'Down to the Countryside' movement, in which students and professionals were encouraged to resettle so that they could work alongside and learn from the peasants, who were considered to be more ideologically pure.

So it was that, in late November, Wang Yam and his mother said goodbye to their friends in Beijing and made their way to the city's main railway station. The train carriage they boarded lacked seats or benches; it was more like a freight container than a passenger compartment. Thirty other people were already sitting inside and more would join before they departed. Finally, after waiting for a few hours, the train pulled out, heading towards Wang Yam's former home, the city of Xian.

As they trundled through the outskirts of the capital city, the seven-year-old Wang Yam looked out through the cracks in the wagon's wooden sides. He saw the sides of buildings, bridges and snow on the ground. Before long, there were fields, farm buildings and cattle. His mother told him to sit down, it would be a long journey. They had brought some bread and were able to make hot tea on a small stove, but without blankets or a proper fire, they soon became extremely cold. All they had with them was a small bag containing a few clothes, no bedding. Anything considered bourgeois was prohibited: the Cultural Revolution was, after all, anti-intellectual. His mother hadn't even brought her doctor's bag; she was told that the village hospital would have everything she would need. Eventually, Wang Yam fell asleep on his mother's lap.

Finally, after a gruelling two-day journey, they arrived in Xian. Having disembarked, they purchased some food from a kiosk in the station, and then walked a short distance to the bus depot. They then headed further south, travelling another 250 miles into Shaanxi's hilly southern region. A day later they arrived at Tao Yuan Cun, or Peach Orchard village, a remote settlement located on the banks of the Dan Jiang river and surrounded by dense forest. With only five hundred households, the village seemed tiny compared to Beijing, or even Xian. There were no buildings higher than one storey, there were no electricity pylons or telegraph poles. The roads were unpaved and potholed.

Wang Yam stood by as his mother asked for directions, and then followed as she made her way through the unfamiliar streets. A few minutes later, they arrived at a small, one-room house made of mud bricks and roofed with grey tiles. Inside, they met the female doctor and her teenage son who they would be living with. She too had been resettled from the city.

The next day, Xiulan started work at the village medical centre. With its basic medicine and handful of beds, it could not be considered a hospital. She found the residents nervous about her 'western medicine', preferring the traditional herbal remedies that had been handed down the generations. It wasn't long before the young doctor learned to hold her patients' wrist as if to feel their pulse, a central part of the diagnosis in traditional Chinese medicine, as she proffered her conclusions.

Meanwhile, Wang Yam attended the village school, a one-room building with a single teacher and a handful of children. As one of the only children not to be locally born, he was treated differently, but tried to fit in. Like most of the region, the village was rife with poverty. During the Great Leap Forward the small family farms had been collectivised, resulting in plummeting crop yields and widespread hunger. By the end of the first month, Wang Yam noticed that he was dressed better than most of his classmates and he ate better as well. This was partly because his mother was well educated, but also because they received financial support from his father. Somehow, his father saved up enough to send them the equivalent of £2 each month, which at that time was a significant sum.

Xiulan was fully aware of her son's economic advantages. If she saw another child without clothes or shoes, she offered those belonging to Wang Yam. When neighbours offered food to her son, which was often, she scolded him and instructed him to return it. 'She was a kind woman,' Wang Yam recalled, 'hard working and with a big heart.'

One day, Wang Yam was eating his packed lunch in the schoolyard along with the rest of the pupils. Having had enough, he threw a chunk of bread to a dog that was lingering close by. Before the dog could grab the food, a classmate rushed forward, seized the bread from the dog's mouth and ate it. Wang Yam had never seen anybody so hungry that they would act in this way.

Occasionally, when she travelled to other villages even more remote than where they lived, Xiulan brought her son with her. Wang Yam loved the adventure, walking along the narrow paths that cut through the rice fields, crossing rickety wooden bridges that spanned wild rivers, climbing steep hills sporting breathtaking views across the valleys. Most of the time, however, he remained in the village. Although he was lonely when his mother was away, he kept his emotions to himself, and was proud that he never cried. Each day he went to school, did his best in class, and returned home where he was looked after by the woman with whom they shared the small house. He was relieved, however, when his mother returned to the village. Soon they were back to their old routine: her going off to work, him to school, coming together in the evening for a meal. Yet, even this simple rural life, which he was slowly adjusting to, was soon to be disrupted.

Since Mao's seizure of power in 1949, and up until 1968, middle and high schools had been dominated by the Communist Party's Youth Pioneers of China. Now, with Mao's call for a fundamental shift in society, a wave of anti-intellectual sentiment swept the country. One of the results was the emergence of a new, radical youth movement called the Red Guards. Within weeks, Chairman Mao's support to this network of teenage fanatics was reported on the national radio. Days later, Wang Yam and the other pupils at his primary school were formed into a junior equivalent, known as the Little Red Guards. Though there was no official uniform, most Little Red Guards wore khaki trousers and jackets, a red armband featuring the words 'Red Guard', and a khaki cap.

Whereas in previous months, Wang Yam had studied Chinese calligraphy, history and philosophy, scorn was now poured on Confucius and the other 'old thinkers'. School was no longer compulsory, and when lessons were held they were poorly attended. While many teachers in other local schools suffered public humiliation and even violent attacks, Wang Yam and his classmates limited themselves to verbal abuse. They called their teacher a 'capitalist' and a 'reactionary' – even though he was an ill-educated peasant – and insisted that he focus on teaching them about communist ideology. When the teacher read a traditional story like the hare and the tortoise, the children screamed until he recited a story from the Long March or Mao's epic victory against the Japanese invaders.

Later that month, the father of one of his classmates was publicly criticised for being of 'rich peasant' background and politically unreliable. Wang Yam heard that such 'criminals' were sent for re-education, which meant time away from work, a reduction of income and a loss of status within the village. He worried what might happen to his mother. As part of his schooling, he now spent at least half a day every week working in the nearby farms, carrying heavy boxes of fertiliser from the village to the fields, gathering wheat during the harvest, reinforcing the riverbanks or picking apples from the orchards. At meetings of the Little Red Guards, Wang Yam and his friends sang revolutionary songs and recited long passages from Mao's *Little Red Book*. Sometimes, the political rallies turned violent.

One day when he was eight years old, Wang Yam witnessed a public mass execution by the riverbank. Thirteen village men had been working together to move a statue of Chairman Mao when it had slipped from their grasp and broke on the ground. Without trial the county's party secretary used this as an excuse to sentence them to death by firing squad. Hearing about the execution, Wang Yam snuck out the house and ran down to the river. He watched as the soldiers let off their rounds. The accused were shot in the head; brains and blood spurted from their skulls and their bodies fell to the ground. One of the mothers rushed forward with tears in her eyes and held her dead son in her arms. Seeing the woman, the officer in charge said that she shouldn't cry because her son was anti-Mao, an enemy of the state, and that if she didn't remove herself she too would be shot. The mother ran away. 'At that time you just followed the system,' remembered Wang Yam. 'We didn't have an idea of what to believe and what not to believe. We were too young.'

A few weeks after the public execution, Wang Yam returned home from school and was told that his mother had been taken to the medical centre. Rushing over, he found Xiulan in bed, recovering from an emergency operation. He learned that she had contracted an acute gastrointestinal infection and that they had tried to remove part of the lower intestine. Standing next to his mother, he tried talking to her but she didn't respond. That day and the next, he sat with her, waiting for her to wake up. Every few hours, a nurse would come and check on his mother's progress, but her condition remained the same. Then, on the morning of the third day, he noticed that her chest had stopped rising and falling. A nurse came in, checked the patient, and then told Wang Yam that his mother had died. He ran into the woods behind the clinic until he found a small wooden hut. Inside, he sat on the dirt floor, buried his face in his hands, and cried.

By the evening of 19 June 2006, and with Wang Yam's whereabouts unknown, Peter Devlin needed to understand more about his prime suspect. What had been his recent activities? Who were his last known associates? What was his background? From this they might be able to track him down.

Gathered around a table at police headquarters in Colindale, the investigators looked through the green rubbish bags that they had collected from Denning Road. There was much of interest. Inside they found a number of photographs, old clothes, computers and assorted papers including bank statements and property brochures, along with a diary filled with Chinese characters, telephone numbers and what appeared to be appointments. These items would need to be photographed, tagged and stored for later examination.

Most interesting of all, they found a CV that catalogued Wang Yam's education and employment history. It appeared that the suspect had grown up and attended school and university in China. For reasons unexplained by the CV, Wang Yam seemed to have arrived in the UK sometime in the early 1990s, and then attended university in London, before working for various defence contractors.

As they worked through the papers, Devlin jotted down the basic facts in his notebook, and then added new lines of inquiry. They would have to contact people who knew Wang Yam, who could confirm his work history, and perhaps offer an explanation for why this man was caught up in the murder of Allan Chappelow.

Following his mother's death, Wang Yam remained in the remote village for another year. He stayed with the doctor who had looked after him when his mother had been away. In the spring of 1970, he moved in with his mother's sister Zhang Xuying and husband Ren Li Yi who lived 40 miles north of Xian.

Like many local inhabitants, Wang Yam's aunt and uncle lived in a *yaodong*, a cave house that had been built into the side of a hill. Yaodongs were common in this part of Shanxi province; indeed, Mao Zedong had maintained his pre-revolutionary headquarters in a network of similar caves near the city of Yan'an. Though his new home was a little primitive, Wang Yam received love and support from his uncle and aunt, and for the first time since he had left Beijing, he felt happy.

Having lost more than two years of schooling during his time in the village, Wang Yam now threw himself into his studies. By this point, the fanaticism of the Cultural Revolution had waned and the traditional curriculum was returning. Wang Yam's favourite classes were mathematics and physics, subjects in which he excelled. Spotting his abilities, his teachers pushed him and he was sent to a more prestigious institution.

On 9 September 1976, now aged fifteen, Wang Yam returned home to find his aunt in a state of excitement. She had just been listening to the news on the radio, she said, Mao Zedong had died. Wang Yam was shocked and upset. 'I loved Chairman Mao,' he remembered. 'There was no reason not to love him. In our mind he had saved the country and its people and established the communist regime.' That night, his aunt made dumplings, a dish usually served to celebrate Chinese New Year. When the neighbour learned of their menu, she reported this to the local police. Apparently, their dinner choice was insufficiently sombre. They were given an official warning to eat more appropriately in future.

A few days later, on 18 September, Wang Yam lined up on the school exercise yard along with the rest of his classmates. Everyone wore white trousers and a white shirt out of respect for the dead leader. For two hours, they remained standing while funeral music was played over loudspeakers. At one point a boy kicked Wang Yam in the shins. 'You are not crying enough,' the boy said, 'cry harder.' Wang Yam tried to cry as hard as the other children but the boy kicked him again. Tears never came, but he looked in enough discomfort that he wasn't reported.

Late in the evening of Monday 19 June 2006, Peter Devlin sent an alert to the major airlines and train operators. He provided them with Wang Yam's description, gathered from the staff at Curry Paradise and his neighbours on Denning Road, and urgently requested information on the subject.

The next morning, the security office at Eurostar sent word that a train ticket from London Waterloo to Brussels had been booked in Wang Yam's name at 3.15 p.m. on the previous Thursday, 15 June. The representatives at Eurostar could not say who had used the ticket (tickets are not checked against identification documents at this station), but the police were confident that it was Wang Yam.

By the morning of 15 June there had been a large number of policemen milling around 9 Downshire Hill. The property had been cordoned off, men and women in white suits were carrying rubbish out of the house and dumping it into a skip on the road. A tent had been set up in the garden where investigators examined evidence. Other uniformed police officers were going door-to-door and interviewing neighbours. Anyone walking past would have been aware that a major police investigation was under way.

It appeared that the prime suspects for the murder of Allan Chappelow were now on the run.

CASE NOTE

I met Lansdown again in Colindale. After showing me around the murder investigation team's offices, we had tea in the cafeteria. I asked what he thought about Wang Yam leaving the country on 15 June 2006, a day after Allan's body was found. 'I'm certain that the police activity triggered his flight,' Lansdown told me. 'They knew the game was up,' said Lansdown. 'We spooked them.' I then told him about some of my research, about my growing doubts about the case. He again mentioned the 'building blocks'. He was confident they had the right man. He believed Wang Yam was a 'pathological liar' – 'Somebody murdered Allan Chappelow,' he said, and there was no 'viable alternative'. 'If it looks like a murderer and smells like a murderer, it is a murderer.'

But in the defence files, I found a copy of Wang Yam and Dong Hui's Easyjet plane ticket to Zurich on 4 January 2004, proving that they had previously travelled to Switzerland. I also found a statement given by Deborah Sheppard during Wang Yam's first trial. A landlord in Hampstead, Sheppard had shown Wang Yam around a flat on 7 June 2006, a full week before Allan's body was found by the police. She remembered Wang Yam telling her that he would be 'out of the house travelling a great deal', supporting his story that he had indeed planned to travel to Switzerland.

Went to the London chambers of Kirsty Brimelow QC, the barrister who has represented Wang Yam for over ten years and was still working on his appeals. She said that from the start she and the other defence lawyers did not believe many of Wang Yam's claims. They had not been able to verify, for example, that Wang Yam had studied at Imperial College as he had reported on his CV. She added that Wang Yam was 'not a straightforward character' and that from early on in the case the defence team had considered him to be a 'fantasist'.

Received an email from DC Francesca Spennewyn from Homicide and Serious Crime Command. She said that they would 'not be able to return any of Mr Chappelow's property to you at this time, due to Operational enquiries' related to Wang Yam's ongoing appeal. More than a decade after his murder, the Metropolitan Police were still to return Allan Chappelow's clothes, books, letters and address book to his family.

Wang Yam called at 5 p.m. as usual. When I asked what he would do when he was released from jail, he said that he'd been researching ways to improve the internal combustion engine. 'I have developed a new engine based on hydrogen power,' he said. 'It will revolutionise the way that cars are built.' It's hard to imagine how he could have done this from prison.

9

THE EVIDENCE

In September 1987, having completed high school and graduated from Northwestern University in Xian, and now aged twenty-six, Wang Yam moved to Beijing to study a masters degree at the University of Science and Technology. His focus was solid state engineering and physics. In his spare time he studied English, which was useful for understanding computer coding and for reading overseas academic papers.

It was around this time that Wang Yam met Zhu Xiaoping, also a student at Beijing University. When she said that she was the granddaughter of Ren Bishi, Wang Yam was astonished and declared that he was the grandson. From that point forward whenever they socialised, Wang Yam introduced Xiaoping as his 'first cousin and the granddaughter of the famous Ren Bishi'. Xiaoping preferred to refer to him simply as her 'friend'.

Soon after this first meeting, Wang Yam learned that Xiaoping's boyfriend needed a room to rent so he invited him to come and live in his student dormitory. The three young friends became inseparable, spending long hours playing table tennis in the student halls and drinking beers in the local bars. From time to time, Wang Yam visited Xiaoping's mother, who appeared delighted to have found a long-lost relative. Though keen not to take advantage of his new connections, Wang Yam was pleased to have become close to Xiaoping and her family.

In the spring of 1989, forty years after Chairman Mao and his fellow communists had seized power, pro-democracy demonstrations erupted across China. The protesters called for an opening up of the regime, for freedom of assembly, freedom of speech and a loosening of control of agriculture and industry. The protests had been triggered by the death of Hu Yaobang on 15 April 1989. As general secretary of the Communist Party Hu had championed economic liberalisation and called for the reform of the one-party state until he was forced to resign by a group of party elders and military officials in January 1987. Over the next days and weeks, the protests grew in size and confidence. The lack of government response was interpreted as a signal that free expression was not only possible, but encouraged. Now emboldened, the students began meeting in public spaces, holding up banners calling for change in Mandarin and English and speaking candidly about their concerns to foreign correspondents. Through late April and into May 1989, student organisations staged demonstrations, rallies and teach-ins in over 300 cities across the country. The epicentre of the protests was Tiananmen Square in Beijing.

Measuring more than 100 acres, the capital's Tiananmen Square carried great symbolism for the communist regime, for not only was it here that Chairman Mao first proclaimed the creation of the People's Republic of China on 1 October 1949, but it was also the location for the nation's parliament and the Chairman's mausoleum. At the demonstration's peak, over a million protesters gathered in Tiananmen Square.

Finally, on 20 May, the government decided to act, with the Senior Leader Deng Xiaoping announcing the imposition of martial law. More than 250,000 soldiers were transported into Beijing; some arriving by road, others by rail and air. During the next few days, the students repelled the government forces with over 100,000 protesters gathered in Beijing's city centre. For the moment, there was a stand-off.

At the start of the unrest, Wang Yam had been a member of the official government-sponsored student association, marking him as a supporter of the communist regime. While the protests were barely covered by the state-owned media, he had heard about them from his friends and colleagues. By the end of May, Wang Yam had become worried that the government was taking too harsh a line against the protesters, so he resigned his membership. Now he began spending increasing amounts of time with the dissidents, participating in the workshops and teach-ins that occurred daily around the university.

On 2 June, while pushing his bicycle around Tiananmen Square and enjoying the positive and hopeful atmosphere, Wang Yam spotted Major General F., a family friend in the People's Liberation Army. Chatting with him, Wang Yam was surprised to learn how little the soldier knew about the unfolding political events. They were not allowed to read the newspaper, F. said, or watch television. Once he understood what was going on in the square, the major general appeared to share Wang Yam's concerns about the army's presence in Beijing and agreed that the soldiers should not interrupt the protests. Soon after saying goodbye to the major general, Wang Yam bumped into a journalist named Caroline from a Dutch media company. In Mandarin she asked him for his views on the protest and what he believed would be the likely outcome. 'I hope that the government will see reason,' he told her. When she asked to meet some of the student leaders he agreed, and a short while later he made the introduction.

After lunch on 3 June, Wang Yam biked over to a friend's apartment where he met a 24-year-old student called Li Jia. Finding her both attractive and intelligent, he spent the rest of the afternoon talking to her. She told him that she was a leader in one of the student associations and was studying a masters in economics. Li Jia said that she also supported the protests. After three hours or so, Wang Yam excused himself and returned to his own room.

Later that evening, Wang Yam joined a crowd in front of Beijing University, reading newsletters that had been pasted on its walls. Troops had moved into ten key areas in the city, he read, and student protesters were calling for roadblocks to be set up to stop them approaching Tiananmen Square. There was talk of an even larger demonstration that evening, and of a violent crackdown. Though such threats had been heard before, Wang Yam hoped that the government wouldn't make any rash decisions. Turning around, he caught sight of Li Jia, who had also come to read the posts. After reminding her to be careful, he left, promising to see her again soon.

He spent the rest of the evening with a professor and his family at their flat. Then, around 11 p.m., the professor's wife urged them to see the news. The government was warning that if the protesters did not leave the square they would face dire consequences. Throughout the night Wang Yam heard gunfire and saw white flashes illuminating the sky.

Early the next morning, having slept little, Wang Yam rode over to the square. It was light now, and the streets were littered with the previous night's debris: a sea of bicycles discarded on the ground, bags, cameras, empty tear gas canisters and bottles. Something terrible had happened here. The owners of these cycles must have fled in panic. Looking around more carefully, he noticed bullet holes in the walls and broken windows. Then he saw two children lying on the ground, a boy and a girl. Kneeling down to help them he realised that they were not breathing. He saw gunshot wounds.

Driven by anger, he cycled to a nearby hospital. There he saw hundreds of people with cracked ribs, broken arms and bloodied faces. There were also scores of bodies, all with bullet wounds, some shot in the back. It was obvious to him that the army had marched on the square, shooting as they went. On his way back to the university he bumped into a colleague who told him that amongst the dead were two of his friends, shot by soldiers. Another had been crushed by a tank. They were only able to identify him by matching a key to his university locker that they found near his body.

Now fearful for Li Jia's wellbeing, he raced over to her room in one of the university's female dormitories. On arrival, he found her door locked and received no answer. With rising concern, he wrote a note and stuck it to her door: 'I am not dead, come find me, Wang Yam.'

Worried about staying in the university accommodation, he rode over to his cousin Xiaoping's house in central Beijing, which was located in a gated compound and protected by armed guards. Xiaoping was there, as was her mother, the daughter of Ren Bishi. Together they spent a fitful night, watching the news to see if they could glean any more about the days' events, talking in whispers, reassuring each other that things would get better.

The following morning, 5 June, Wang Yam returned to Li Jia's dormitory. Seeing her bike outside, he realised that she hadn't gone to Tiananmen Square after all. Later that day, one of his classmates told him that Li Jia had been picked up by her father and was at home with her family. Still incensed by the previous days' events, Wang Yam confronted a policeman he saw in the street. 'How many more people will die?' he asked angrily. 'The central government is a mess!' Before he could say any more, a stranger pulled him away. He was lucky not to be arrested.

The next morning, Wang Yam was working in his university office when two uniformed policemen walked in without knocking. They wanted to know about the major general he had spoken to in the square, what they had spoken about, and if the soldier had sympathies for the protests. They also wanted to know what he had said to the Dutch journalist. Wang Yam wasn't sure how they'd known about his activities in the square; most likely there were thousands of informers who had infiltrated the demonstrations and reported back to their party bosses. Despite the policemen's repeated questions, Wang Yam refused to provide any information.

Over the next weeks, he was interrogated three times by his department's security officer along with the vice chairman of Beijing University. Even when he was threatened with exile to a coalmine for 'worker re-education' he remained silent. When the questioning was over, he was left deeply troubled. He had grown up loving his country, but if the government was willing to fire upon unarmed civilians, what else could happen? What future did he have in China?

The London heatwave continued into the third week of June 2006. Normally temperatures never rose above 25 degrees at this time of year, but some days the thermostat on Pete Lansdown's car registered in the thirties. While tourists sunbathed in the parks and ice-cream sellers enjoyed a spike in sales, the man in charge of the Chappelow murder inquiry was getting anxious.

The biggest problem facing Lansdown was that he still didn't know the whereabouts of Wang Yam or Dong Hui. The last known location of Wang Yam was the Eurostar terminal in Brussels on 15 June, while the last confirmed sighting of Dong was at Luton Airport on her way to Zurich on 16 June. Lansdown was desperate to issue a 'Red Notice' through Interpol, which would have alerted the world's police forces to the dangers posed by Wang Yam and called for his arrest. Frustratingly, however, he had been told by his superiors that he could only issue Red Notices if he believed there to be an imminent threat to life. He believed it probable that Wang Yam had murdered Allan Chappelow, but he didn't think he was likely to kill again.

He was allowed, however, to add the suspect's name to Interpol's criminal database, which he did, informing his international colleagues that Wang Yam was wanted in the United Kingdom. As a last-ditch effort, he also sent a request to the Chinese authorities through the Foreign Office, asking if they had any information on Wang Yam, a background check perhaps, or a copy of his criminal record.

While they waited for a response from Interpol, Pete Lansdown and Peter Devlin now focused on confirming exactly how Chappelow had been killed. From the pathologist's report, they knew that the victim had received numerous blows to his head and neck. No murder weapon had yet been found at the crime scene, but they hadn't given up hope that one would be located. They understood, however, that the search would take at least another week. Lansdown had also been handed a report from a blood scatter expert, who found that there was no blood trail near the front door, the hallway or main corridor. The conclusion was that Allan had been beaten to death in Room Six. This begged the question: why, if there had been a bungled burglary, was there no forensic or DNA evidence found (proof of a struggle) between the front door and where the body had been found?

The forensic reports raised more questions than they answered. What did the wax mean? Why was Allan buried under half a ton of paper? Could a single assailant have moved such a load? More positively, the crime scene investigators had found eight cigarette butts near Room Six. These would have to be sent off for DNA testing. They had also identified a series of footprints on the undersides of the manuscript pages that had covered the body as well as blood samples near the front door handle. Such evidence might prove helpful once they identified a culprit.

Having spoken to Allan Chappelow's neighbours and acquaintances over the previous few days, it had become clear to Lansdown and his team that the only person with access to the property was the handyman, Thomas Carr. As such, Carr was considered to be a possible suspect. Devlin's suspicions were strengthened when the forensics team found Carr's DNA on a latex glove and on a tissue that had both been found metres from the body.

Two detectives were dispatched to interview Thomas Carr. A few hours later his statement was on Devlin's desk. Carr had said that on 8 May 2006 he was fixing a downpipe at home. After a few minutes, he started to feel unwell so he went upstairs to lie down. 'I think I called the ambulance about 11.40 a.m.,' he said. He was taken by ambulance to the Royal Free Hospital in Hampstead. After conducting some tests, the attending doctor told him that he had suffered cardiac arrest and Carr remained at the hospital for four and a half weeks. Devlin knew that Chappelow had been alive on 8 May because they had a recording of him speaking to the Inland Revenue. The homicide investigation had just lost their only other suspect.

Lansdown and Devlin's next task was to determine when the victim had died. This line of inquiry would allow them to establish what some call 'opportunity', ruling in or out a potential suspect depending on whether they could provide a credible alibi. To establish a time of death they turned to Samantha Pickles, the entomologist who had collected blowfly and pupa specimens from 9 Downshire Hill.

On 24 June, Pickles met with her supervisor Dr Martin Hall in the lab of the Natural History Museum, and together they examined the samples. After a person dies, his or her body immediately begins to decompose. Typically, within twenty-four hours of death, blowflies find a cadaver and lay their eggs around its orifices, including the mouth and nostril, and any open wounds. These eggs develop into larvae or maggots, which grow rapidly and then migrate away from the body (but typically nearby) to find a safer place to pupate. After a number of days, the adult fly emerges, and the cycle begins again. The speed of the cadaver's decomposition, and the time it takes for a blowfly to emerge, varies depending on the weather conditions. The hotter the temperature the faster the process occurs. Pickles and Hall immediately observed that the samples belonged to the urban bluebottle blowfly (*Calliphora vicina*). One of the flies was male. From its bent and wrinkled legs the scientists concluded that it was newly emerged. They also identified two pupae that were in the final stages of development, their red eyes and dark hair-like bristles clearly visible.

Now using data supplied by the Meteorological Office, which provided the average temperatures for the previous two months, and relying on standard germination times listed in textbook tables, Pickles and Hall determined the development cycle in order for a blowfly to emerge on 16 June.

In his report delivered to the homicide team, Dr Hall said that, working backwards, the latest likely time of death was 16 May. Though he acknowledged that this was speculative, the scientist suggested that the murder had therefore likely taken place sometime between 9 and 16 May. Given that the police had found his body on 14 June, this meant that Allan Chappelow had lain undiscovered for at least four weeks. It also meant that whoever had called the victim's banks and visited 9 Downshire Hill to collect the PIN codes had done so well after the murder had taken place. The killer must be particularly cold-hearted, Devlin thought, to return to the house while the body lay rotting under a pile of papers.

Throughout the summer and into the winter of 1989, Wang Yam and Li Jia saw each other often. Li Jia told him that she had graduated in the top 5 per cent of her university class, that she specialised in British economic history and was currently working on two chapters for a book entitled *The Grand Dictionary of Economy*.

After meeting each other's families, they moved into a small flat, and soon after decided to marry. On 17 September 1991, they were granted a marriage licence by the Beijing Xicheng District. The document declared: 'this marriage is in conformity with the provisions on marriage in the Marriage Law of the People's Republic of China'. Wang Yam was thirty years old, Li Jia was twenty-six. With the papers now in order, they were married in a short ceremony and held a small party at a local restaurant for a few friends and family members. 'We were happy together,' Wang Yam later recalled. 'We were in love.'

Since the authorities appeared to have lost interest in him, Wang Yam returned to his job at the Beijing Technical University. Based at room number 230 in Building 10, he worked as a researcher developing electrical sensors for China's burgeoning nuclear research programme. Meanwhile, Li Jia started work at the International Trade Research Institute within the Ministry for Foreign Economic Relations. Her main task was researching foreign trade within the European single market, particularly that involving China and Britain.

In the period following the Tiananmen Square protests, the Chinese government was overtaken by hardliners who were opposed to both political freedom and free market enterprise. Deng Xiaoping stepped back from his position as Senior Leader and several members of the politburo were replaced. Meanwhile, China was shunned by the international community, reducing international exports and slowing foreign trade agreements. Among those most affected were members of the trade ministry, particularly those who specialised in British and US relations. So it was that in early 1992, Li Jia heard that she might be relocated to Fushun City in Liaoning province, southern Manchuria, as part of a re-education programme. Dismayed by this prospect, she told Wang Yam that she wished to leave the country. He agreed that it was time to go.

Since the 1949 revolution, the government had restricted foreign travel, causing resentment particularly in the population's more educated sections. In 1986, the People's Congress of China had responded by passing an emigration law that enshrined a citizen's right to leave the country. From 1982 to 1990, the number of people annually emigrating quadrupled to 234,000. The new law required one of two reasons for travel: to participate in an overseas student programme or to join family overseas. Wang Yam and Li Jia, however, didn't know anyone overseas nor had they been accepted into a foreign university.

In the first week of August 1992, Wang Yam took a plane from Beijing to Shenzhen in Guangdong province. Located in China's south-easterly corner, Shenzhen provided the main transit route to Hong Kong. Arriving in the city, Wang Yam booked himself into a hotel. The next day, he called on the offices of the city mayor and family friend, Li Hao, who offered to help him obtain entry papers for British-controlled Hong Kong.

Two weeks later, Wang Yam checked out of his hotel and took a taxi to the Hong Kong border. He did not tell Li Jia of his plans in case she was questioned by the police about his disappearance. All he had with him was a small briefcase, in which he carried his wallet, passport and a few family photographs. He didn't want to give the impression that he was seeking an extended stay. When it was his turn, he handed his papers to the Chinese passport control officer, who glanced at them, checked them against his computer screen and, after a brief pause, waved him through. A hundred metres down the road he was stopped at another checkpoint, this time manned by members of the Hong Kong border police.

After taking Wang Yam's passport, the guard asked in Cantonese the purpose for his visit. Wang Yam replied in English that he had 'political problems' and that he 'wanted to leave China'. The guard was a little surprised. 'You speak English?' he said, and then suggested that he should go back to China. Wang Yam replied that he couldn't, that it wasn't safe and that he wanted to get his wife out of the country as well. The guard consulted with one of his supervisors and then Wang Yam was told to climb into a car so that he could be driven to the city centre for a more extensive interview.

Looking through the police vehicle window as he drove through the streets, Wang Yam was stunned. This was his first time out of China, and he was amazed by the tall glass and steel office towers, the flashing neon advertising hoardings, the streets filled with Western cars, and the luxury goods displayed in the shop windows. He felt tremendous relief, 'as if a pile of bricks had been removed from my shoulders', he later recalled. 'It was a free land.'

Over the next three days, Wang Yam was questioned by an assortment of officials. Some clearly belonged to the Hong Kong police force, others to its immigration department.

While he was being questioned, his captors took his address book and placed calls with various people in an attempt to verify his story. His uncle and aunt confirmed his basic biography, as did his wife. When they spoke with Wang Yam's university professor, they were told that his colleagues had alerted the authorities that he'd gone missing and that the Beijing police force was looking for him.

'Where would you like to move to?' his interrogators asked him. 'Any country', he replied, 'that speaks English.'

It is common for a defence lawyer to criticise the way in which a police investigation is handled. The detectives have been too aggressive with a witness, they might say, or maybe the forensic data has been sloppily gathered, or perhaps the chain of evidence has been broken. One of the most common complaints is that the police rush to judgment. They quickly identify their culprit, goes the argument, and then construct their case around him or her.

Peter Devlin was more than aware of these potential accusations. He had been present in sufficient courtrooms to know that the remedy was to present a watertight case to the Crown Prosecution Service, or CPS. His colleagues would keep looking for Wang Yam, but in the meantime he would build the evidence. So it was that, as the spring of 2006 turned to summer, statements were collected from airline staff, bank clerks, estate agents, telephone sales representatives and medical professionals who had come into contact with Wang Yam or Dong Hui.

From HSBC bank, Devlin obtained CCTV footage of a man depositing four cheques at their Tottenham Court Road branch, which included Allan Chappelow's refund from the Inland Revenue. The man was wearing a beige jacket and carrying a bag over his shoulder. He looked similar to the photographs of Wang Yam that the police had found at the flat in Denning Road. Next, Foyles bookshop delivered a still image of a man purchasing two books using Allan Chappelow's credit card. It looked like the same man. Finally, CCTV footage was obtained of a man using the victim's Sainsbury's card at an ATM machine in Kentish Town. These images were less clear, but perhaps they could match the suspect's description.

By early July, Devlin felt comfortable that a decent barrister would be able to persuade a jury that Wang Yam had handled items stolen from the victim. What was less clear was the motive for murder. Why had he beaten an elderly man to death? Why did he brazenly return to the property after the crime? Devlin realised he needed to understand how Wang Yam had attempted to steal money from Allan Chappelow's deposit account.

From his conversations with the security officers at RBS and ING banks, Devlin learned that £10,000 of the victim's money had at one point passed through Money TT, a small private clearing bank owned by a certain He Jia Jin. After a little more research, the detective discovered that He Jia Jin was one of Chinatown's most colourful characters.

The 43-year-old He Jia Jin controlled a number of London businesses in addition to the Money TT company. He had been vice-president of the Chinatown Chinese Association, published a fortnightly newspaper and had connections with the Chinese Embassy. He also attended parties and socialised with diplomats, though he claimed he did not work with members of the Chinese military. In 1997, He Jia Jin was convicted of forgery and counterfeiting by the British authorities. According to various press accounts, he was also convicted in Greece and Hong Kong, but didn't serve time in either country. In 2004, the police had seized £150,000 from him, but the funds were returned with interest after they failed to present sufficient evidence of wrongdoing. More recently, £1.5 million of his assets had been frozen by a High Court judge, which he was currently contesting. Over the years, he had been suspected of human trafficking, money laundering, tax fraud and being a member of the 14K Triad, the world's second largest Chinese gang. At one of his court appearances, He Jia Jin admitted that some considered him to be 'the Chinese Osama Bin Laden'.

Having updated Lansdown on this new line of inquiry, Devlin and Pickering drove to Kennington in south London to interview He Jia Jin. They met at his workplace, a one-storey building on a quiet shopping street. The Chinese businessman kept the police officers waiting for a few minutes before inviting them into his office. He Jia Jin was short, with closely cropped dark hair and a round face, and dressed in an expensive suit. 'He was very intelligent,' recalled Devlin, 'not charming, but helpful.' Throughout the interview, one of He Jia Jin's associates stood watch at the door.

He Jia Jin told Devlin that £10,000 was transferred out of Allan Chappelow's RBS account and into Wang Yam's Money TT account on Friday 9 June 2006. Concerned that this might be fraudulent, He Jia Jin had asked RBS to reverse the transaction. A few hours later, He Jia Jin had received a call from Wang Yam on his mobile phone. The man on the line introduced himself and asked for the £10,000 transfer to be reinstated. This surprised He Jia Jin as the transfer had been in the name of Wang Yam. The customer was angry, he recalled, demanding that Money TT fix the problem immediately. He Jia Jin tried putting the customer off but he called back numerous times. Indeed, Wang Yam called so frequently that He Jia Jin found it hard to work. Finally, he agreed to meet the following Monday, at Money TT's office in Kennington.

Wang Yam and He Jia Jin got together for an hour at 10.30 p.m. on 12 June 2006, around the same time that the police were concluding their first day's search of 9 Downshire Hill. While He Jian Jin was making a copy of his passport, Wang Yam said that he had attended Imperial College and that he was a barrister at a well-known firm of solicitors located at 80 Shaftesbury Avenue in London. He then criticised Money TT for being a poorly run organisation and offered to register it on the London Stock Exchange. He Jia Jin listened politely but made no comments. He didn't trust this man, he told the police. He knew the building at 80 Shaftesbury Avenue and didn't think any lawyers worked there. For some unexplained reason, Wang Yam or John Wong appeared to be trying to befriend him.

At the meeting's end, He Jia Jin recalled, Wang Yam grabbed a pen and wrote his email on the ink blotter that lay on the bank manager's desk: johnwongmbox@hotmail.com. Wang Yam said he would transfer the funds again to Money TT the following day, and said that the reference would be his friend's name, 'Jenny'. As soon as the money arrived he wanted to be notified.

'On the face of it,' Devlin said, 'He Jia Jin was very helpful.' He didn't appear to hide anything, but Devlin admitted being 'tainted' by what he knew about the businessman. He was wary, yet there was no evidence to back up his suspicions. The one key lead was 'Jenny'. Devlin didn't think it was Dong Hui, who also went by

'Vivien'. Jenny's name had come up once before in the investigation relating to another of Wang Yam's transactions, when Wang Yam had deposited four of Allan Chappelow's cheques into his bank account at HSBC. He had then attempted to transfer a little over £14,000 to a Bank of China account, also in Jenny's name. It was time, Devlin decided, to visit this Jenny. First, however, they needed to speak with Wang Yam's first wife, Li Jia.

CASE NOTE

Went to the Natural History Museum to meet Dr Martin Hall, the entomologist who had prepared a time of death report for the police. Hall said that blowflies find rotting flesh typically within the first twenty-four hours of death. To confirm this he had recently left a pig's head on the roof of a nearby building and observed that the flies arrived within hours. In another experiment, Hall left a pig's head in a suitcase and was surprised to find that the blowflies were able to lay their eggs through the zip to drop onto the carcass. He said that determining likely dates of death when a body has remained undiscovered for so long becomes speculative. I mentioned that Jane Ainger had recalled seeing Allan Chappelow at the start of June 2006, at least two weeks after the entomologist's latest date of death. Hall said that perhaps he had the time of death wrong for Allan Chappelow as the corpse would have been hotter under all the manuscripts, which may have accelerated both decomposition and the blowfly life cycle. This would have put the time of death closer to start of June 2006.

Still looking through defence files (I have over 1,000 pages from James Mullion's office). In his police statement, Thomas Carr confirmed that he sometimes worked as Chappelow's handyman and had access to 9 Downshire Hill. He also said that he didn't smoke, and that he had been taken to hospital on 8 May 2006. Carr's medical records confirmed that Carr had indeed suffered 'chest pains' and been admitted to the Royal Free, but according to the time stamp on the Accident and Emergency report, he'd arrived at 14.46 on 9 May 2006. This means there are almost twenty-four hours unaccounted for between Chappelow's last known act (his call to the Inland Revenue on 8 May) and Carr's arrival in hospital. Is this important?

I asked Wang Yam's barrister Kirsty Brimelow about Thomas Carr being an alternative suspect. Witnesses often make mistakes in their statements, she said, adding that when she saw him in court (old and frail) she had discounted him as a potential suspect. She asked what Carr's motive would have been for killing Allan Chappelow?

Spoke again with Wang Yam's solicitor, James Mullion, who said that WY had now put me on visitor's list. When I called the prison, however, they had no records of me. I called the press department at the Ministry of Justice saying that I'd been unable to get anywhere with the prison authorities and could they help arrange a visit with Wang Yam? They told me to write a formal letter, which I did (again).

Have hired a researcher in Beijing to help me track down Wang Yam's background. She said that it is very hard to find paper records in China, especially those dating back to the 1960s and 1970s. She did manage to speak by phone with WY's former academic supervisor, Professor Chen Nanxian. The details 'are lost to memory', Chen stated, because Wang Yam 'left the Chinese university twenty years ago'. Chen also said that his former pupil was 'very strange'. When pushed on what he meant by this, all he would say was 'Truth and lies, truth and lies'. The professor refused to speak further. Beginning to worry that I am being manipulated by Wang Yam.

IO

ARRIVAL

———————

On 27 August 1992, Wang Yam drove to Hong Kong Airport and then took an overnight flight to London. All that he had with him was his suitcase filled with a few clothes provided by the Hong Kong authorities, along with the small collection of personal items that he had brought from China.

Early the next morning, Wang Yam landed at Gatwick Airport. After a brief stop at immigration control, he took a taxi to the Cricket Field Hostel run by the Refugee Council located at 244 Sebert Road in Forest Gate, in north-east London. He checked in with a friendly Kenyan woman at the front desk, and was then taken up to his room on the third floor. It was small, with two single beds, two chests of drawers and a window overlooking a cemetery. The carpet was worn and the wildlife posters on the walls were peeling at the corners. He would be sharing with a refugee from Somalia, he was told by the Kenyan lady. This would be his home for the next few weeks until he could find more permanent accommodation. Wang Yam was now a guest of Her Majesty's government.

As soon as he had unpacked, Wang Yam returned downstairs and asked how he could make an overseas call. He wanted to make contact with Li Jia. The woman at the front desk pointed to a pay phone in the lobby and explained that he would need a large number of coins if he wished to call China.

A few minutes later, and now with a pile of £1 coins neatly stacked on the phone, he dialed Li Jia's number. It was the first time he had spoken with her in almost a month. 'I'm safe and I'm in London,' he told her. 'I'm well and I'm not in prison.' His wife, however, was furious. He had left Beijing without telling her where he was going. It had been a terrifying few weeks. She was convinced that her phone was bugged and that her letters were being opened. If she had known what he was up to, she said, she would have stopped him. After a few minutes, they agreed to speak in a day or so. Wang Yam hoped he would have a better lay of the land by then.

The following morning, he woke up refreshed and ready to explore London. After eating breakfast downstairs, the first thing he wanted to do was to deposit his money, so he asked directions to the high street and set off in search of a bank. It was all very unfamiliar. He'd never been to Europe and for the first time in his life he felt like a minority. After a few hours walking, he entered a pub for a drink, his first English pint, and was surprised that it was populated by old men. In Beijing, the bars were full of students and bachelors, while the old men stayed at home. Where, he wondered, were all the young men? Next he tried to open a bank account, but found the branch closed. Again this came as a jolt; in Beijing the banks were open all day on Saturdays.

Early on Sunday morning the following day, Wang Yam took a train into central London and walked up and down Oxford Street, a shopping district so famous that he had heard about it as a child. Again he was surprised. The street felt abandoned, most of the shops were closed and the pavements were empty. He managed to find one shop open, an auction house that was selling electronic and other consumer goods. The man outside appeared friendly and encouraged Wang Yam to come in. He did need a few things, he thought to himself, as he had been able to bring so little from Hong Kong. A few minutes later, he left the shop carrying a large black rubbish bag filled with merchandise. As soon as he arrived back at his room in the hostel he started playing with his new toys. There was a digital watch, a radio player and a camera, but after fiddling with them for a while he realised that none actually worked. 'I felt so stupid,' he remembered. 'My English was not very good and I didn't understand the men at the auction house.' By Monday he had run out of cash. It was a bank holiday and Wang Yam borrowed some money from the nice lady at the front desk to buy some food. It felt like an inauspicious way to start in his new country.

When he came down for breakfast on Tuesday, there was a message waiting for him at the front desk: he had an appointment that morning with a tax lawyer in central London. An hour later, Wang Yam arrived at 3 Field Court, the offices of Philip Baker QC. A rotund man with rimless glasses, a grey beard and a kind face, Baker was married to a Chinese woman and since 1989 had helped over 300 Chinese nationals apply for political asylum in the UK. Like Wang Yam, many had connections with China's pro-democracy movement.

Wang Yam spent the afternoon with the barrister, recounting his story and filling out his application for political asylum. 'Mr Yam now fears very serious consequences for himself if he were to return to China,' Baker wrote. 'It seems almost certain that the Chinese authorities are aware of his activities in 1989. He has escaped from the country without permission, at a time he was working on a top-secret military project. He is also concerned for his former supervisor and Major General F. if he were to return to China. If he were interrogated he might be forced to reveal their involvement in the events of 1989. The consequences would then be extremely serious for these persons.' By teatime, they had completed his form and sent it by mail to the UK Immigration and Nationality Department at Lunar House in Croydon, south London.

Over the next weeks, Philip Baker helped his new client in other ways. He introduced him to a network of Chinese immigrants. He answered questions about how to apply for housing benefit and how to open a bank account. Perhaps most importantly, with Baker's letter of support and introduction, Wang Yam was able to obtain a researcher's job in the physics department at Queen Mary and Westfield College in Mile End, east London. Then, in October 1992, just a few weeks after arriving in the UK (which was unusually fast), Wang Yam received his refugee status papers from the Home Office. 'The UK government', he said, 'looked after me very carefully.'

Through his new contacts, Wang Yam became involved in Chinese pro-democracy politics in London. He attended rallies and handed out leaflets in Chinatown. It was here, at one of these events, that he met a young woman call Jia Zhao, also known as Jenny Zhao. Like Wang Yam, she had been radicalised by the Tiananmen Square protest. They struck up a friendship and before long were sleeping together.

Early in December 1992, and feeling guilty about his affair with Jenny Zhao, Wang Yam spoke to Li Jia about joining him in London. She was initially unconvinced. Though she had been worried about being relocated to the provinces, her position at the International Trade Research Institute had become more secure. She had received a considerable sum for her new book on English trade practices and she had recently been promoted to manage trade licences with Taiwan. In spite of her success, however, she wanted to be with him. After another week's discussion, they finally agreed that she should fly to London as soon as possible.

On 18 December 1992, Wang Yam wrote to Philip Baker. Having thanked him for all his 'kindly help', he reported that he had received a letter from his father, via Hong Kong, which encouraged him to 'study hard and reback [sic] China at suitab [sic] situation in future'. Wang Yam then told Philip Baker that 'it is hard time for me alone. I want my wife to come here as soon as possible. I know this is very difficult but I will try at my best.' He suggested that perhaps Philip Baker could forward Li Jia's work history to his 'friend at Oxford University'.

To travel to the UK, Li Jia had to first apply for a passport from the Beijing authorities, which she did but was turned down. She tried again, making use of her business and family connections, but once more she was rejected. At that time, Beijing was one of five cities that were bidding for the 2000 summer Olympics. The winner was to be announced at a gala ceremony to be held in Monte Carlo at the end of September. Incensed that his wife was trapped in China, Wang Yam 'called a senior government official in Beijing' and promised to 'make a noise' if Li Jia didn't immediately receive a transit visa. A few days later, she received word that she was free to fly to England. Hearing the news, Wang Yam wrote to Philip Baker. 'I just receive the news that my wife has gotten passport. I'm and my whole family really very happy this,' adding, 'Very thank you for your help and concerning.'

So it was that on 23 September 1993, Li Jia passed through the arrival gates at London Heathrow Airport. Wang Yam was excited to see his wife and walked towards her open-armed and ready for a hug. Instead, she pushed him away. 'She was very upset,' Wang Yam recalled. After a testy exchange, they travelled by Underground to Finsbury Park where Wang Yam had rented a room in a boarding house.

The following day he wrote again to Philip Baker.

> Dear Philip Baker
> My wife has arrived here yesterday night. I have arranged every-
> thing ready now. Very thank you for your help. We want to visit
> you at your convenient time.
> Yours sincerely
>
> Wang Yam

'We spent the week in bed,' Wang Yam said, 'catching up, talking about the time we had missed.' Apparently, ever since her husband's flight from China Li Jia had found it hard to sleep. She said that the security police had called asking where he'd gone. The police seemed to be looking for someone to blame for his absence. He told her about his time in Hong Kong, how he had crossed the border, his interviews with the British officials and his first days in London.

Within a few weeks, Li Jia enrolled in a master's degree course at the London School of Economics. When she finished, a year later, she secured a job at the Bank of China in central London. Meanwhile, Wang Yam moved to Imperial College and started a PhD in the electronics department.

When they visited their friend Philip Baker at his house for tea, Wang Yam and Li Jia appeared comfortable together. 'They clearly loved each other,' Baker recalled. 'One had a good job at a bank, the other was studying at one of the best universities in the world. Their English was excellent. They were on the up and up.'

Having been unable to reach her by phone, Peter Devlin decided to visit Li Jia at her house in Wimbledon. If he wanted to piece together Wang Yam's early years in Britain, he needed to take a statement from his wife.

An hour after leaving Colindale, DS Peter Devlin and PC Rob Burrows pulled up outside a two-storey home at 18 Melrose Avenue. Pressing the buzzer, the door was opened by a thin Chinese lady. She looked unhappy that they had come to her house and did not invite them inside. Once Devlin had explained that he was leading the investigation into the murder of Allan Chappelow he asked her to confirm her identity. 'She appeared paranoid,' he later said. 'Her English was good but she didn't want to speak with us.' They asked her a few simple questions – When did you and Wang Yam first meet? When did you last speak with him? Do you know where he is? – but her answers were rambling and confused. It appeared to the policemen that she didn't want to help. A few minutes later, the door was closed and they returned to the car. 'That was a complete waste of time,' Devlin said when they were back in the vehicle.

A few days later, Peter Devlin and Gerry Pickering drove to Merseyside to speak with Jenny Zhao, the name listed in Wang Yam's Money TT and HSBC transactions. They found her in Wallasey, a run-down neighbourhood of Wirral, near Liverpool. She worked at Jia Min's Chinese Medical Centre, a small two-storey red-brick building on Poulton Street, located opposite a chip shop and a beauty parlour, and only a few hundred metres from Central Park, a public space known for its drug users and vandalism.

Walking into the shop, the policemen were greeted by a tall, slender and attractive Chinese woman who was standing over a seated client. As she was with a customer, the officers allowed her to finish her treatment. While they were waiting, Jenny's husband arrived; he was perplexed by the presence of the two police officers, but took his wife's cue and waited like everyone else. When she had finished and the customer had paid and left, Gerry Pickering stepped forward. 'Are you Jenny Zhao?' he asked. 'Yeah, that's right,' she said, her London accent still containing a trace of Beijing. 'I am arresting you for conspiracy to defraud,' continued Pickering, 'involving our investigation into the murder of Allan Chappelow, where cheques stolen from Mr Chappelow had been paid into an account intending to go into your account.' Devlin watched carefully for a reaction and noted that Jenny seemed unsurprised, as if she had been expecting their visit. The police then escorted Jenny and her husband to the nearby police station on Manor Road.

Jenny said that she had first met John Wong, as she then knew Wang Yam, in 1993, two years after her arrival in England. They both lived in Finsbury Park, north London; he was an IT consultant at the time, she was starting out as a Chinese medical practitioner. They lost touch after she moved to Liverpool in 1999, until the spring of 2006, when she had called him to ask if she might be able to stay with him in London. When the police asked for a specific date, she checked her diary and said that it was 5 May 2006. She picked him up at Holloway Underground station and he then directed her to his flat on Denning Road in Hampstead. During the car journey, she remembered, he said that he was now in the mortgage business. Dong Hui was waiting for them when they arrived home. He introduced her as his 'flatmate'.

That evening, over dinner, Wang Yam had explained that he was trying to help a Chinese relative obtain a work visa in the UK and that he needed someone to guarantee his stay. To demonstrate their financial stability, this guarantor needed a bank account with at least £10,000 in savings. If he transferred the funds into Jenny's account, he asked, would she be willing to help? When she enquired why he couldn't do this himself, Wang Yam said that, unlike her, he didn't have a regular income. She agreed to help, and they laughed when Wang Yam said that of course she would have to return the funds. The next day, she phoned him with her Bank of China account details.

Three weeks later, he called saying that he had transferred funds from HSBC to her account at the Bank of China. The amount was a little over £14,000. When Jenny telephoned the Bank of China, however, she was told that the funds had never arrived. Wang Yam said that perhaps he had entered incorrect account information and promised to speak with his bank.

It was in the second week of June, Jenny said, that Wang Yam called with the news that he and Dong Hui were 'leaving London'.

Would she mind, he asked, helping Dong Hui pack? He didn't give a reason, but Jenny assumed it was because he would be out of the country. On Saturday 17 June, she drove to London and over the weekend she helped Dong Hui transport nine suitcases and twelve rubbish bags to the Safestore warehouse in north London. At the warehouse, Dong Hui filled out an application form, giving her name as 'Vivien Don' and saying that she would be back in two to four weeks to pick up her belongings.

Before saying goodbye, Jenny Zhao lent Dong Hui £250 so that she could fly out to Wang Yam. Sometime during this weekend, Jenny again spoke to Wang Yam. He thanked her for her help and told her that he had now found a job in Europe and would be 'staying there for some time'. Jenny did not know in which town or city Wang Yam lived.

With the interview complete, Devlin asked Jenny to sign a witness statement. He then told her that she was free to go home and that they would soon be in touch. If she heard from Wang Yam or Dong Hui or she remembered any further details, he told her, she must contact them. Two hours after the interrogation had begun, Jenny grabbed her bag, put on her coat, returned to her husband in the waiting room, and walked out of the police station.

CASE NOTE

_____

Wanted to check claims on Wang Yam's CV. I emailed Centerprise International, which he had mentioned as one of his employers, attaching a list of all the names Wang Yam had used. Their human resources department wrote back, 'We have checked our system files, and there are no records of any of the names.'

I also contacted Imperial College (which Wang Yam also listed on his CV) to see if he had studied there. The alumni office said they would look into it.

Called Peter Devlin and asked him about Wang Yam's state of mind. 'I have as good a nose as anyone,' he said, 'and I have been right more times than I have been wrong.' It is easier, he believed, to tell if someone is innocent than guilty. When arresting someone for murder and they don't ask who the victim is, then that is a sign that they are involved. Equally, if they say 'no comment', that is another bad sign; if people are innocent they are desperate to say so. Devlin didn't place much weight on physical signs such as sweating, tics or eyes moving upwards when telling lies. He said that the telephone cell tower, bank and CCTV camera evidence proved that Wang Yam was a liar. 'I never believed the facts that he gave,' Devlin said. 'Nobody could understand why he did things. He was a Walter Mitty type.'

Having a hard time speaking with people who knew Wang Yam in the UK. Managed to find Jenny Zhao's mobile phone number, but she refused to talk with me. Have made contact, however, with Philip Baker, the QC who helped WY when he arrived in UK, and arranged a time to meet.

My researchers in Beijing and Xian are also finding it difficult to confirm Wang Yam's backstory. Everyone they approach either denies knowing Wang Yam or is reluctant to speak. That he has been out of the country for ten years is bad enough, I am told, but the fact that he is a convicted murderer – in China having a relative in prison is shameful to the family – makes it close to impossible. Researchers have tracked down Ren Jining, who Wang Yam told me is his half-brother. Ren Jining has written books about his famous grandfather Ren Bishi. It took a few phone calls to make him feel comfortable (at first he denied he was even Ren Jining), but eventually he agreed to talk. He said that Wang Yam was not the grandson of Ren Bishi, nor was he the son of Ren Yuanyuan, nor a cousin. If he continued to spread such 'lies', said Ren Jining, he would sue Wang Yam.

Wang Yam has finally given me the name of someone who knows him in the UK: Xing Sheng He. We met at a beautifully decorated restaurant in Richmond, Surrey. Xing ordered a huge amount of food and he appeared keen to be friendly towards me. The son of Chairman Mao's bodyguard, Xing left China more than twenty years ago. He said he first met Wang Yam in the early 1990s when he went to a shop in south London to have his computer repaired. Over the next few years they saw each other occasionally; Wang Yam helped Xing's wife open a bank account in London and they invited him to their home for dinner. Xing said that in one of their early conversations Wang Yam told him that he was the grandson of Ren Bishi and the son of Ren

Yuanyuan. As it happened, Xing was a friend of Yuanyuan and had visited his house many times in Beijing. He remembered his friend having small children but could not recall their names. Xing asked Wang Yam a couple of questions to double-check his story. What was your father's address in Beijing? he asked, and what was your grandmother's name? Not only did Wang Yam answer both correctly, he cried at the mention of his grandmother (just like his father) so Xing concluded that he was indeed a member of the famous Ren family. He had last seen Wang Yam in the early 2000s and was shocked to hear that he was in prison for murder. Xing didn't think Wang Yam was capable of killing anyone. Who should I believe, the alleged half-brother or the family friend?

I I

EXTRADITION

By the mid 1990s, with Li Jia now earning a sizeable salary from the Bank of China, Wang Yam's financial situation improved. They moved out of their one-bedroom flat in Finsbury Park and into the leafy suburbs of south London. First they rented a home on Stuart Road in Southwark, and then they purchased a two-storey terraced house at 18 Melrose Avenue, Wimbledon. It was a charming property, with a large garden, modern kitchen and a living room with bay windows.

To pay for the deposit on the new home, Wang Yam borrowed money from contacts in the Chinese community. The loan terms were onerous and he soon felt under pressure to make more money. In 1997, Wang Yam said that he left Imperial College without completing his PhD, and set up a number of business ventures. First came Quantum Electronics Corporation Ltd, registered at Companies House as 'maintaining office and computer machinery'. Other corporations followed, including a computer repair company, a mobile phone business, and a photocopying firm.

In early 1998, Li Jia became pregnant and, nine months later, on 13 November, she gave birth to a daughter. They gave her an English name, Angela, meaning messenger from God. In many Chinese families, it is traditional for grandparents to help with the childcare and, given that Li Jia was soon back to work at the Bank of China and Wang Yam was busy with his business ventures, they arranged for Li Jia's mother to visit them in England. When her tourist visa expired six months later, Li Jia's mother took Angela back to China, where she would remain for the next year. It was hard for Wang Yam and Li Jia to be away from their child, but they were glad that she was being well looked after and exposed to Chinese culture.

Upon his return from interviewing Jenny Zhao in Liverpool, Peter Devlin focused on collecting more evidence about Wang Yam and Dong Hui. Now that they had identified a number of witnesses, along with photographs of the suspects, the next priority was to establish whether everyone was talking about the same people.

In traditional identity parades, a witness or victim was brought into a police station, ushered into a small dark room and encouraged to look through one-way glass. On the other side, five or more members of public waited patiently next to a suspect. Usually, the police already had a strong sense of their criminal's identity and used the parade to confirm their suspicions. Yet while such parades frequently proved useful, they also had their problems. Many victims felt upset and intimidated by being in close proximity to their assailant. Moreover, the parades took considerable time to organise, with police officers having to round up similar-looking people from the local town or city. Even worse, these lineups gave police numerous opportunities to interfere with the outcome, sometimes making subtle or not-so-subtle suggestions as to which of the options might 'look right'.

In March 2003, in response to these and other criticisms, the Yorkshire police force, and then later twenty other UK police forces including the Met, had introduced a digital version of the identity parade. Now victims and witnesses sat in front of a computer screen – either at a police station or on a laptop – and were presented with a series of clips taken from a large database of over 20,000 people. Known as the Virtual Identity Parade Electronic Recording system, or VIPER, it was quicker, less emotionally stressful and, at a quarter of the price, cheaper than the traditional method. It was also, according to the Home Office who oversaw the system, less susceptible to police interference. Upon VIPER's inauguration, the Home Secretary David Blunkett had told the *Yorkshire Post*, 'The system has proved particularly useful in identifying street robbers,' adding that it will 'bring these criminals to justice much more quickly and take them off the streets where they are causing so much harm'.

So it was that on the morning of 4 July 2006, the 'designated showing officer' Sergeant Nigel Green prepared the VIPER suite at Kilburn police station in north London. The interview would be filmed and neither Peter Devlin nor any of his colleagues would be present. At 11.22 a.m., the first witness was shown into the identification suite: the postman, Nicholas Sullman.

Since making his first statement the day after Allan Chappelow's body was found, Sullman had made an additional statement to the police in which he provided new details to the inquiry. The postman now reported that the man who had stopped him while he made his rounds was 'sort of half Chinese and half English' and that he was '80 per cent sure' that he had 'an English accent from the south-east' and that he 'definitely didn't have a regional accent'. If he saw him again, he added, he would 'definitely recognise him'. He also said that he wore 'thick glasses like the comedian Eric Morecambe used to wear'.

Sullman's evidence was considered crucial. Yet this last detail, that the Chinese man wore thick glasses, had troubled Devlin for some weeks. Sullman was the only person who remembered Wang Yam – if indeed that was who Sullman saw – wearing glasses in public. Anna Toma the landlady had been clear that she never saw him with glasses. The same was true for the other witnesses. Equally, the CCTV footage of Wang Yam at the bank didn't have him wearing glasses and his optician reported that his only prescription was for reading spectacles, which were grey. This was another reason why today's VIPER interview was so important, to establish who the postman had actually seen.

'You've been asked here today', said Nigel Green from behind a computer terminal to Nicholas Sullman who was sitting opposite him, 'to see if you can identify the person that you saw on a date you can't recall but believe to be in the last two months and [who] spoke to you regarding post at a particular address.' Green then explained that he would show nine video clips and that the person that the witness had seen 'may or may not' be on the film. When Sullman said that he understood the process he was shown clips of nine possible suspects, and after a brief pause, he was shown the images again. The only clip that had an unshaven Chinese man wearing a beige jacket was the first: it was Wang Yam.

Once the presentation was over, Green said formally, 'If the person you are here to identify was shown on the film, please state the number that was shown on the screen when that person was displayed.' To this Sullman replied, 'I'm not positive, but number one is the only person who is like the vision in my head.' Though Green considered that the witness had demonstrated a 'strong element of recognition', he did not believe this to be a 'positive identification'.

The landlady Anna Toma and Ali Shahid, the manager at Curry Paradise, were also interviewed that morning. In contrast to the postman, these two witnesses clearly recognised Wang Yam and Nigel Green believed that they were confident in their identification. At

12.06 p.m., two hours after starting, Green concluded the VIPER presentation, placed a video of the witness responses inside an envelope, labelled it and typed up his notes.

When he read the VIPER report, Devlin was pleased that two of the key witnesses could positively ID the suspect. But he was troubled by Sullman's less-than-certain answer. Sullman was the only person who could place Wang Yam near 9 Downshire Hill, and given that they had no forensic evidence linking the suspect to the scene of the crime, this felt like a real blow to their investigation.

By early 2000, most of Wang Yam's business ventures had either failed to generate significant money or closed. One company, Quantum Electronics Corporation Limited, had even filed for bankruptcy. A few of his fellow directors were so outraged that they filed suit against Wang Yam in civil court. Meanwhile, Wang Yam continued to receive weekly calls from the lenders who had financed his house.

With Angela's return to 18 Melrose Avenue in the spring of 2000, the family mood shifted for the worse. Though able to secure a Chinese nanny through their contacts, Li Jia and Wang Yam seemed unable to adapt to the responsibilities of new parenthood or how this affected their relationship. According to Wang Yam, Li Jia complained about a stalker who was bothering her at work. He suspected, however, that his wife was having an affair with a German who worked at Commerzbank. 'Honestly I had more affairs than her,' he confessed, but nevertheless his 'heart sank' at the thought of her with another man. When he accused her of hacking into his emails and mobile phone, trust between the two of them broke down.

Shortly after, Wang Yam moved out of 18 Melrose Avenue and into a flat in Hampstead in north London. 'Li Jia didn't accept it,'

Wang Yam recalled, 'she cried and cried. She wanted me back. She kept calling me on my mobile phone. It was all very hard.' It wasn't long before the couple agreed to a divorce.

Hoping to improve his financial situation, Wang Yam attended a training workshop for new mortgage lenders and then set up a complicated web of financial services companies with names like First Credit International Limited, Global Combined Services, and Credit General Group Plc. He rented an office in central London, printed business cards, registered domain names, created email addresses, and then began looking for customers for these businesses. One marketing tool he used was taking out advertisements in local newspapers in which he offered attractively priced Sun Life mortgages to Chinese nationals.

In the autumn of 2001, one of Wang Yam's adverts was seen by a Mr and Mrs Lee who lived in Market Drayton, a small town near Stoke-on-Trent. They made contact with Wang Yam through his company First Credit International Limited and a few days later, on 3 September, he travelled north from London to see them at their home. Having filled out a mortgage application to Sun Life, he collected three cheques, two for Sun Life to pay for the mortgage application fee, and one to cover his train fare.

Arriving back in London, Wang Yam realised that he'd made a mistake in the paperwork and called the Lees to fix the problem. He told them that one of the processing fee cheques should have been made out to his company First Credit International Limited, and he asked permission to change the name written on the cheque. Growing suspicious, the Lees asked for their money back, but Wang Yam refused, saying it was non-refundable. By the conversation's end, neither party felt satisfied. Nevertheless, Wang Yam changed the name on the cheque and deposited it in his bank account.

A few months later, the Lees called Wang Yam and asked for help with a new mortgage application. When he asked if they were sure they said yes, and Wang Yam again took the train north. This time he was met at the station by two police officers, who took him in for questioning. Having explained his side of the story, he was cautioned and released without charge.

The trouble with the Lees was not the only time Wang Yam came to the police's attention. In 2002, bailiffs arrived at the house in Melrose Avenue looking to seize property to cover unpaid debts. While they were inside they found five credit cards that belonged to neither Wang Yam nor Li Jia. This time, Wang Yam was taken to Wimbledon police station and questioned. He said that he was holding the cards for his friends and was released once again without charge.

In addition to selling mortgage loans and repairing people's computers, Wang Yam also speculated in domain names. At this time, it was possible to purchase a domain name for a small amount of money and then sell it for a large sum to a company desperate to protect their brand. Names like sex.com, money.com, and marijuana.com sold for millions of dollars. Given that it could cost as little as $10 each to register a name and around $15 a year to store the domains at a hosting site, such domain name speculation promised enormous potential profits.

By 2003, Wang Yam had amassed over 600 domain names. Many of these – such as jamboreefoods.com, mygroceryads.com and higdonsfoods.com – were long shots. A few, however, had real promise. Bankofhongkong.net, for instance, might be of interest to Hong Kong and Shanghai Bank (HSBC); StandardLife.cn would surely be desired by the Standard Life bank; while food4less.com echoed the name of a grocery chain owned by Kroger – which with $60 billion sales in 2005 was one of the USA's largest supermarket companies. Similarly, fleming.com sounded close to Robert Fleming & Co., a Scottish bank which in 2000 sold to Chase Manhattan Bank for over $7 billion. In many ways, these domain names offered Wang Yam his only real hope of amassing significant and legal earnings. Despite this, he failed to capitalise on his investments. Either he held on too long, rejecting the few low offers that arrived in his inbox, or he failed to attract the necessary interest.

Then, the food giant Kroger sued for 'food4less.com'. In their claim, Kroger said that the domain name had originally been registered with another supermarket behemoth, and when this firm had filed for bankruptcy in July 2003, it had been agreed that the domain name would be acquired by an intermediary company who would then sell it on to them, Kroger. During this period, however, Wang Yam's 'company' Star Asset Management had seized the name and registered it. 'The record is unclear', stated the lawsuit, 'as to how [Star Asset Management] became the registrant of record'. Kroger reported that it had attempted to reach Star Asset Management, a.k.a. Wang Yam, 'via all the contacts listed with the domain registrar', but had heard no reply. Shortly afterwards, an arbitration panel awarded the domain name 'food4less' to Kroger. A few months later, another arbitration panel handed the 'StandardLife.cn' name to Standard Life. Any opportunity to settle out of court, possibly for hundreds of thousands of dollars, had been missed.

Throughout the summer of 2006, Peter Devlin gathered information on Wang Yam's business history. Companies House had a record of all the businesses that he had set up, the names, dates of birth and addresses of the directors involved, copies of the accounts and any dissolutions. Trickily, Wang Yam had used different names when registering as a director – Wang Yam, Yam Wang and Wong Yam – but by tracing companies associated with his fellow directors (who luckily kept their names), Devlin was able to compile a comprehensive list. Tracking down Wang Yam's history as a domain speculator was equally straightforward. A simple search on the 'Whois' website revealed a long list of domains that had been registered to Wang Yam, Ren Hong, and his other aliases.

Far more complicated was the task of reconstructing Wang Yam's movements during the spring of 2006. Peter Devlin and his team contacted the suspect's banks, credit card companies and internet service provider. The work was painstaking and required considerable attention to detail. Each organisation demanded a separate official request form that needed to be filled out and approved. When the evidence arrived, it had to be logged and numbered before it could be reviewed. If any useful intelligence emerged it had to be cross-referenced against the growing inventory gathered from other sources.

The mobile phone data was perhaps the most difficult to assemble. In addition to tracing the phone calls made on Allan Chappelow's handset, the police had to gather the calls made on phones belonging to Wang Yam, Li Jia and Dong Hui, along with other witnesses including Jenny Zhao and He Jia Jin. From this vast pool of information, they would need to identify when each took place, which cell towers were used (so they could determine the location of the caller) and, where audio recordings were available, transcribe conversations. This task was made onerous as telephone calls were protected by stringent privacy laws and each line required a separate application, necessitating hours of paperwork.

The gathering of all this information would take months to complete.

In the summer of 2004, Wang Yam flew from London to Shanghai to do business with some Chinese insurance companies. Though he was travelling on a British passport and under his adopted name, he was nervous about arriving in China. Might they recognise him at passport control, take him aside for questioning, ask him about his role in the 1989 student protests?

As he was waiting in line, he noticed a small, pretty young Chinese woman standing next to him. They started talking. Her name was Dong Hui. She also lived in London where she was studying marketing at Middlesex University. She was back in China to see her parents and the rest of the family. As the line snaked forward, they continued chatting, and before it was Dong Hui's turn, they agreed to meet up later that week. After a few minutes, and having picked up his luggage and passed through customs, Wang Yam was seated in a bus on his way to the city centre. He had made it.

Shanghai had changed dramatically since he'd last seen it in the early 1990s. Massive cranes towered over the skyline. Whole swathes of the city had been cleared to make way for a forest of apartment blocks and its streets were teeming with cars, motorcycles and electric bikes. Even from inside the bus he could tell the pollution was oppressive. A gloomy grey miasma filtered the weak sunshine while many pedestrians wore face masks.

While he was in Shanghai, Wang Yam visited his elderly grandmother in hospital. Standing next to her, Wang Yam realised that she was too weak to recognise him. The 94-year-old wife of China's great hero Ren Bishi had been ailing for many months and was now close to death. Wang Yam loved his grandmother and was deeply sad to know this was likely to be the last time he would see her.

A few days later, Wang Yam called Dong Hui on her mobile phone. They met up the next day, and the day after that. It turned out that she was seventeen years younger than him. She told him that she liked to play table tennis, and that both she and her father had been table tennis champions. Wang Yam said that he also liked to play, and that as a boy he had been coached by a famous player who knew her father. According to Wang Yam, she said that her family had roots in Taiwan and she had cousins in Germany and the USA, one of whom was the tennis player Michael Chang (winner of the French Open and Wimbledon quarter-finalist). Her family was conservative and wealthy by Chinese standards. Earning an annual salary of 150,000 yuan, her father's income was six times the national average.

Dong Hui's parents lived in Wuhan, the capital of Hubei, China's landlocked central province. As he didn't have enough time to fly out to meet them before returning to England, Wang Yam called Dong Hui's father. Introducing himself on the phone, Wang Yam said that he lived in London and ran a successful business, and that he was interested in a romantic relationship with Dong Hui. Her father thanked Wang Yam for the call and promised to speak to his former coach so that he could verify his character.

According to Wang Yam, Dong Hui's father was displeased with what he heard: Wang Yam was politically unreliable, financially undependable, divorced, and even had a young daughter. Once she graduated, he wanted Dong Hui to move to the USA, where she could take advantage of opportunities and be helped by family members who lived there. He didn't want her to be stuck with this older man with poor prospects. Dong Hui, however, was unrelenting. She said that she liked Wang Yam and wanted to see him in England. It would be hard for her parents to exert control when she was eight time zones and 5,000 miles away.

In September 2004, Dong Hui flew in to London for the second year of her marketing course and to complete her master's dissertation. Before long, Wang Yam and Dong Hui were in a relationship and, despite the age difference, they fell deeply in love. In her 6 January 2005 diary entry, Dong Hui recorded her feelings for Wang Yam:

Another New Year has come. I have spent nearly two years in London and still have not succeeded in anything at this moment. My dissertation is on hold and I don't have a mind to go to work. However, my love life has gone through earth-shaking changes – heart-melting pain and perseverance. I know that he is the man I am madly in love with. The madder I am the more scared I am. I am scared that he will no longer belong to me one of these days. I am not talking about his person, I am talking about his heart. In front of him I feel like a wilful princess, on other occasions I feel a mature woman. Sometimes I am like a docile bird whilst other times I am like a mother. He always wants me to love him with full intensity and to possess him. I know he is the first man whom I love with all my body and heart. Mum once said, 'Don't expect a lot,' but I always hope to get what I want. How much I want to put on a wedding dress. This is my dream, my dream.

A short while later, Wang Yam and Dong Hui agreed that they should move into a flat together and discussed the best location. He travelled by bus to his office in central London and she had to take the Underground every day to her classes, so they opted for a one-bedroom flat at 49 Gayton Road in Hampstead, as it was affordable and equidistant for their daily commutes.

Nevertheless, not all was rosy for the London couple. Dong Hui didn't like her boyfriend's weekly visits to his six-year-old daughter. She didn't like that in order to do this he had to go to 18 Melrose Avenue in Wimbledon, where his ex-wife lived, the house that they still jointly owned. And she didn't like the letters and phone calls she received from her parents, exhorting her to leave Wang Yam. But she persevered. She loved him and vowed that they would always stay together.

In the spring of 2005, Wang Yam and Dong Hui decided to find a new flat. Her mother would be visiting in the first week of June and they would need more space. Though her parents disapproved of the relationship, they missed their daughter. 'Her parents had no choice,' Wang Yam later said. 'They had to accept me.'

Despite the tensions, Dong Hui was upbeat. On 26 May 2005, she added another note to her diary:

> I went to the park today on my own and stayed there for ages. There were many children playing happily in front of me. I saw a girl sitting on a swing. Her swing went up really high in the wind. She was so happy and was enjoying herself to the full. Her long hair was also floating freely in the light wind. She was completely immersing herself in the beautiful sunny afternoon.

In a later entry she confessed to her diary that 'I really want to have a little baby'. Soon, she hoped, she too would have a 'calm and warm family', be a mother and able to visit the playground with her husband and children.

It had been a long, tiresome few weeks for Peter Devlin. While the rest of his team caught other jobs, he, Rob Burrows and Gerry Pickering continued to focus on the Allan Chappelow murder. By the World Cup final on 9 July 2006, a thrilling game in which the French captain was sent off for head-butting his opponent and which was eventually won by the Italians on penalties, Devlin wondered if they would ever find Wang Yam. He could be anywhere.

Frustrated, he asked his boss again if they could issue a Red Notice, but still Lansdown's answer was a firm 'no'. Instead, he was told to redouble his focus on the bank, telephone and internet evidence which might help them locate their prime suspect.

Then they caught a break. Early on in the investigation, Devlin had asked Police Constable Rob Burrows to speak with Iomart, the company managing Wang Yam's domains. During these inquiries, Iomart said that the account was in the name of 'Ren Hong' and that it was still active. It was Burrows who now suggested that maybe they could track the suspect when he next attempted to renew one of his domains.

On 24 July, Iomart passed on the information that three domains had been recently paid for on Wang Yam's account: americabancorp. com, Fleming-china.com, and London-re.com. On their Apache server logs, they traced the online activity to an IP address registered as 212.4.86.73. This, Iomart informed PC Burrows, belonged to a computer located in the canton of Zug, Switzerland. A few days later, Iomart received a call regarding the Ren Hong account. The UK telephone number captured on the customer representative's screen was '+44 765 253 888', which Burrows discovered was being forwarded to '+41 417 116 767', a Swiss number. They now had two pieces of evidence suggesting Wan Yam's whereabouts. Hearing this news, Pete Lansdown asked Peter Devlin to prepare an international arrest warrant request to be submitted to the Swiss authorities.

Meanwhile, Devlin continued gathering information about the suspect's financial background.

On 19 September 2005, Wang Yam had applied for personal bankruptcy at the Royal Courts of Justice in central London. He filled out Form 6.28, paid the filing fee of £310, and was told the case was to be heard in room 211 on the second floor of the Thomas More building. In his filing, Wang Yam stated that he was unemployed and that he owed over £1 million. The bankrupt's list read like a litany of past cons.

Many of the debtors were familiar. He owed £10,000 to his first wife Li Jia, for instance, as well as £3,000 to her mother. He also owed £50,000 to 'Jessie' Li Ping Chan, the owner of a Chinese restaurant in south London whose husband, like Wang Yam, had been a director of Sun Life Financial Limited. He owed £57,000 to Tae Young Jung (aka 'Tyger Jung'), the owner of a London fashion company. Jung had helped finance the purchase of 18 Melrose Avenue and had never been reimbursed. Most astoundingly, Wang Yam claimed that he owed £250,000 to Dong Hui's father, 'a loan to purchase a wine company', read the complaint. When he was asked by the court why he was filing for personal bankruptcy, Wang Yam wrote that 'the creditor push me too hard and not give me more time', and that 'I try to set up Business make the Money pay them Back. But have struggled near 3 years. It is failed.' The bankruptcy now granted, Wang Yam was effectively destitute.

As part of his investigation, Devlin also visited Dong Hui's doctor in Hampstead and gathered her medical records. From these he discovered that she had become pregnant in January 2006. Presumably she would have told Wang Yam by early March. Given the bankruptcy, the lack of a job, the problems with Anna Toma the landlady, and then the baby, Devlin thought that by early spring 2006 the suspect must have been feeling desperate.

It came as a surprise, therefore, when the detective learned that it was around this time that Wang Yam offered to purchase a house in Hampstead Village for £1.6 million. The property was located at 48 Gayton Road, the same street where he and Dong Hui had first lived together. As part of this new transaction, Wang Yam left proofs of funds with a Chestertons sales agent. The documents included a bank statement from Credit Suisse showing that he had over £34 million in his account. Inquiries to this Swiss bank, however, failed to confirm whether Wang Yam had ever been a client.

From his discussions with other estate agents, Devlin learned that the house on Gayton Road was not the only property Wang Yam had made offers on. Indeed, he had left his details with at least ten estate agents in north London and viewed more than twenty flats and houses. To bolster his *bona fides*, he had told some agents that his family owned a bank in Hong Kong and others that he worked for Credit Suisse bank in Mayfair. He offered different email accounts to the branches he visited. To Goldschmidt and Howland he gave the address JohnWong@axasunlife.com. To Savills he gave John-Wong@fleming.com, JohnWongmbox@yahoo.com to Winkworths and Johnwong@swissbanktrust.com to Chestertons. He added that he was a cash buyer and explained that he had many offshore accounts.

Wang Yam had informed one agent at Foxtons in Notting Hill Gate, for instance, that he was interested in buying properties priced between £3.5 million and £8 million. They even discussed the purchase of Montpellier Hall, which was on the market for £20 million. Wang Yam said he would have to 'check his finances'. He looked at two properties on Prince of Wales Terrace valued at £4 million each, and told the agent that he wanted 'his people to see it'. He also viewed a small Georgian house at 40a Downshire Hill, less than 100 metres from Allan Chappelow's home.

Devlin had discovered that Wang Yam had made an offer for £960,000 on another house on Gayton Road, this time number 56. The offer was submitted to the estate agents TK International, accepted by the buyer, and a surveyor was sent to examine the property. The deal fell through, however, as the 'purchaser was unable to produce funds because of problems with his estranged wife'. When Wang Yam's cheque to the surveyor bounced, the estate agent went to his flat at Denning Road but Dong Hui said that her boyfriend was out, and she didn't know when he would return.

It was through further interviews and by poring through reams of financial records that Devlin was able to reconstruct the suspect's last few days in England. On 5 June, the same day that £20,000 was transferred out of Allan Chappelow's ING account, Wang Yam had visited the HR Owen car dealership in Euston Road and said that he wanted to buy a Volvo estate. He left a cheque with the salesman for £500, a deposit on a car that was worth £23,000, but again this cheque bounced and Wang Yam never returned to the car dealership. The next day, 6 June, he viewed yet another flat in Hampstead. He gave the owner, Sarah Jacobs, a cheque for £1,850, representing the deposit and three weeks' rent for the property. This cheque also bounced.

Wang Yam's final property search took place on 13 June 2006 (a day after PCs Mike Cole and Sam Azouelos first entered 9 Downshire Hill). Sometime that afternoon, Wang Yam walked into the TK International estate agents in Hampstead and said that he was 'still looking'.

Forty-eight hours later, he would be on a train to Brussels.

In 2006, when a suspect was arrested there had to be a 'reasonable suspicion', which is a fairly low burden of proof. They were told why they were being arrested, read a caution, and then typically released pending further investigations and trial (though many were remanded in custody). The intervening period gave the police an opportunity to interview the accused and other witnesses, as well as gather as much evidence as possible. When it came to an international arrest warrant, however, the Crown Prosecution Service, or CPS, had first to be persuaded that there was sufficient evidence that there was more than a 50 per cent chance that they would win in court. It also meant that the police would not be able to interview the suspect after arrest.

Devlin and Lansdown were convinced that they had found their man. They had motive: there were numerous reports of Wang Yam's financial troubles. They had opportunity: Wang Yam lived around the corner from Allan Chappelow and, despite his uncertainty, they believed that the postman Nicholas Sullman linked the suspect to the scene of the crime. And they had plenty of evidence: perhaps best of all, Wang Yam captured on CCTV depositing the victim's cheques in his own bank account. It was more than enough, they thought.

If Wang Yam had been traced to a member country of the European Union, they could have issued a European Arrest Warrant but, as Switzerland was not part of the EU, the arrest warrant would have to be channelled through the International Criminality Unit at the British Home Office and then forwarded to the Swiss authorities. Normally, the request for an international arrest would take weeks, even months, as the complicated form had to be first approved by the CPS and then translated into French. Luckily, however, Devlin had recently submitted a warrant to the French authorities and was able to reuse much of the material for this case.

With the paperwork now filed, Lansdown and Devlin waited for a response. Weeks passed. Lansdown asked the International Criminality Unit to chase their Swiss counterparts, yet still there was no news. He had so many questions – was Wang Yam really living in Zug? Had the Swiss Federal Police spoken to him? Was Dong Hui with him? – but they went unanswered. 'We got nothing,' Lansdown later said. 'It was like a black hole. The Swiss are very secretive.'

CASE NOTE

_____

I received a call from Thomas Carr's wife. I had left a few messages on her voicemail and she wanted to know what I wanted. She said that her husband had known Allan and helped from time to time with odd jobs around the house. 'He was very sad', she said, 'when he learned of Allan's death.' She then told me that her husband had died in 2008, of a heart attack. I tried to keep the conversation going but she refused to answer any more questions and then asked me not to call again. Feel awful for having intruded, and for my initial suspicions about Carr.

Wang Yam called me as usual at 5 p.m. I asked him about the property deals he had attempted just after he declared bankruptcy. Surely he had no hope of affording any of the houses he made offers on. He was quick to respond. 'The money did not come from me,' he said, 'I had a cousin in Xian who was quite rich. He wanted to send his children to the UK, and he had some cash available.' This type of proxy purchase wasn't particularly common back in 2006, he said, but was widespread today. 'London property is a safe bet for overseas investors,' he added. This makes a little more sense to me.

At 7.30 p.m. Wang Yam called me again. I was in the kitchen having dinner with my family. He has started doing this more often, phoning without an appointment. 'I want to tell you something else,' he said. A few years ago, he'd become friendly with an inmate who was also serving time for murder; they'd played table tennis together, they'd grown to trust each other. One day, they were sitting in Wang Yam's prison cell reading newspapers, the inmate on the bed, Wang Yam on a chair. The inmate was looking at a story about the murder of BBC TV presenter Jill Dando when, out of the blue, he said: 'I did it.' The inmate reported that he'd ridden up to Jill Dando's house on a scooter (she was opening her front door) and aimed a pistol at her head. 'Bam, bam,' he said. Two shots (the newspapers reported only one shot fired). He then sped away. Unlike reports in the press it had nothing to do with Bosnia, Wang Yam remembered the inmate telling him. Instead it was connected to the British criminal underworld, which Dando was known to expose in her television show Crimewatch. *The conversation then moved on to other matters. Wang Yam said that following the inmate's confession, he had provided the details in a letter to Philip Baker, but the lawyer had warned Wang Yam that he might be at risk if it became known that he was a jailhouse snitch. Despite Baker's warning, Wang Yam also sent the inmate's confession to a court official. He was surprised when nobody came to interview him. Maybe Wang Yam was looking for attention (from me), or perhaps the inmate really did tell him (but was insane). Maybe it is true. I have to get this information to the police, but don't want to make a fool of myself.*

12

THE FUNERAL

_____

On 25 September 2006, detective Gerry Pickering emailed an update to Patty Ainsworth, Allan Chappelow's American cousin. 'We now have sufficient evidence to charge our main suspect and are waiting for the completion of an international arrest warrant,' he wrote. 'Once that has been approved by a judge, we will be going abroad to arrest him and bring him back to England.' He added that Allan's letter that she had provided to the Metropolitan Police 'has helped' as it showed that her relative was alive on 5/6 May. 'I can't say too much about the rest of our findings but once our suspect is charged I will be able to tell you more.'

Pickering also explained that Allan's Danish relatives were now taking responsibility for the estate. A funeral would be held in four days' time in London. Patty hadn't visited the UK since the 1970s, and the ticket would be expensive, but given the time she had spent with Allan that spring, she felt she had a duty to be there.

The service was held at 2.30 p.m. on 29 September 2006 at the Hoop Lane chapel in Golders Green, where George Bernard Shaw had been cremated in 1950. Allan Chappelow's body lay in a dark wooden casket in the back of a large black hearse which had transported him from the morgue in St Pancras. As family and friends arrived, he was guarded by six undertakers from Floyd and Son dressed in black suits and silky top hats.

The meagre funeral party gathered outside in the chapel's courtyard and introduced themselves. In all there were fewer than twenty people. The family was represented by four of Allan's cousins who had flown in from Copenhagen (including Torben Permin and Merete Karlsborg), along with his two distant English relatives, Michael Chappelow and James Chappelow, as well as Patty Ainsworth from the USA. Allan's friends John and Peggy Sparrow were there, as were the chairwoman and secretary of the George Bernard Shaw Society. There were also a number of Allan's Downshire Hill neighbours, including Peter Tausig and Lady Listowel. The local journalist Dan Carrier was also present.

Pete Lansdown stood at the edge of the gathering, looking on. It was rare for a senior investigating officer to attend a murder victim's funeral. So many things could go wrong. He could be bombarded with questions, he might say something inappropriate, or a family member might consider his presence an intrusion. For Lansdown, however, staying away would have been a mistake. He wanted to make sure that Allan Chappelow had a good send-off. Hearing an American accent, Lansdown walked up to Patty Ainsworth and introduced himself. As Gerry Pickering had arranged, she handed him the original letter that Allan had sent to her after his trip to the USA. Lansdown thanked her and said that it would be entered into custody for possible later use at trial.

One of the mourners asked who was going to deliver the eulogy. It quickly became clear that nobody knew Allan well enough to give a proper tribute. The priest who had been hired by the family offered to say a few words and wondered if anyone had any suggestions. Again, there was an awkward silence. One of the Danish cousins had brought with him a copy of Allan's book *Shaw – The Chucker-Out*, and suggested that this might be used as a source.

A few minutes later, the group was steered into the chapel. As they took their seats, they saw Allan's wooden casket was now sitting on metal rollers on the hall's left side. After the organ stopped playing, the priest stood up and read the author's biography that was printed on the back cover of *Shaw – The Chucker-Out*. 'Allan Chappelow was an MA and twice prizeman of Trinity College Cambridge,' he began. 'He has travelled widely and his book *Russian Holiday* (1955), in which he described his experiences as one of the very first visitors to the Soviet Union a few months after Stalin's death, achieved wide acclaim . . .' The mourners listened on as the priest valiantly attempted to deliver an emotional eulogy from the marketing material's cold words. 'In *Shaw the Villager*, a work of entirely different nature, Mr Chappelow showed himself equally the master of his material,' the priest pressed on, '*Shaw – The Chucker-Out* is complementary and deals mainly with the public Shaw. It is a commentary in which Shaw's views are presented and their controversial and paradoxical nature critically examined.'

When the priest sat down, a small bearded man dressed in dirty clothes and with yellowed fingertips rushed forward and began speaking loudly from the podium. 'Allan would not have wanted this,' he shouted. 'He didn't believe in religion.' The man's words became rambling and incoherent. Someone whispered that he was a homeless person from Hampstead. After it became clear that he showed no sign of stopping, Pete Lansdown stepped forward, gently took the man's elbow and led him to one side. As they walked past, Dan Carrier smelled alcohol on the heckler's breath.

The organ started again, mostly hiding the sound of a machine humming into motion. The metal rollers propelled the coffin towards two small wooden doors which opened, revealing flames inside, and then shut, consuming the body of Allan Chappelow. After a brief pause, an usher opened a large wooden door at the rear of the hall. The entire service had lasted less than ten minutes. Afterwards, the four Danish cousins, the neighbours, Michael and James Chappelow and the other mourners drank tea and ate biscuits in a small room next to the chapel. Most were relieved the service was over. It had been uncomfortable, Patty Ainsworth remembered, and 'a little sad'.

As he was leaving Allan Chappelow's funeral, Pete Lansdown felt his phone vibrate in his pocket; it was Peter Devlin. 'They've got him,' said Devlin. 'The Swiss have arrested Wang Yam.'

PART III

PROSECUTION

'*The trouble with all police prosecutions is that, having once got what they imagine to be their man, they are not very open to any line of investigation which might lead to other conclusions. Everything which will not fit into the official theory is liable to be excluded.*'

Arthur Conan Doyle, *The Case of Oscar Slater*

13

THE ARREST

_____

It took a while for them to work out what happened, but having spoken to their contacts in the Belgian, German and Swiss police, Pete Lansdown and Peter Devlin were eventually able to piece together Wang Yam and Dong Hui's movements.

On 18 June 2006, three days after leaving London, Wang Yam took the ICE train from Brussels to Frankfurt am Main in Germany, and then boarded an express train to Basel and on to Zurich, the economic capital of Switzerland. The journey took a little over ten hours. On arrival, he checked into the Apart-Hotel on Karistrasse, a small family-run establishment that cost £150 a night. The next day, 19 June, he collected Dong Hui, who had flown in from Luton to Zurich Airport. They paid for the hotel room using Dong Hui's credit card.

The following day, Wang Yam and Dong Hui visited the British consulate in Zurich to obtain a Swiss marriage licence. Wang Yam explained that he was in Switzerland to carry out business and that he had visited many times before. They had wanted to marry in the UK, he continued, but they had been told that because Dong Hui was a Chinese national and had entered the UK on a student visa, they would have to marry outside the country and then re-apply for entry.

The consulate official informed them that they would first need to fill out a document from the UK General Registrar which would demonstrate that they were free to marry. Wang Yam wrote that they lived at 49 Gayton Road in Hampstead and that he had never before been married. Making a copy of Wang Yam and Dong Hui's passports, the British official said that hopefully their papers would be ready by the end of September.

In late June, Wang Yam and Dong Hui moved into a room above the Peking Duck restaurant in the town of Oberägeri. With a population of a little under 6,000 people, Oberägeri was located within the canton of Zug, some 30 miles south of Zurich. Sitting on the shores of Lake Ägerisee and with glorious views over the lower Alps, Oberägeri attracted summer visitors from across Europe. The room was small with a single window overlooking the main street. They shared a bathroom and kitchen with the other tenants. The restaurant was well situated; nobody would notice another two Chinese people going in and out of the Peking Duck.

Occasionally Wang Yam visited a local library to check the news and keep an eye on his internet portfolio. During this time, he used Dong Hui's credit card to renew 127 of his existing domains through his online Iomart account and registered more than twenty new names, including flemingtrust.com and beijingwatch.org. When he was not in front of the computer, or on the phone talking to customer service representatives at Iomart, Wang Yam spent time at the lake. Unlike the pressure that he had felt in London, Wang Yam now had plenty of time on his hands. Half-naked, he stood in the water, rod in hand, and waited for a fish to take a nibble at the small chunk of bread dangling from his hook. If he became too hot, he put down the rod and went for a swim.

Now five months pregnant, Dong Hui didn't like to swim, nor did she like the heat or the tourists who gathered in the cafés dotted around the lakeshore. Instead, she stayed in the room above the restaurant reading books and talking to her friends in England and China. She was eager to get the marriage licence sorted out so she could return to London in time for the birth. It was critical that their baby was born in England so that he – the doctors had told them it was a boy – qualified for European citizenship.

A few weeks before Allan Chappelow's funeral, the British Consulate in Zurich had called Wang Yam saying they'd received the documents showing that he was free to marry. Then, on 20 September, Wang Yam and Hui had applied for a marriage licence at the registry office on Kolinplatz in Zug. There, they were told that they must first register with the Swiss police.

The next day, 21 September, Wang Yam and Dong Hui paid a visit to the Zug police station, a three-storey white-stone building topped by a red-tiled turret. They registered with the sergeant in reception. Wang Yam said that he was in Switzerland on business and he intended to marry his pregnant girlfriend. When the police officer ran a check on the Chinese couple, she was surprised by what she found. 'The British police', she said, 'are looking for you.' Wang Yam replied that he had no idea why this was, and the officer said that she would look into it and would be in touch.

A week later, on the evening of 27 September, Wang Yam and Dong Hui were in their room preparing dinner when they heard their door open. Three Zug police officers walked in – black boots, black trousers, blue shirt, blue cap – each with a gun on their belts. 'We need to talk with you,' said the female officer who they had seen the previous week. 'You have to come with us.' 'All right,' said Wang Yam, a spoon still in his hand. 'What about?' 'We will tell you at the police station,' replied the female officer.

One of the policemen told Wang Yam to put his hands behind his back and then placed a pair of cuffs around his wrists. The others conducted a rudimentary search, removing various items including a mobile phone, his passport and a hard drive. All the while, Dong Hui looked on without speaking. Wang Yam was then roughly escorted downstairs into a waiting vehicle.

An hour later, he was sitting in an interview room with the female police officer at the Zug police station. The interrogation was conducted in English. Wang Yam felt relaxed; this was probably about Dong Hui's immigration status, he thought to himself, or something similar. The officer then repeated that the London police were looking for him and this time gave him the reason: he was wanted for murder.

'I was shocked,' Wang Yam later claimed. 'I didn't know what they were talking about.' He said that his mind raced trying to figure things out, to catch up with what was happening, that he was confused. He decided that it was best just to tell his story. 'I can clear it up straight away,' he said and suggested that he speak to the British consul in Zurich, but the policewoman declined his offer and said that the interview was now terminated.

He was booked and then led to a cell housed in the basement of the police station. Next door was a large German woman who had been arrested for drug dealing. After chatting for a short while, he said good night and tried to get some sleep on the thin mattress that lay on a metal-framed bed.

The following day, Wang Yam met with his lawyer who had represented him in previous business dealings in Zug. He was then taken for his first hearing in a room that looked more like an office than a courtroom. The judge wore a dark suit and sat behind a simple desk, a recorder and a translator beside him. The judge explained that the Metropolitan Police had requested, via the British Home Office, that Wang Yam be extradited to England to face charges of fraud and murder. If he so wished, he could challenge the extradition in federal court. What did he have to say?

Wang Yam declared he was innocent of all charges but he would not fight the extradition. The judge said that he would give the accused twenty-four hours to reconsider and, if at any time he changed his mind, he could call the court. After that it would be too late. The next morning, Wang Yam informed the judge that he had decided to return to England to clear his name. In response, his jailers told him that he would remain in the Zug police cell while the extradition papers were being prepared. It would likely take between one and two months.

In the early afternoon of 8 October 2006, just under two weeks after Wang Yam's arrest, Peter Devlin, Gerry Pickering and DS Tressey Clarke drove from Colindale to Heathrow Airport. They were dressed in plain clothes and in an unmarked car. It was a big moment for Operation Barnesdale. They'd heard that Dong Hui was returning to England so that she could give birth in a London hospital. They would greet her upon disembarkation.

Arriving in Terminal 2, the homicide investigators were escorted airside by immigration officers. When Swiss International Airlines flight 324 landed from Zurich just after 4 p.m., they were waiting at the gate. The pilot asked that all passengers remain in their places with the exception of the woman sitting in seat number 12F. A few seconds later, a small, sturdy and heavily pregnant Chinese lady exited the plane and stepped into the terminal. 'Are you Dong Hui?' asked Clarke, recognising her from a photograph. When the passenger confirmed her identity, Gerry Pickering presented his warrant card and said, 'I am arresting you for conspiracy to defraud and conspiracy to steal, and on suspicion for the murder of Allan Chappelow.' Dong Hui appeared shocked. 'Murder!' she yelled. 'My partner Wang Yam has already been arrested in Switzerland for murder!'

Having collected Dong Hui's luggage, they waited while she was processed by immigration officials and then passed into the arrivals hall. Pickering asked if she was expecting anyone to collect her from the airport. Dong Hui said she was hoping that her friend Jenny Zhao would pick her up, but as there was no sign of her they decided not to wait. The police then escorted Dong Hui out of the airport.

The officers then drove Dong Hui to Holborn police station in central London, arriving a little after 7 p.m. Having offered her something to drink, Peter Devlin now sat across from Dong Hui in a small room and began the interview. What was your relationship with Wang Yam? Have you ever visited 9 Downshire Hill? Why did you leave England so quickly in June?

When she spoke, the woman's English was 'fine but not perfect', recalled Devlin, and from time to time she consulted an electronic dictionary to check a word's meaning. It became clear that she had not spoken with Wang Yam for a few days and was anxious to know how he was faring. She explained that she had returned to London so that her child would be born in the UK and gain British citizenship. Other than that, she was 'very difficult' and her answers were 'all over the place', Devlin said. 'We could not get her to give a coherent account. She talked, but said nothing. She appeared lost. She was scared.'

Eventually, around 9 p.m., Devlin brought the interview to a close. Dong Hui looked exhausted and he didn't think he would get any further by keeping her any longer. She gladly accepted his offer to find her somewhere to spend the night, and an hour later he said goodbye to her at the entrance to a nearby hotel. Tomorrow, she would go and stay with one of her friends in Finchley, north London. Then she would book an appointment with her doctor in Hampstead.

A few days later, Peter Devlin received a translation of Dong Hui's personal diary that had been seized when she was arrested. One entry was written just six days before her arrival back in London.

2 October 2006

I'm on the verge of a breakdown. My fiancé has been arrested by the [Swiss] police. They said it has to do with a murder case. I cannot see him and I want to know whether he is OK and how is his health. Whenever I think about our past time together, tears start streaming down my face. Only now do I realise how much I love him. Although everyone else doesn't think he is an ideal husband, I know deep down that he is, and I love him so very much. This is why, beyond being pregnant, I am now in so much pain. I must learn to be strong, to face the emotional pain, even more courage to accept the mental blows that are to come. Even possessing nothing, one must not lose belief.

Over the next few weeks the police kept a close eye on Dong Hui, but were unable to collect another statement more useful than the first. 'I always suspected that she knew more,' Devlin later recalled, 'but we could find no evidence beyond her association with Wang Yam.'

A month later, on 11 November, Armistice Day, Peter Devlin was once again at Heathrow Airport, this time at the Bath Road police station near Terminal 2. A little after 2.30 p.m., he received a call telling him that the prisoner was on his way. He walked outside and stood waiting in the yard for the extradition squad to arrive. The wind had picked up, and though he had his coat on, he hoped they wouldn't be too long.

A few minutes later, a police van pulled up. An officer hopped out and opened the back door. Out stepped the prisoner, a slim, medium-height man of Chinese descent, with short greying hair: Wang Yam. The prisoner seemed calm, confident, apparently unworried about what was going to happen to him. 'It was nice to have him back in England,' Peter Devlin recalled. 'There was sufficient evidence to think that he did it, and a certain satisfaction to having him in custody.'

Having handed over the prisoner, the extradition escort then passed Devlin a sealed box of exhibits of evidence collected in Switzerland. Amongst other items inside the box were a single pair of size-46 shoes, a silver Safecom mobile hard disk drive and Wang Yam's passport. The Swiss authorities also handed over three mobile phones that had been retrieved from the room above the Peking Duck. Taking him by the arm, Devlin walked the prisoner into the police station's front reception area. There he was checked in and his fingerprints were recorded. The prisoner was then led into a custody suite and told to sit in a chair.

A few minutes later, Peter Devlin was sitting across from Wang Yam. 'I am charging you', he said, 'with the murder of Allan Chappelow, and other frauds. You do not have to say anything, but it may harm your defence if you do not mention, when questioned, something which you later rely on in court. Anything you do say may be given in evidence.'

'I reject to that,' said Wang Yam. 'I want to speak to a lawyer and I [then] will be interviewed and take you through it step by step.' As he didn't have a lawyer, he was provided with a list of possible firms whose bills would be paid by the government's Legal Aid scheme. Soon he was speaking with James Mullion, the on-call lawyer at the London-based Janes Solicitors. Wang Yam was also allowed to speak with Dong Hui. On the telephone, he told his girlfriend that he was back in London, he was unhurt and in police custody. She said that everything was okay with the pregnancy, though she felt a little uncomfortable, and promised to visit him soon.

Later that evening, James Mullion arrived by car from central London and spent the next two hours in a conference room with his new client. During this conversation, Wang Yam told his lawyer that he had indeed been in possession of Allan Chappelow's cheques and tried to deposit them at HSBC but that he did not kill the man, nor did he ever visit his house. Mullion asked why he had the victim's cheques. Wang Yam explained that he had been mixing with a group of Chinese gangsters – men involved in identity theft and money laundering.

As Wang Yam proceeded to tell his story, Mullion made rapid notes. He was surprised by what Wang Yam disclosed, but also sceptical. This was not the first time that he had heard outlandish claims from those accused of serious crimes. Some were mentally ill, others were playing games. At the same time, he didn't discount Wang Yam's story, nor did he tell him he was being ridiculous.

The conversation quickly moved on to what would happen next. Mullion explained to his client that after they'd finished their meeting, he would be interviewed by the police and their exchange would be recorded on tape. Don't say anything, Mullion told his client. They needed time to prepare their defence. He would be held in custody until his committal hearing, and then, pending the start of the trial, he would be assigned another prison, probably a 'Category A' facility given the murder charge. His firm, Janes Solicitors, would provide advice and would represent him at no cost. The lawyer then invited Wang Yam to fill out the legal aid forms.

At 10.10 p.m. that same evening, Devlin met with the prisoner again, this time with his lawyer present, as well as a Chinese interpreter. When he was given an opportunity to respond formally to the charges, Wang Yam declined to comment. Devlin gave Wang Yam his business card and told him to contact him anytime if he wanted to talk. The conversation ended after only six minutes.

With the official proceedings now over, Wang Yam was invited to say goodbye to his lawyer – who promised to stay in touch – and was then driven to HMP Pentonville in north London. There, he was checked in at reception, searched and handed a temporary prisoner number (TX6281), before being led off to a cell where he would spend his first night in an English prison.

On 18 November 2006, a week after arriving at Pentonville Prison, Wang Yam received word that he was needed in the governor's office.

A female prison guard escorted him to the administration wing where he was directed to the telephone. It was Dong Hui, calling from her bed at the University College London Hospital. She had given birth that morning, she said softly into the receiver; it had been a long and painful delivery but she and the baby were safe. It was a boy, she added, his name was Brian Ren Dong. Her mother had been with her, but she wished that Wang Yam had also been present.

Standing in the prison office, Wang Yam felt a mixture of emotions: joy at his son's birth, sorrow that he couldn't see him. Dong Hui reported that she was being well cared for by the doctors and nurses, for which Wang Yam was relieved. They were letting her stay in hospital for another night or two, she said, as they realised that her partner was in prison. Leaving the office, Wang Yam thanked the guard for allowing him to speak to Dong Hui and said that it was a boy. 'Congratulations,' replied the guard, and walked him back to his cell.

Two months later, Dong Hui came to visit Wang Yam. It took her less than an hour to travel from her flat in Finchley, north London, to Pentonville Prison. She brought Brian with her though it wasn't easy with the pram and changing bag. They met in the starkly lit visiting room; around them other prisoners were noisily talking with their relatives. Brian looked just like him, Wang Yam thought. The baby slept throughout the entire meeting.

Dong Hui told Wang Yam that her love for him was constant and that she would come and see him again soon. She believed in him, she said, and while she was confused and frustrated by his being in jail, she trusted that he would receive a fair hearing in the British justice system. Surely he would be acquitted at trial. After all, this was not China.

CASE NOTE

I have been trying to understand the background to Wang Yam's secret trial, but the key players are reluctant to talk. After several attempts I managed to make contact with a former British Foreign Secretary and asked if he could provide any information on the process. He asked why, and when prompted said that he remembered Wang Yam's story but: 'I was not aware that you were writing about a specific case (one on which I have no detail to hand). I am afraid therefore that there is too much room for misunderstanding for me to get into this.' I also contacted former Home Secretary Jacqui Smith via Twitter, sending her a Direct Message and requesting an interview. A response came through surprisingly quickly. She asked me what it was about, and when I answered, she went silent. I also emailed the former director of public prosecutions, Ken Macdonald, via Wadham College Oxford where he is now warden. At first he said, 'I'm afraid I have little or no recollection of this case and don't recall being involved in any of the decision making, so I doubt it would be of any use to you,' then when I said I was only looking for generalities, he replied, 'I'm afraid I can't really say much without revealing the sensitive material, which is obviously out of the question.' I need to find someone who can explain why and how in camera trials are put together.

Still looking into claims made by Wang Yam on his CV. It took more than ten telephone calls and emails to the alumni affairs office at Imperial College, but eventually I received the following reply: 'Dear Mr Harding, Your query has been forwarded to me as the College's Data Protection Officer. I can confirm that Wang Yam studied at Imperial College between 1993–1997.' WY was telling the truth about being a student at Imperial.

After repeated requests, I finally secured an interview with the founder and CEO of Centerprise, Rafi Razzak (son of 1960s Iraqi prime minister). Despite his human resources staffer categorically denying Wang Yam had ever worked at the company, Razzak now set the record straight. 'Mr Wang did work in Centerprise,' he wrote. 'I did not know Mr Wang as he was not in any managerial or important role.' He added that Wang Yam had been paid £20,000 a year. Again, Wang Yam was being honest in his CV. Shows how hard it is to nail down facts, especially from twenty years ago.

Trying to confirm Wang Yam's explosive revelation about the murder of Jill Dando. From news articles, it appears that his inmate friend was arrested for drug smuggling in Bolivia in the late 1990s but it is unclear whether he was in the UK in April 1999, i.e. had the opportunity to commit the murder. Also, spoke to Met Police advisor who said that it is quite common for inmates to falsely confess to high-profile murders. They either wish to improve their status within the prison or are psychopaths tormenting grieving families. He reassured me, however, that I was right to pass on the information. There's enough here, he said, to look into. He will reach out informally to his friends in the police force.

Spoke to WY and asked him for a favourite memory with his daughter Angela – who he has not seen for over a decade – he remembered when she was a toddler and he was pushing her around Wimbledon Park. 'Oh Daddy,' she said, 'I will push the pram for you when you are an old man!' He also recalled a time when they were still living at 18 Melrose Avenue, Angela was a toddler and bouncing up and down on the bed. She stopped for a moment, peed on the coverings, and started laughing. Angry, Wang Yam stepped over to her and slapped her bottom. 'I must have used too much force,' he said. 'She saw me as a stranger. I said, "Don't worry, I am so sorry about that." ' She never cried, and Wang Yam never did it again. Strikes me that a cold-blooded murderer would not show empathy and remorse. Has an innocent man been jailed for ten years for a crime he didn't commit?

The story keeps expanding. It's hard to contain. Every time I think I understand it, I discover another witness to speak to, another lead to follow, another legal submission to review. And looming ever larger is the possibility of another appeal. I wonder what it must have been like for the investigators, for the judge, for the members of the jury? They at least had the ability to review all the available material – but how can you be certain about a case when there are so many questions to answer? A case that is still unfolding. This is not a story that stops in 2006; this is happening now.

I keep having a recurring fantasy. I am in the Royal Courts of Justice on the last day of the final appeal. All arguments have been heard. The judges ask Wang Yam to stand. The original conviction is declared unsafe. There is another suspect to pursue. Wang Yam walks through the giant wooden doors of the Royal Courts of Justice, arms raised, grinning at the crowd of photographers and journalists gathered below. He has spent ten years in prison for a crime he did not commit, but for now he is happy. For the first time in a decade he can eat in a restaurant, take a bus ride, visit his children. This daydream keeps coming back to me.

14

IN CAMERA

On 19 February 2007, Wang Yam was driven from Pentonville Prison to London's Central Criminal Court for a bail hearing. Awaiting his arrival was the local reporter, Dan Carrier. 'I didn't know what to make of him,' Carrier recalled. 'I was looking for signs of a man who had committed a heinous crime, but was surprised because he looked fairly nondescript and mild-mannered.'

The hearing was brief. Wang Yam's lawyers argued that their client be released on bail in light of his lack of previous convictions, and so that he could spend time with his newborn son. The judge refused the application, saying that there were substantial grounds for believing that the accused would not attend court. As Wang Yam was removed, Carrier observed him closely. 'He looked like he hadn't washed or kipped in a while,' the journalist recalled. 'He appeared thoughtful and very scared.' Wang Yam was now transferred from Pentonville to Belmarsh, a 'Category A' prison in Woolwich, south-east London.

Opened in 1991, Belmarsh was considered a modern facility. Within minutes of his arrival, however, Wang Yam realised that this was going to be unlike any jail he had seen before. Home to just over 900 prisoners, many of whom were serving time for murder, and more than fifty of whom had been found guilty of terrorism, Belmarsh felt like it was under martial law. Less than a year earlier, a riot had rocked the facility. Four prison officers had been seriously injured. According to independent reports, the staff were aggressive and there was widespread use of force to control the inmates. That year, 2007, four inmates would commit suicide, well above the national average. Some people called it 'Britain's Guantanamo Bay'.

Having been processed, Wang Yam was shown his cell in House Block 2, one of four residential buildings, which he would be sharing with one other inmate. There was a lot to take in. Each prison had its own rhythms and eccentricities, and Belmarsh was no different. He had to learn the daily schedule, where to eat, where to work, where to exercise. He already knew that the best way to get along was to keep a low profile, to speak only when spoken to, and keep answers brief.

Over the next few weeks, Wang Yam met his legal team, the senior barrister Geoffrey Robertson QC and his junior Kirsty Brimelow. Robertson – a handsome, garrulous man with a quick wit – was a celebrity both in legal and media circles, regularly appearing in front of the cameras as he defended free speech and human rights. In 1992, he had famously argued in *Regina v Ahluwalia* that a battered woman has a right of self-defence. He successfully secured the rights of journalists to protect their sources during the 2002 Yugoslav war crimes trials in The Hague. And he represented the main defendant during the 1978 'ABC' case, which led to the government admitting to the existence of its secret surveillance site GCHQ. He was known for his ability to master even the smallest detail of a case and his capacity to savage a witness during cross-examination. The 37-year-old Brimelow had more than fifteen years' experience working in criminal law and was featured in *Management Today*'s list of '35 Most Influential Women Under 35'.

Meeting in the small, windowless room set aside for lawyers and their clients at Belmarsh Prison, the barristers now encouraged Wang

Yam to provide a full and detailed account of his story. Had he known Allan Chappelow, they wondered, and why had he been caught on CCTV depositing the victim's money into his account?

The reason that he had been in possession of Allan Chappelow's cheques and credit card, Wang Yam said, and the reason that the victim's SIM card had been used in his telephone handsets, was that he had become involved with a group of Chinese gangsters in London. When the lawyers asked for more information, he said that he had been given the deceased's cheques, credit cards and banking information by men known to him as Gaz, Zhao Dong and Ah Ming. He provided their physical descriptions and the places that they frequented. He said that it was these gangsters who were responsible for the theft of the deceased's identity. He said that they must have shadowed him, committed the murder, and framed him.

On 29 March 2007, Wang Yam's solicitor wrote to the Crown Prosecution Service requesting a number of disclosures relating to the case, including copies of Allan Chappelow's telephone records, details of the criminal activities of Money TT boss, He Jia Jin, a copy of the items seized at Denning Road and a copy of the letter to Patty Ainsworth.

Two months later, on 31 May, Wang Yam's barristers Kirsty Brimelow and Geoffrey Robertson QC prepared an internal document entitled 'Advice on Evidence'. Having summarised the case, the lawyers reported that they had hired a private detective who had been unable to confirm many of the details provided by their client. Wang Yam had said, for instance, that one of his associates had run a noodle bar at Greenwich DLR station, but the detective could find no noodle bar at that location. He said that another of the gangsters ran the Digital Vision computer repair shop in Camden Town, but no shop of that name could be traced. Equally, no newsagent in Hampstead recognised his photograph, despite him saying that he placed an advertisement in one of their shop windows. Brimelow and Robertson concluded that 'Mr Yam does not seem to understand the weight of evidence against him' and 'it is very difficult to make him focus'. They went on: 'All [his] instructions appear to lead nowhere. Often he presents as a fantasist.' After further discussions, the legal team arranged for a psychiatrist to evaluate Wang Yam's mental state.

'They thought that I was mad and I tell lies from the beginning,' Wang Yam later recalled. 'If the solicitors won't trust me how can they work for me?' He added that talk of a psychiatric evaluation made him 'very upset'. Yet, when he spoke with other inmates in Belmarsh, they warned him not to miss the appointment. If he refused to see the doctor, they told him, then maybe the lawyers would believe that he was in fact insane. 'I could be locked up in a mental hospital without trial,' remembered Wang Yam. 'I might never come out.'

On 10 September 2007, Wang Yam met Dr Warren Dunn, a consultant forensic psychiatrist, at Belmarsh Prison's outpatient clinic. They spoke for an hour in a small interview room. When Dr Dunn asked about his family background, Wang Yam recounted his early childhood years in Xian and his time in Beijing as a student. He added that his father had criticised him for 'doing too much' and added that 'his father believed that he would not be a success for this reason'. He also said that he didn't receive much maternal attention, as his biological mother died at a young age, that he was 'breast fed by a number of different nannies throughout his childhood'.

Having asked Wang Yam to provide an extensive account of his work history, the doctor pulled out two documents that had been retrieved from Wang Yam's computer entitled 'Objectives and Study Plan' and 'Study and Work Plan'. These were lists of his life and career aims. His top objective was to become prime minister of China. Immediately embarrassed when confronted with the documents, Wang Yam acknowledged their over-ambitiousness and said that they were for nobody but himself. At the session's end, the doctor asked the prisoner to take part in what he called a 'Mini Mental State Examination'. Wang Yam made only one error. In addition, he found the recollection of three new items in five minutes 'quite difficult'.

In his report, Dr Dunn began by explaining the background to the examination. Wang Yam's lawyers, he said, had voiced concerns about their client's mental health, in particular that 'he has expressed paranoid ideas relating to his cell mate, the evidence and the police' and had shown 'grandiosity in relation to his account of his life and history'.

Having noted that 'there was no history of mental health problems on either side of the family', Dr Dunn reported that Wang Yam was 'cheerful', 'polite', 'engaging' and, 'if anything, he appeared rather unconcerned about his predicament'. He said that the prisoner was 'cognitively intact' and presented no 'psychotic symptoms at interview'. He went on to say that 'I too have been unable to verify his personal history'; however, 'his account of his academic training and education had a ring of truth and consistency about it'.

Finally, Dr Dunn wrote:

I was left with the impression of a man who exaggerates and extrapolates factual events as a way of maintaining his inner sense of ambition and need for achievement. He has the self-confidence and sense of entitlement of a man from a privileged background. I do not think that he manifests grandiose or paranoid delusions.

In conclusion, Dr Dunn said that there would be 'insufficient medical evidence on which to base an argument in support of an abnormality of mind' when considering a defence of diminished responsibility under the 1957 Homicide Act.

Following the psychiatrist's report, the defence lawyers appeared to have even less confidence in Wang Yam's account. Through September, October and into November 2007, however, Wang Yam persisted with his story. The lawyers again wrote to the CPS on 8 November, providing the names of defence witnesses they intended to call at trial. They heard nothing in reply.

In early November 2007, a letter arrived by government car at the Home Office. Inside was a request that the Home Secretary Jacqui Smith approve a Public Interest Immunity (PII) certificate. If signed it would call for some or all of Wang Yam's trial to be held *in camera*, or in secret.

A PII certificate is a government document allowing a court to prevent evidence from being disclosed either to one of the participants or to the public, or both. Previously known as 'Crown privilege', one of the earliest uses of a PII was in 1939 after the bereaved families of a capsized submarine claimed damages, and the government issued a certificate to prevent the disclosure of the vessel's architectural plans. The rules governing PIIs were enshrined in Section 3 of the Criminal Procedure and Investigations Act 1996. While each year the police and intelligence services sent about a thousand low-level requests to the Home Office – to protect informants, children or other sensitive witnesses in court – only twenty or thirty high-level PII certificates were annually submitted to ministers of state.

Before reaching the Home Secretary's desk, an independent counsel for the Crown Prosecution Service had decided that the sensitive material attached to the PII was relevant to the Wang Yam prosecution. Now, in evaluating whether to approve the PII, Jacqui Smith had to conclude that two additional criteria were present. First, that disclosure would likely lead to real damage to the United Kingdom's national security or economic interests. And second, that this damage outweighed the public interest in open justice.

The certificate itself comprised two main parts: an open schedule which did little more than refer to the need to protect national security interests and certain witnesses, and a highly sensitive closed schedule which contained an extensive summary of Wang Yam's case. Though Smith had help from legal advisors from both inside and outside government, in the end the choice was hers. After considering the arguments and reviewing the documents for some hours, she approved the application by adding her signature to the end of the certificate.

So it was that on 30 November 2007, just six weeks before the trial's scheduled start, Wang Yam's team were told that the trial might be held *in camera*. When they asked why, the CPS resisted disclosing their reasons. After a few days of increasingly fierce exchanges, the CPS relented and explained that they could not proceed if the trial took place in open court 'in the interests of national security and to protect the identity of a witness or other person'. Geoffrey Robertson, Kirsty Brimelow and Janes Solicitors were puzzled by these revelations.

There was one more stage before the PII came into effect. The prosecution had to make an application to the court. If the trial judge ruled in favour, this would be the first murder trial in modern history to be held in secret.

On 13 December, the *Evening Standard* published a story under the headline HOME OFFICE WANTS MURDER TRIAL HELD IN SECRET, describing the murder and ongoing case in close detail. The following morning the *Daily Mail* ran a similar story, explaining that 'the CPS refused to discuss the reasons behind the application', and adding that 'the highly unusual move is thought to be the first where a such a "gagging order" has been sought in a murder trial.'

The restrictions on reporting were decried by the British media at large. It was an unprecedented action, and a gag the press were not willing to accept. Within a few days of the order being released, a group of Britain's leading newspapers including *The Times*, *Guardian*, *Independent*, *Telegraph* and *Daily Mail*, along with the BBC, agreed to work together to challenge the closed court hearings. They hired the veteran freedom of speech barrister Gavin Millar QC to intervene in the case. A pre-trial hearing on media access to the murder trial was scheduled for 15 January 2008 at the Old Bailey.

In response to the PII, the *in camera* hearing request, and the press coverage that followed, the defence team scrambled to react. How would they best mount a defence that was held in closed court? And could a closed trial be fair?

The pre-trial hearing for the murder of Allan Chappelow began on 15 January 2008. Officially known as *Regina v Wang Yam*, this proceeding focused on one question: should the trial be held in secret? While the Home Secretary had approved the PII, the judge was empowered to accept, reject or partially accept it with some modifications.

The hearing was held at the Central Criminal Court, also known as the Old Bailey. A grand, white-stone building located in the heart of the City of London, the Old Bailey is situated only a few streets from St Paul's Cathedral. Above its domed roof stands Lady Justice, a bronze statue with eyes wide open, a sword in her right hand and a balanced scale in the other. Over the entrance to the building are carved the words 'Defend the children of the poor and punish the wrongdoer'.

At the front of number 14 court were seven dark wooden desks; behind each a high-backed wooden chair inlaid with green-coloured mallard leather. Sitting on one of these was the 68-year-old Sir

Duncan Brian Walter Ouseley, his head covered by a white wig, his dark suit shrouded by a red robe. Ouseley would be the judge for the entire trial, and since he was the most senior justice sitting at the Old Bailey that day, the gold-plated Sword of State hung vertically on the wall behind him. According to his authorised *Debrett's* listing, Ouseley had been a judge for eight years and his recreations included 'family, sport, music, wine'. It also mentioned that he was a member of the Garrick Club in central London, whose alumni include William Makepeace Thackeray, Charles Dickens, T. S. Eliot and Sir Alec Guinness. In their assignment of national security cases, the government often selected Mr Justice Ouseley; he was known to many in the establishment as a safe pair of hands.

To the left of the judge was the jury box, filled with two rows of empty wooden benches as the jury would only be empanelled once the main trial started in a fortnight's time. Below the judge sat one shorthand transcriber, along with a clerk who would help with the administration of the proceedings.

In front of the judge sat the bewigged barristers and the wigless solicitors who supported them. Representing the defence were Geoffrey Robertson QC and his junior barrister Kirsty Brimelow. On the same row and to the judge's left sat the prosecution, led by Mark Ellison QC. A graduate from University of Wales, Ellison had made a name for himself prosecuting complex fraud and financial cases. He was assisted by the 41-year-old Bobbie Cheema-Grubb. Born in Leeds, she had become the first Asian woman to be appointed a Junior Treasury Counsel in 2006. Also present at this pre-trial hearing was Gavin Millar QC, representing the media. Today, he was irritated as, unusually, the CPS were still refusing to tell him why they were asking for parts of the trial to be held in secret. The defence knew – but were unable to tell their colleague. 'It was like driving in the dark,' said Millar.

Above the defendant's dock (which was empty) was the crowded public gallery. The run-up to the case had been widely covered by the media and there were few seats available. Also in court were a number of journalists including Dan Carrier from the *Camden New Journal* and a crime reporter from the *Guardian*. They sat on the cramped press bench in front of the judge, their knees squashed against a wooden wall, so close to the barristers they could read the writing on the notes passed between them. There were no members of Allan Chappelow's family in court, nor were there any family or friends supporting Wang Yam.

The judge opened the hearing and explained that if the CPS's application was successful then the press and the public would be excluded from parts of the trial, but the jury, the defendant and his lawyers would hear the whole of the evidence and any cross-examination in relation to it. Geoffrey Robertson stood up for the defence and argued that public interest and the principle of open justice all required the trial to be held in public. His client would not receive a fair trial, he said, if it were held in secret. 'He wants the public to hear his defence and have his name cleared. His defence – the defence the Crown wishes to suppress – will explain why he has fallen under suspicion.' One of his particular concerns, he continued, was that if key parts of the defence were held in secret, the press would be unable to fully report on the trial, and new witnesses would be less likely to come forward.

The principle of open justice, Robertson continued, had been paramount in England for centuries. He then quoted the radical author John Lilburne who had stated at his libel trial in 1649:

> The court must uphold the first fundamental liberty of an Englishman, that all courts of justice always ought to be free and open for all sorts of peaceable people to see, behold and hear, and have free access unto; and no man whatsoever ought to be tried in holes or corners, or in any place where the gates are shut and barred.

Robertson said that the seventeenth-century judges had agreed that hearings should be held in public so 'that all the world may know with what candour and justice the court does proceed'.

Next to speak was Gavin Millar on behalf of the media. 'There have been plenty of trials in the past', Millar said, 'in which issues have been raised about national security material,' and then listed a number of cases when allegations about the intelligence agencies had been made in open court. The anonymity of witnesses called by the defence could be assured, he added, by simple use of a screen or other similar device. 'The strong presumption', Millar proclaimed, 'was that the press, as watchdog of the public, may report everything that takes place in a criminal court.' He then added that it was impossible to argue against the CPS's request for a closed trial since they refused to give their reasons, placing his media clients and the defence at a disadvantage. After all, how could he forcefully argue for an open trial if they did not understand the details of the alleged national security threat?

Mark Ellison's submissions for the prosecution was brief. He explained that if the trial was held in the open then they would drop all charges (fearing the disclosure of various national secrets), allowing a potential murderer to roam the streets. At this, Geoffrey Robertson bolted up and with indignation declared that Ellison's argument was a form of 'forensic blackmail'. Noting his point, the judge asked the prosecutor to resume his arguments. Mark Ellison spoke a little more about the importance of protecting the nation's security and then added that the Home Secretary Jacqui Smith supported their request to hold the trial *in camera*.

In his ruling, the judge acknowledged that trials should in general be held in the open, and that this served justice, not least so that the general public could understand the consequence of wrongdoing. There were exceptions however, he said, where national security was at stake, and he worried that the Crown Prosecution Service (CPS) would drop the case if the trial proceeded in the open. He also didn't believe that the national security issues could be dealt with by voice distortion or by standing behind screens. The problem was protecting the identity of those involved as well as the activities in which they engaged. 'The circumstances', he said, 'point unerringly to an order that part of this trial be heard *in camera*. I am quite satisfied that the defendant can have a fair trial with the order that the Crown seeks.'

In a separate order, which was handed out to the members of the media, the judge said that not only were they to be excluded from the *in camera* portions of the trial, but they were forbidden from speculating why the trial was being held in secret. He added that any speculation would amount to a contempt of court punishable by a fine, and possibly even a prison sentence.

CASE NOTE

Met Philip Baker QC at his chambers in Gray's Inn. He handed me a copy of Wang Yam's asylum file from 1992 detailing much of WY's China back-story. Baker had kept in touch with WY, though he felt guilty that he had only visited him once while at Whitemoor Prison ('It's an awful place,' he confessed). Of the 300 or so Chinese nationals who Baker helped in the 1990s, WY was not one of those he expected to get into trouble. 'There were a couple of thugs', Baker said, 'who I wouldn't have been surprised if the police had called regarding a murder inquiry. When they asked about Wang Yam I was surprised.'

I met with my publishers to discuss an early draft. They said that I cannot explore Wang Yam's defence in any detail as to do so would be in breach of Mr Justice Ouseley's order. I asked if there was some way around it. But there wasn't. Wang Yam's defence, they said, was heard in private at trial, and 'to this day is covered by reporting restrictions'. By complying, I worry that I become an accessory to the gagging of the press, craven to the establishment. It is so frustrating that I will not be able to tell Wang Yam's story in full. But better to tell it partly than not at all.

One thing really bothering me: if it was a bungled burglary, why was there so much violence? Struggling to get the horrific images of Chappelow's mutilated body out of my head. Surely, after a scuffle, even a blow to the head, the thief would flee, rather than bludgeoning and burning the victim and then covering him with 560kg of paper? I needed to speak with someone who understood criminal behaviour. Via Twitter, I contacted ex-FBI 'profiler' Bill Fleischer, then spoke by phone with him at his office in Philadelphia, USA. I gave him the police theory: a thief who was desperate for money was stealing mail from a front hallway when he was interrupted by the elderly homeowner; a struggle ensued; the criminal became carried away and brutally bludgeoned the victim to death. Bill said that he thought this was very unlikely. 'It sounds too personal to be a bungled burglary,' he said. 'There was too much violence in this case', referring to the repeated blows to the victim's head and the caving in of his skull. It was unlikely that the murder had been committed by a stranger and the killer was most likely an assertive type. 'Covering the face of the victim', he added, 'is most always a signature of a retaliatory rage killer.' As to why the body was covered by the victim's own manuscripts, he said, 'Sometimes a cigar is just a cigar. The manuscripts were probably at hand and abundant.'

Wang Yam called me. He said that he had heard from his Chinese contacts: Triad gangsters had collected evidence that someone else committed the murder of Allan Chappelow, and that they are expecting him or his family to pay them to release this evidence. He says that this form of extortion, or 'evidence kidnapping', is common in China. When I asked my Beijing researchers, they said that they hadn't heard of 'evidence kidnapping', but that didn't mean it wasn't possible.

Spoke to James Mullion by phone, he said that the Camden New Journal had published an appeal and a new witness had come forward. He told me that he wasn't sure if this man was credible, reporting that the witness had said that over 300 men regularly gathered on Hampstead Heath for public sex. Mullion didn't sound as if he believed this. Nevertheless, he passed along the contact details for 'Serpico'.

15

THE TRIAL

The trial of Wang Yam started on 28 January 2008. Mr Justice Ouseley welcomed the jury to the Old Bailey and explained how the case would unfold. The defendant was charged with six offences, he said, the most serious being Count One: murder. He was also charged with two counts of burglary, including breaking and entering a property, and three counts of handling stolen goods.

Opposite the judge, and behind the line of lawyers, was a raised wooden dock that was enclosed at eye-level by a sheet of glass. Inside sat a young female Chinese interpreter, a guard and Wang Yam. The prisoner was wearing a grey suit, dark tie and brown shoes, which Dong Hui had brought to him earlier that week. He'd changed out of his prison clothes before travelling to court that morning. Ten metres to his left sat his lawyers. All he could see were their backs as they, like him, faced the judge. To pass a note to his barristers, Wang Yam had to catch a bailiff's attention and then ask them to carry it over. His lawyers would be unable to place a reassuring hand on his arm or share a friendly smile.

There were twelve members of the jury, all British citizens and all obliged to serve having being issued with a formal court summons.

It was a diverse group. Nine men and three women. Eight members were white, two were black and two were of Asian extraction. As was typical for such cases, each had been told that they should not attend if they worked as lawyers or for the Crown Prosecution Service.

Now seated, the judge explained that the jury could find Wang Yam guilty of all, some, or none of the counts. The prosecution would present their case first, and introduce witnesses who could be cross-examined by the defence. Then it would be the turn of Wang Yam's legal team. They too would introduce witnesses, and the prosecution would also have the chance to cross-examine. Once all the witnesses had been heard, both sides would make their closing arguments and then he, Mr Justice Ouseley, would spend some considerable time summing up the case for the jury. Only then would they retire into a separate room to see if they could agree a verdict. If they could find him guilty on any of the counts, the judge would then decide the sentence. The trial, he said, could take between four and six weeks. Given that it was the first day, little more was accomplished, and the judge told the court that proceedings would start at 9 a.m. sharp the following morning.

Before adjourning, Mr Justice Ouseley reminded the assembled media representatives of the strict reporting guidelines that had been agreed at the pre-trial hearing. There would be no coverage of the closed court sessions or speculation as to why they were taking place. To do otherwise would make them liable for being held in contempt of court.

That night, BBC's flagship news programme, *Newsnight*, ran a six-minute report on the trial. First, they explained the background to the case, showing pictures of the dilapidated house at 9 Downshire Hill and interviewing a member of the Shaw Society who spoke warmly about Chappelow's books. They then spoke to Allan's friend John Sparrow. 'He would start a conversation with you,' said Sparrow. 'He would be very interested in what you had to say and this little bit of flattery always managed to hook you in, that's how he did it.'

The report also featured Malcolm Rifkind, secretary of defence from 1992 to 1995 under Prime Minister John Major, who had approved a number of Public Interest Immunity certificates. 'There is a legitimate public interest', said Rifkind, 'that certain highly sensitive documents cannot be put in general release. There is also a public interest that people facing criminal charges should have access to the information they might need for their defence. There is a conflict, and the question is who is the best person to resolve that conflict? It cannot be a politician,' he concluded. 'It must be someone impartial, like a judge.'

After the end of the pre-recorded package, the show's presenter Jeremy Paxman led an in-studio panel discussion with two lawyers seated at an oval table in front of a mauve-washed backdrop. 'What do you make of it?' Paxman gruffly asked the human rights barrister Alex Bailin. 'Clearly, the presumption is in favour of open justice, no one is going to dispute that,' said Bailin. 'The difficulty is what to do in the exceptional cases. If it's genuinely the case of state secrets that need protecting then clearly it is possible that some of the trial will have to be in private, otherwise state secrets are revealed to everybody and there is no point trying to protect them by prosecuting somebody. The question as to whether this [case] falls into that category is where it gets hard.'

'And we can't speculate because we don't know,' Paxman jumped in, aware of the judge's warning not to guess what might be disclosed during the closed court sessions. 'It's a pointless thing to do,' Bailin responded. 'What you have to look at more closely is whether in fact the claim for secrecy is based on genuinely protecting state secrets or something less, like prohibiting the government from revealing embarrassment. That's the real issue.'

Then, turning to Dr Michael Powers QC, the presenter asked, 'But it is surely more important that justice is done than it is merely seen to be done?'

'Yes, certainly,' said Powers with a wry smile, 'but in the end isn't it a choice between deciding whether you throw the secrets away in the hope of getting a conviction or whether, on the other hand, you retain the secrets and abandon the prospect of getting a conviction?'

'Are there no circumstances in which a decision like this is permissible?' Paxman pushed his guest. 'Yes, of course,' replied Powers, 'there will be some circumstances, but the very reason you are holding this discussion tonight is because of the concern which everyone will feel about having a murder trial which is at least partially held in private . . .'

'But also,' Paxman interrupted, 'because it is so extremely rare.' Powers concluded this thought, 'If it remains extremely rare I suspect Alex and I will be very happy . . .' The studio director cut to a shot of Alex Bailin smiling and nodding his head. ' . . . But if it becomes a more common practice,' Powers continued, 'for whatever reason, then we have a great need to have concern about it.' Seeing a good out-point, Paxman then wrapped up the discussion and thanked his guests.

The following day in court, the BBC received word that they had trodden dangerously close to contempt of Mr Justice Ouseley's restrictions. The judge had sent a clear message to journalists: follow my rules or suffer the consequences.

In his opening speech, Mark Ellison QC set forth the prosecution's main argument, a theme he would return to frequently. The accused was financially desperate, the lawyer said; he stole the victim's mail, killed him, and then fled the country when he realised that a police investigation had begun.

In a flat and dry voice, Ellison moved on to the details of the case.

He said that at the time of the murder the defendant was 'in deep financial difficulties' with debts of more than £1.1 million. This was the motive, said the prosecutor: 'The evidence shows that even when Wang Yam started to steal the victim's post he was in real problems.' He then pointed out that CCTV footage had captured the defendant depositing the victim's cheques into his bank account at HSBC, taking money out of an ATM in Kentish Town (using Allan Chappelow's credit card) and purchasing books at Foyles (again using Chappelow's card). Though grainy, the images clearly identified a Chinese-looking man with a small bag over his shoulders.

Over the next week, the prosecution paraded a series of witnesses who were all cross-examined by the defence: the owner of the Curry Paradise restaurant, Anna Toma the landlady, Lady Listowel the neighbour and the postman, Nicholas Sullman. The pathologist Dr Chapman was called to the witness box, graphically describing the nature of the wounds inflicted upon Allan Chappelow and the manner of his death. He was followed by the entomologist Dr Hall, who explained how he used the life cycle of the blowfly to determine Allan Chappelow's likely date of death.

A number of forensic experts also spoke, who confirmed that there were no DNA, fibres or other substance that could link Wang Yam to 9 Downshire Hill. Though he would have liked to have offered forensic evidence connecting the defendant to the crime scene, Ellison continued, he was unable to given the terrible state of the house. The lawyer was laying the groundwork for the jury to find the defendant guilty based only on circumstantial evidence.

When it was his turn, Detective Sergeant Peter Devlin provided a detailed account of Wang Yam's financial situation, which he categorised as dire, and said that he believed that Wang Yam would have gone on to try and sell Allan Chappelow's house if the body had not been found. He admitted, however, he had no evidence to support this claim.

One of the most compelling witnesses was Beverley Young, who worked for a non-profit organisation dedicated to preventing financial crime amongst high-street banks and credit card companies. She explained that the mail thief or 'facility hijacker' involved in this case showed 'persistence and confidence which is higher than we normally see'. Typically, she said, when a hijacker is challenged by a bank – as was true of the person who was in possession of Allan Chappelow's credit card – they withdraw. Facility hijackers normally remain anonymous, she added, preferring to work by internet, mail or phone. Yet, in this circumstance, the hijacker frequently returned to 9 Downshire Hill to collect a new PIN number and credit card, risking discovery by the owner. The prosecution explained that the reason why the mail thief went back to the property so many times was because he was confident that he would not be disturbed by the owner, and the reason for this was that he knew that the occupant was dead.

The following week, a number of witnesses were called from telephone companies and internet service providers who detailed the time, length and location for innumerable phone calls and internet sessions during the months of May, June and July 2006. Mark Ellison started by explaining that the police had tracked the usage of four different telephone handsets and the same number of SIM cards, which were used at different times in different handsets. To keep things clear for the jury, the prosecution presented what they called 'Appendix A', a chronological list of all the phone calls with a multi-coloured key explaining which handset and SIM was used, who the calls were made to, which cell tower relayed the call and how long the call lasted. In all there were 550 calls listed.

The prosecution argued that Allan last used his mobile phone on 8 May 2006 to call the Inland Revenue. The call started at 9.43 a.m., lasted 6.18 minutes, was made using Allan's black Nokia phone ('Handset 1') and his SIM card (ending 8642), relayed via the cell tower located at the Royal Free Hospital in Hampstead. The next use of Allan's SIM card, they said, took place twelve days later on

20 May. At first, the SIM was used in a different phone, named Handset 2, a silver LP flip-phone that belonged to Wang Yam. Then, twenty-five minutes later, Allan's SIM was used twice more with Handset 1, Allan's handset. All three calls were made to retrieve voicemail messages from Allan Chappelow's account. The prosecution reminded the jury that Allan had reported his missing cheques to the police. Surely he would have done the same if he had believed his mobile phone had been stolen. It could be deduced, Ellison continued, that his handset and SIM card had remained in the victim's possession until his death, and that someone had removed both items from 9 Downshire Hill in early May. He added that it looked like whoever was using Allan's SIM card in the third week of May 2006 had been trying to see if anybody had attempted to get in touch with the deceased.

Then the prosecution played a number of telephone conversations that had been recorded between the man using Allan Chappelow's SIM card and various bank customer service representatives. There was complete silence in the court as everyone strained to hear. The voice on the phone sounded Asian, probably from China. While the tape was being played many of the jurors looked at Wang Yam.

When Dan Carrier returned to the *Camden New Journal* offices that evening, he was asked for an update on the trial. The day's telephone evidence had been dramatic, Carrier said, and the sense that Wang Yam had been involved in some way with the hijacking of Allan Chappelow's identity was overwhelmingly convincing.

Starting in the third week of the trial, it was the turn of the defence. Geoffrey Robertson's manner was different from his even-tempered colleagues over at the prosecution's bench. A brilliant orator, he played to the house, used grand hand gestures and colourful language. At one point, for instance, Robertson compared Allan Chappelow's murder to being clubbed 'like a seal pup on an ice floe' and 'with more blood than Sweeney Todd' splattered on the walls and floors. His argument was that it was inconceivable that his unremarkable and placid client had carried out such a dastardly act. Sometimes Robertson's theatrics went too far and Mr Justice Ouseley told him to 'get to the point'. 'The judge held his own,' Carrier noted from his bench nearby. 'He was very learned; a bit of a beak.'

Most of the defence would be heard in open court, and their strategy revolved around three main arguments: that there was no forensic evidence linking Wang Yam to 9 Downshire Hill or the body that was found there, that he had never shown violence in the past, and that other potential suspects had been at the scene of the crime. Robertson was trying to raise doubt in the jurors' minds. Could the crime have been committed by someone else, he wanted them to ask themselves, and if so, who? In his opening remarks, therefore, Robertson referred to statements made by Allan Chappelow's neighbours, including Lady Listowel, who recalled seeing various nondescript characters entering and leaving the garden of 9 Downshire Hill while the occupant had been away in the USA. Robertson also mentioned the possible involvement of the Israeli intelligence agency, Mossad, Allan Chappelow's handyman, as well as various Albanian and Chinese gangsters. Beyond quoting his client, however, Robertson provided no evidence to bolster such claims nor, as far as Mossad's alleged involvement was concerned, did he offer an explanation.

Wang Yam's lawyer friend, Philip Baker, was a key witness for the defence. Having explained how he had first come to know the defendant shortly after his arrival in the UK, Baker gave an account of Wang Yam's family background in China, including his being the grandson of the famous Ren Bishi. This was the equivalent, Baker said, of being the grandson of Sir Winston Churchill. When asked if he had ever known the accused to show signs of violence or acts of aggression, Baker said, on the contrary, Wang Yam had always presented himself as a calm and even-keeled individual, who was eager to assimilate into British society. He said that Wang Yam had received approval for political asylum within weeks, which was highly unusual, adding that Wang Yam must have been a good friend to the British government. For the jury's sake, Robertson repeated the witness's conclusion: Wang Yam had been a good friend to the British government.

When he returned to the *Camden New Journal* at the day's end, Dan Carrier had a different answer for his colleagues. He was no longer sure of Wang Yam's guilt. Now he was persuaded by Robertson's arguments. The hacks in the newsroom laughed at him for changing his mind.

The following day at 10.40 a.m. on 7 March 2008, Wang Yam went into the witness box. The court was still open to the public. Geoffrey Robertson QC got straight to the point, asking a series of rapid-fire questions:

Robertson: Mr Wang, did you kill Allan Chappelow?

Wang Yam: No.

Robertson: Did you know Allan Chappelow?

Wang Yam: No.

Robertson: Did you ever to your knowledge meet Allan Chappelow?

Wang Yam: No.

Robertson: Did you ever enter the property at 9 Downshire Hill?

Wang Yam: No.

Robertson: It may be suggested to you that, in the course of stealing Allan Chappelow's mail, he surprised you, you assaulted him and later killed him. Is there any truth in that proposition?

Wang Yam: No truth.

Robertson: Did you burgle that house?

Wang Yam: No.

Robertson: Were you the man in the Eric Morecambe black glasses, the Chinese man who accosted Mr Sullman the postman?

Wang Yam: No.

Robertson: Did you ever clear trees from the path up to the door at 9 Downshire Hill?

Wang Yam: No.

Robertson: Have you ever resorted to violence?

Wang Yam: No.

Robertson: Hurt anyone?

Wang Yam: No.

Taking a brief pause, Robertson then suggested that his client sit down and have a drink of water as 'you are going to be there for a while'. For the next hour, the defence barrister took Wang Yam through his family history, asking about his grandfather Ren Bishi and his childhood in Xian. When he came to his mother's death during the Cultural Revolution Wang Yam paused, stuttered, 'I will not like to . . . I don't like to speak,' and then burst into tears. Seeing his client in distress, Robertson asked if he would prefer to speak through an interpreter. 'No, it is OK,' said Wang Yam. 'It is not the business here.'

A few minutes later, the defendant again broke down when he started speaking about the 1989 Tiananmen Square protests. 'Just pause, Mr Wang Yam,' said the judge. 'Take your time.' Then seeing that the defendant needed a moment more to recover, the judge suggested that the court take a short break. With the jury absent, Robertson suggested that a cup of tea be brought in for his client. 'I am not in charge of that,' the judge replied curtly. 'Water is the normal sustenance.'

After a brief adjournment, Robertson invited his client to speak in Mandarin with the help of an interpreter, and for the next few hours, the testimony continued, sometimes in English and sometimes in Mandarin. Seeing that the jury had difficulty understanding what was being said, the judge frequently asked the defendant to repeat himself and to speak more slowly and louder. When he believed that Wang Yam was 'getting to the stage when we cannot afford to miss the detail', the judge insisted that Wang Yam speak through an interpreter. Even then, the defendant often reverted to English, much to the frustration of the judge and members of the jury. Some of his sentences were partly in English and partly in Mandarin, confusing matters still further.

Later in his evidence, which the judge continued to allow to be in open court, Wang Yam described how he tried to 'get alongside' the Chinese gangsters. He said that he had been handed the cheques and credit card by three gangsters whom he had come to know, and that he was playing them along as a means of assembling evidence against them and reporting them. He named them as Gaz, Zhao Dong and Ah Ming and he gave descriptions of them, of the places they frequented and, in the case of Ah Ming, where he worked. They had wanted him to take part in illegal immigration and other crimes, he said, and Gaz had handed him the cheques and asked him to pay them into the bank.

Wang Yam also admitted making 'dodgy documents' after he had been declared bankrupt so that he could rent a flat. He went on to tell the court that he couldn't lift heavy objects because of his weak heart, which is why he asked for help when moving house. From this, the defence hoped, the jury would infer that Wang Yam could not have lifted 560kg of paper onto the murder victim. According to Dan Carrier and others present in court, however, the defendant's testimony became increasingly rambling, unintelligible, at times contradictory and most of all unconvincing.

Sometimes, while Wang Yam was mid-sentence, the judge brought the proceedings to an abrupt halt and warned the defendant not to talk about such sensitive matters in open session. The clerk then called for the court to be cleared. The journalists, police officers and any members of the public were ushered out of the courtroom, and the heavy oak doors were locked by the bailiffs. These breaks in the procedure lasted just a few minutes, and each time the judge instructed the recorder to redact from the transcript whatever was said during this period. His client's stop-and-start testimony didn't faze Geoffrey Robertson, though he believed that it was very important to keep the jury from investing too much importance in the secret evidence. His strategy was to keep their minds focused on the defence narrative, not to be distracted by the court interruptions.

At one point during his cross-examination by the prosecution, Wang Yam said that he could prove that he was not a murderer. Removing one of his shoes and offering it to the jury for examination, he said that nobody had compared his footwear to the marks found on the papers that covered the victim's body. As they could see, he continued, waving his shoe in the air, his size-46 shoes were far larger than the footprints found at the crime scene. Mr Justice Ouseley reprimanded the defendant for his antics and told him to put his shoe back on and, once calm had returned to the court, the prosecution explained that a number of experts had failed to identify the size of the footmarks and that this issue was of no significance. While Wang Yam appeared annoyed that this evidence was not being taken seriously, his lawyers appeared irritated by their client's unruliness.

Starting on the morning of 10 March, and continuing into the next day, Wang Yam's testimony was heard *in camera*. To ensure that journalists and members of the public were barred, the courtroom door was locked. In all, less than nine of the thirty-four days that made up the trial were held in closed court. In addition to Wang

Yam's *in camera* testimony, the defence called four witnesses who provided their evidence in closed sessions on Wednesday 20 and Friday 22 February. These secret hearings formed no part of the prosecution case against Wang Yam.

Finally, at the end of March 2008, the defence closed its case. For those seated in the gallery hoping for a mention of safe houses, dead-drops or secret disguises, the trial had been a disappointment. There had been little mention, at least in the open session, of any matters relating to national security. Over fifty witnesses and experts had been called by the prosecution and defence. It had been ten weeks since the trial's start.

It was now the judge's turn to sum up the evidence. Over the next three days, he gave an overview of the law and then carefully repeated what each side had presented during the trial. Once he had finished, he told the jury that it was now up to them. Before he released them, however, he gave the following direction: if they could not find the defendant guilty of theft of mail from 9 Downshire Hill they should not find him guilty of murder. The jury then left the courtroom.

That night, Carrier once again reported back to his colleagues. He was worried that the evidence presented in court was only circumstantial and he was frustrated that he had been unable to hear the closed court testimony. Over a beer that evening he told his colleagues that if he'd been on the jury he would have needed an extremely charismatic foreman to have persuaded him that Wang Yam was not guilty. Whatever the outcome, it had been fascinating. It was the most interesting case he'd ever worked on.

On 2 April, after four days of deliberations, the jury returned to the courtroom. The clerk asked Wang Yam to stand. The defendant showed little emotion, looking deadpan towards the jury box as the foreman was asked for the verdict. The jury found Wang Yam guilty of three of the charges, declared the foreman, including the illegal transfer of £20,000, the theft of £20 cash from a cash machine and the handling and receiving of stolen goods. As to the other charges of burglary, mail theft, and most importantly murder, the jury could not all agree on his guilt. The foreman then sat down, as did Wang Yam. With only the briefest of pauses, the judge thanked the jury for all their efforts and then discharged them as they had been unable to reach a verdict. There would be a retrial, he declared, later that year. Until that time Wang Yam would remain in custody.

The defendant was then led out of the room and down to the holding cells in the basement. A few minutes later, he was brought into a conference room where he was joined by his legal team. What did this mean? he asked them. His lawyers tried to cheer him up and keep him positive as to what the verdicts meant. Critically, the jury didn't believe that he had gone in the house or stolen from the porch and so hadn't found him guilty of mail theft, let alone murder. They could build on this.

'They had decided that Wang Yam was their man,' Geoffrey Robertson said of the police investigation. 'There was a logic to it. He was difficult to understand, they didn't bother looking much further, and they didn't run down the alternatives.' He was hopeful that they would be even more successful at the second trial.

While he was of course disappointed that he would be returning to Belmarsh Prison, Wang Yam was also relieved. After an almost three-month-long trial, a jury had been unable to find him guilty of murder. He trusted that over the next months, his lawyers would hone their arguments so that the next jury would deliver an even more favourable verdict.

CASE NOTE

Interviewed Philip Baker again at his chambers. I played him the audio of a Chinese man pretending to be Allan Chappelow on the phone to the credit card companies and he said he was sure it was not Wang Yam. Even in 2006 Wang Yam's English was much better than that of the person speaking on the phone. The phone is key. The police assumption had been that Allan Chappelow had his phone with him when he died, so only the killer could be in possession of it. If Wang Yam didn't use Allan Chappelow's phone or SIM, then there was nothing connecting him with the crime scene (he or his associates could have removed the mail from the front hallway without entering the house). Finally, I asked Philip Baker if he thought WY had killed Allan Chappelow. 'I don't think he did it,' he said, 'but it's just a gut thing.'

Following James Mullion's introduction, I met 'Serpico' at Villandry restaurant near the Haymarket. A tall, thin man in his sixties, he was upset by the price of the wine, but relaxed after a few sips. Serpico told me that he had cruised the West Heath section of Hampstead Heath for decades. Between 2000 and 2006, he had frequent encounters with a man dressed in black trousers, black shirt and a black hat. This man had facial hair, perhaps a beard, moved about quite gingerly, spoke with a posh accent and was called 'Allan'. Serpico said that

'Allan' disappeared from the West Heath in the spring of 2006. When asked why he did not come forward earlier, Serpico said that he believed that the police had arrested a culprit so there was no need to provide testimony. Did the victim have a second hidden life? And if so, does Serpico provide an alternative theory for the murder of Allan Chappelow?

Called Allan Chappelow's Danish cousin Torben Permin. Wasn't sure how he would respond, but asked anyway. Did he think that his cousin might have been gay? Apparently unfazed by my question, Torben said that the police had told him that various sex-related paraphernalia had been found at 9 Downshire Hill. Among the items was a video of a gay pride march in Hampstead and a condom. Torben believed that Allan's sexuality was the cause of the tension between him and his conservative father. 'I think Allan was gay and Archie disapproved,' Torben said. 'At that time it was not good for a family [to have a gay son]. It was not accepted. In my opinion, Archie was quite traditional.'

Also spoke with James Chappelow, one of Allan's English cousins. He said that both he and his brother Michael (who died in 2012) were gay and that he thought it quite likely that Allan, who had never had a female relationship and lived by himself, was also gay. 'It's all hints and whispers with this kind of stuff,' he added. Patty Ainsworth, Allan's American cousin, also thought it probable that Allan was gay, and that this could not have been easy for him growing up in 1930s and 1940s Britain. Allan's family's assumption seem a bit tenuous to me, but when taken together with Serpico's testimony, perhaps there is something to it.

I called Peter Devlin who said that he had not thought Allan's sexuality significant to the case and that it had not played a part in the investigation.

Was there another side to Allan Chappelow? I booked a flight to Austin, Texas.

16

THE VERDICT

In April 2008, two weeks after the first trial's end, Dong Hui came to see Wang Yam in Belmarsh Prison.

She came with a friend. The two women wore flowery shirts and matching ankle-length pink skirts. They had white flowers in their pinned-up hair, heels and make-up. Around Dong Hui's neck hung a simple pearl necklace. After a short wait in the reception area, the two visitors were escorted by a guard to the prison chapel. There they met Wang Yam, who looked stiff and formal in his dark suit, blue shirt and diamond-patterned tie. His receding hair had streaks of silver and had been recently cropped. They greeted each other and were still chatting when the governor walked in. He asked Wang Yam and Dong Hui to stand in front of him and then read a series of lines from a printed brochure, which they repeated sombrely. Wang Yam and Dong were getting married.

Fewer than a hundred prison weddings take place every year in the UK. Most inmates are granted temporary release and allowed to hold their services outside of prison. As a 'Category A' prisoner, however, Wang Yam's wedding had to take place inside Belmarsh because of security concerns. Even though he had declared himself to be a Christian on his prison forms, he was not a religious man, and had asked for a civil ceremony.

Standing at the chapel's front, the governor proceeded through the short service, asking the bride and groom to repeat their vows. Though they were without family, guests and music – besides the one friend – for Dong Hui and Wang Yam the ceremony was deeply meaningful. Having said 'I do', the bride and groom were invited to exchange silver rings and then kiss. They were married.

Next, Dong Hui and Wang Yam signed the marriage certificate, writing their ages – his forty-seven, hers thirty. The governor told them to add Belmarsh's private address so that the name of the prison did not appear on the document. Dong Hui's friend and the governor then signed the marriage certificate as witnesses, before the governor stepped aside to give the wedding party a little privacy. After a few minutes, he suggested that perhaps now was a good time to eat. A plate of sandwiches had been prepared by the prison staff, along with a small white-frosted wedding cake. It even had a scattering of flowers on top.

Dong Hui's friend took some posed photographs. The first image has the smiling couple seated on a pair of blue chairs, one of Wang Yam's arms around his bride, the other holding a pen against the registrar's wedding book. Dong Hui is clutching a small bunch of flowers. Another picture captures the newlyweds standing in front of a set of closed prison wooden doors, again smiling into the camera, their hands gripping a white plastic knife above the wedding cake.

After about thirty minutes, their time was up. The newlyweds had one last kiss and promised to see each other the following week. Wang Yam was then escorted away. Ten minutes later, Dong Hui and her friend walked out of the prison gates and made their way to the bus stop. 'It was very strange', Wang Yam later remembered, 'not to go home with her.'

Soon after the end of the first trial, Geoffrey Robertson announced that he would be unavailable for the retrial since he was committed to working on another case. Another senior barrister had to be quickly found and by the early summer of 2008 Geoffrey Cox QC was selected to lead the defence. The lawyers for the prosecution remained the same as the first trial, as did the judge. Kirsty Brimelow worked once again as the defence junior counsel.

In addition to being a barrister, Geoffrey Cox was also the Conservative member of parliament for Torridge and West Devon in south-west England. Wang Yam worried that he was too busy to do either job well, but Cox pointed out that there were other MPs who worked in more than one job and, furthermore, a recent cross-party commission had concluded that it was better for British democracy if its politicians had real-world experience. Mollified, Wang Yam believed that it might be to his benefit to have such an establishment figure on his side.

As trial preparations continued during the second half of 2008, tensions began to emerge, however, between the defendant and his legal team. Ever since the first trial, Wang Yam had become convinced that forensic evidence was the key to his liberty. Eight cigarette butts had been found near the body of Allan Chappelow, Wang Yam pointed out, but the DNA collected from these did not match the victim, the accused or the only other person with access to the house, the handyman Thomas Carr. The police's DNA expert had even assigned these butts to a person he called 'Male X'. Surely, the defendant argued, this could help their case. Equally, he said, they should make use of a footprint that had been found on the underside of the manuscript closest to Allan Chappelow's body. As he had insisted at the first trial, this footprint did not match his shoe size. Again and again, in long detailed letters written from his prison cell, he asked them to hire additional experts to re-examine these issues. When new professional witnesses were finally found, who concurred with the previous experts' conclusions, Wang Yam was unhappy with the results.

The defendant and his legal team agreed to focus more on the audio recordings that had been played during the first trial. In court, the jury appeared to assume that the Chinese-sounding man pretending to be Allan Chappelow on the phone calls to the banks was Wang Yam. To counter this, the defence now rehired Dr Allen Hirson (who had appeared in the first trial), an expert in forensic phonetics from London's City University, as well as Professor Yi Xu, a new audio expert from University College London.

First, Hirson sent one of his staff members to Belmarsh Prison to record Wang Yam in normal conversation. Various questions were asked which would later be used to ensure that the prisoner was not attempting to mask his voice in order to game the system. Hirson and Xu then compared Wang Yam's speech recorded in prison to the voice captured on the telephone to the banks. In their report to the lawyers, Hirson and Xu explained that Mandarin speakers often make the same mistakes when speaking English. They swap 'police' with 'please', they say 'she love John' rather than 'she loves John', and they add a nasal emphasis to the letter 'a', for example in the word 'ban'. In this case, the sound experts found that the men on both recordings added an incorrect 's' to many of their words and both had a problem with their voiceless dental fricative – when the tip of the tongue is pressed against the teeth – so that instead of 'thing' they both said 'ting'. But again, this was true for many Chinese natives who speak English.

When it came to more subtle sounds, which a layperson might not hear, the experts detected significant differences between the recordings. They found that the voice quality and filled-in pauses ('er' and 'um') did not match. Equally, they heard Wang Yam say 'OK' differently from the man on the phone.

At the end of their joint report, Hirson and Xu concluded it was 'quite unlikely' that the man on the bank recordings was Wang Yam. They also told the lawyers that they had discovered something else in the audio file. It appeared to them that at the end of Allan Chappelow's call to the Inland Revenue on 8 May 2006 they heard a second unknown male voice.

On 13 October 2008, the second trial for *Regina v Wang Yam* began.

Following the judge's opening remarks, Mark Ellison QC once again rose for the prosecution. The jury, comprising a new set of twelve men and women, listened eagerly as he offered a simple explanation for the victim's death: Allan Chappelow had interrupted a burglary that was being carried out by the defendant, Wang Yam. A struggle had ensued, during which the victim had been bludgeoned to death.

Over the next month, Ellison and his colleague Bobbie Cheema-Grubb walked the jury through the evidence. They called over a hundred witnesses, including the police, various Hampstead residents, forensic experts and the pathologist. Handing out large bundles of data, they presented the enormously detailed and at times tedious telephone and internet evidence. The jury was shown CCTV footage of Wang Yam depositing the victim's cheques and withdrawing money from an ATM using the victim's credit card, and they were shown photographs of the body that had been found buried under manuscript pages in Downshire Hill (the most graphic images were not exhibited).

One of the most absorbing witnesses introduced by the prosecution was Dr Holmes, a forensic voice expert. Mark Ellison asked the clerk to play the audio recordings of the man who called Allan Chappelow's various banks. Once the tape had finished, Ellison asked Dr Holmes whose voice was on the recording. Without hesitation, Holmes said that she believed that it was 'quite likely' that the voice was that of the defendant, Wang Yam. Over the course of the next hour, the expert explained the reason why she had reached this conclusion. With her testimony finished it was the defence's turn to cross-examine. After posing a few softball questions, Geoffrey Cox QC asked Dr Holmes if she was an expert in Chinese voices. When the expert said that she was not, Cox said that was all he had to ask, and sat down.

The court was far less packed than it had been for the first trial. There was seldom anyone sitting in the public gallery, and when there was, these were typically tourists who had randomly walked in hoping to witness a piece of Britain's famous fair play in action. Dong Hui came as often as she could, but with a two-year-old at home and having started a new job at a travel agency in north London, she found it hard to find the time to get away. Journalists were rarely seen on the press bench. Even those who had shown the most dedication in covering this case, from the *Camden New Journal* and the *Guardian*, felt that daily reporting of the trial was now unnecessary. The matter of court secrecy had been adequately covered on the previous outing, their editors felt, and it was unlikely that any new evidence would be disclosed.

Once the prosecution had concluded their case, it was Geoffrey Cox's turn to call his witnesses. He offered similar arguments to those deployed by Geoffrey Robertson in the first trial, all supporting the idea that Wang Yam had indeed been involved with the mail fraud but had nothing to do with the murder. Many of the same witnesses were recalled, including Philip Baker. But Cox offered some new theories of his own. The victim's reading glasses were found near his body, he said, implying that he was reading just before he was killed, not answering the door. Equally, there was no DNA or blood evidence found in the corridor leading away from the front hallway, suggesting that the struggle had taken place in Room Six, and not before. Finally, the handyman Thomas Carr was called back to give evidence, confirming it was possible to access the house through the roof – a refutation of the prosecution's argument that the only way into the house was through the locked front door.

The defence then introduced their voice experts, Dr Allen Hirson and Professor Yi Xu. With the help of a computer and projector, the experts talked their way through a PowerPoint presentation titled '*R v Wang Yam*: Voice Analysis' in which they explained the anatomy of the vocal tract, the basics of phonetic science, and the distinctiveness of pitch, accent and speech pattern. In his evidence, Professor Xu said that based on the level of pitch he was 'certain' that the voice on the phone calls was not the defendant. Geoffrey Cox argued that if it was not Wang Yam pretending to be Allan Chappelow on the phone calls to the banks, then there was no proof he had been in possession of Allan Chappelow's phone and SIM card, which were the only evidence linking him to the victim's body.

Cox then asked Dr Allen Hirson to explain what else he had found on the tapes. Hirson said that he had listened carefully to the victim's call to the Inland Revenue on 8 May 2006, focusing in particular on the last few seconds of the call, starting at 6 minutes. A detailed transcript of this part of the call was introduced to the proceedings.

Time	Speaker	Content
06:03	MV1	. . . Just worried that, eh, it might've fallen into the wrong hands. Thank you very much.
	FV1	You're welcome, Mr Chappelow.
	MV1	Yes. Thank you very much indeed. Bye, bye.
	FV1	OK. Bye.

	MV1	Thank you. Bye, bye, (I) thank you.
6:13		[click]
6:14		[signal distorted]
		[Low-level speech babble including at least one female voice]
6:21	MV★	All right then.
		[Low-level speech babble including at least one female voice]
	MV1	(Yes) it would have been, fallen into the wrong hands otherwise.
		[Low-level speech babble including at least one female voice]
	MV1	As you say, I mean, you'd want to have notified. Well I've only just realised that it was one of the things, due to me and eh . . .
		[Very low-level background speech babble (signal distortion)]
6:38	MV★	Mm.
6:39		[Call ends]

Dr Hirson identified three expected sounds: the female operator 'FV1' at the Inland Revenue end of the call, a male speaker 'MV1' who he said was clearly Allan Chappelow, and background 'babble' from the Inland Revenue, the type you might find in an open-plan office or call centre. The voice expert said that surprisingly the recording had also captured a fourth sound. After 06:13 minutes, when the phone call appeared to have come to an end, he observed 'utterances' from a new person, who he called 'MV★'. In his evidence, Hirson explained that two additional utterances originate from an unknown male speaker other than Mr Chappelow and that this male voice was likely to have originated from the distal [Allan Chappelow's] end of the line rather than from the proximal [Inland Revenue] end of the line.

This Inland Revenue telephone call, the defence now argued, suggested that there was a second person in the house with the victim.

Perhaps, they said, this was someone who had befriended Allan Chappelow. This would refute the prosecution's operating theory of a bungled burglary involving a solitary recluse. In summary, argued the defence, 'Whilst there was evidence that Mr Yam was guilty of fraud, the evidence did not drive to the conclusion that he was guilty of murder. The circumstances of the murder alone point away from the prosecution case that Mr Chappelow was the victim of a spontaneous attack at his front door.'

Mark Ellison then rose to cross-examine Dr Hirson. According to Appendix A, Ellison said, the list of telephone calls prepared by the police, all that was known about Mr Chappelow's phone call to the Inland Revenue was that it had been made on 8 May 2006 in the vicinity of Hampstead's Royal Free Hospital's cell tower. It could therefore have been made away from 9 Downshire Hill, he argued, possibly at a post office or shop, and the second voice could have been a shop assistant. When Dr Hirson said he wasn't sure, Ellison then went further. Perhaps the other voice on the phone could have been the elderly victim talking to himself? To this Hirson said that given the speech quality he was confident that the second voice was not Allan Chappelow. The prosecutor, however, felt he had raised sufficient doubt in the jury's mind and, with nothing more to add, he sat down.

The trial rumbled on through November, December and into the New Year of 2009, until it was Wang Yam's time to give evidence. The judge had ordered that because of Wang Yam's difficulty in 'keeping distinct the sensitive and non-sensitive aspects of his evidence' in the first trial, this time his entire evidence would be heard *in camera*. Geoffrey Cox tried to challenge the ruling but failed, leaving the defendant distressed. Wang Yam felt gagged by the judge.

As with the first trial, once Ellison and Cox had closed their cases, Mr Justice Ouseley spent three days giving legal directions and summarising the evidence for the jury. He reviewed the evidence provided by the key witnesses, and methodically laid out the main elements of the telephone and internet evidence. When it came to the voice experts, he pointed out that Professor Xu had changed his evidence from believing Wang Yam was 'quite unlikely' to be the person impersonating Allan Chappelow on the phone calls to the banks to being 'certain' that he was not, and that while the first conclusion was not based on pitch, his in-court testimony was. He cautioned the jury to be wary of such a 'step change' and warned that he believed Professor Xu had portrayed only some of the calls in his presentation and not those that did not fit his conclusion. The judge also addressed Dr Hirson's belief that he had heard an unidentified male voice during the victim's call to the Inland Revenue. The judge observed that the jury had to be cautious also about the extent of Dr Hirson's knowledge of 'whether this 86-year-old man tended or did not tend to talk to himself'.

Finally, at 11.05 a.m. on Monday 12 January 2009, Mr Justice Ouseley announced that it was now the jury's turn to deliberate a verdict. By this point, two of the original twelve jury members had left because of illness, leaving ten. Under English law there was no system for alternates, but since the minimum required number of jury members was nine, the deliberations could proceed. The judge explained that he would prefer a decision agreed by all jury members, but he would accept a majority verdict. 'I look forward', he said, 'to seeing you at the end of the day.'

Five hours later, the jury returned to the courtroom with the news that they weren't close to a decision. 'I am going to say go home now; rest,' said the judge, adding: 'Do not discuss the case either with anybody outside your number or among yourselves until tomorrow morning.'

The jury was unable to reach a verdict on Tuesday and struggled to reach an agreement throughout Wednesday. Late that afternoon, they sent a question to the judge: what does a 'majority verdict' mean? Back in court, the judge explained that a majority decision was reached when at least nine of the jury agreed. Hearing this, the foreman shook his head, appearing disappointed. 'I have a feeling', the judge commented once the jury had been removed from the courtroom, 'that they may have thought a majority was not at least nine.'

The jury spent the whole of Thursday deliberating and then, just before 4 p.m., the judge received a message which he read out in court. 'Jenny the bailiff has just phoned,' he said. 'The jurors would like to be released for the day.'

On Friday 16 January, the ten jury members were once again welcomed by the judge who told them that they were 'not under any pressure' to make a decision, and that they could return the following week. They were then ushered into the deliberation room, but a few minutes later they were back in court. Perhaps they had needed to sleep on a decision that had been reached the night before, or maybe all they needed was one last discussion. Either way, they had reached a verdict.

The public gallery was more crowded today – a few law students wanting to see this historic trial's conclusion, people who had read about the case in the papers, along with the usual smattering of tourists. Busy at work, Dong Hui had been unable to come; there were no members of Allan Chappelow's family present. On the press bench were journalists from the *Guardian*, *The Times* and *Daily Mail*, along with Dan Carrier from the *Camden New Journal*. Sitting in the dock at the back of the courtroom was Wang Yam. He appeared calm, ready.

'Will the defendant please stand?' the judge instructed. 'Madam Foreman, will you please stand?'

Judge : Members of the jury, have you reached verdicts?
Foreman : Yes.
Clerk : Members of the jury, on Count One, do you find the defendant Wang Yam guilty or not guilty of murder?
Foreman : Guilty.

Hearing the news, Wang Yam did not move. Nor did he cry or

let out a noise. He looked around the court until he saw Dan Carrier and locked eyes. To the journalist, the accused appeared angry and intense. Eventually, after perhaps five seconds, Wang Yam looked away.

Meanwhile, the clerk continued asking for the verdicts. The foreman reported that the jury's vote on the murder charge had been nine to one, and that they had all found Wang Yam guilty of burglary. The clerk added that the deliberations had taken twenty-two hours and twenty-nine minutes. The judge then announced that he would adjourn the court while he considered sentencing. After a brief exchange with his lawyers, Wang Yam was escorted to the cells in the courthouse basement, awaiting transfer back to Belmarsh Prison. Kirsty Brimelow and James Mullion spent some time with their client, he was deeply shocked.

Dong Hui was at her desk when she learned of the verdict. The priest of her local church called her and told her that her husband had been found guilty. Hearing this, she collapsed on the ground. For three years she had been convinced that a British jury would find Wang Yam innocent. After being revived with a cup of tea and kind words from her colleagues, she soon recovered. How would the judge sentence her husband? she wondered. How would she take care of their young son by herself?

The next day, 17 January 2009, *The Times* ran a story on the verdict under the headline WANG YAM FOUND GUILTY OF KILLING MILLION-AIRE AUTHOR TO STEAL HIS IDENTITY. In an attempt to protect themselves from Mr Justice Ouseley's ire, the article quoted material previously covered by the other newspapers, but also released information that had not yet been covered by the press: 'His defence also claimed that there were many possible suspects for the murder, including Mossad agents, the Chinese triads . . . [and] a young man that Mr Chappelow had befriended on Hampstead Heath.'

When he read this article, Mr Justice Ouseley was displeased and referred it to the attorney general Lady Scotland, 'for her urgent and serious consideration'. The attorney general informed *The Times* that the article was in breach of the judge's order which had specifically prohibited 'speculation' about why the hearing had been in private, but that it was not in the public interest to pursue a prosecution. In the end, no action was taken, but *The Times* and other publications were yet again put on notice that the *in camera* proceedings were not to be covered.

On 29 January, Wang Yam, his lawyers, the prosecutors, court reporters, bailiffs and judge gathered once again at the Old Bailey for the sentencing.

The judge began by reminding the court of the brutal crime that lay behind the trial. The victim was a 'defenceless man who was semi-conscious at times during the assault', he started. 'He was murdered in the course of burgling of his house for stealing of mail.' Then, looking at the defendant, he said, 'By the jury's verdict, Mr Yam, the man who committed that murder and burglary was you.' According to the government's sentencing guidelines, the judge explained, his starting point must be a minimum of thirty years.

After a brief pause, the judge continued. Given that he did not believe that Wang Yam had intended to murder rather than burgle Allan Chappelow, he was willing to reduce the sentence. 'The victim', he said, 'just unfortunately happened to be there', to Mr Yam's 'surprise'. The judge also discounted the idea that the defendant had tortured the victim with wax, which 'probably had nothing to do with the murder'. He added Wang Yam had no criminal record, and that 'most importantly, it is quite clear that the acts of the defendant were wholly out of character'.

With the defendant now standing, the judge announced his sentence. Having taken account of the mitigating and aggravating factors, 'I have come to the conclusion that the minimum term which I can properly impose is one of twenty years.' He also sentenced Wang Yam to four and a half years for the burglary and two years for the handling of stolen goods, both to run concurrently with the murder.

Wang Yam had been arrested in September 2006 and had been in prison ever since awaiting the outcome of the trial. The twenty-year prison term would therefore be deducted by the 852 days that he had already spent in custody, the judge said, including the forty-seven days he was held in Switzerland pending extradition. He would not be released, therefore, until 27 October 2027, when he would be sixty-six years old. Wang Yam showed no emotion as security led him out of the court.

CASE NOTE

I suggested to Geoffrey Robertson that it had been a mistake to call the defence witnesses that had led to parts of the trial being held in secret – potentially confusing the defendant, jury and press. 'I don't agree on the secret evidence,' he responded by email. 'It gave him [Wang Yam] some credibility. His real problem was his maniacal refusal to plead to the fraud. I spent hours trying to persuade him to do so, otherwise the jury might disbelieve him on the murder. That is why, I think, the second jury, thinking him a liar on the fraud, assumed he was lying when denying the murder!' He then added, 'You can only do what I did – tell him until you are blue in the face to plead [guilty to fraud] in order that the jury will not believe him dishonest. His refusal left doubts about his sanity – hence the shrink report.'

Arrived in Austin, Texas, late at night and checked in at the youth hostel on Lakeshore Drive where Allan Chappelow had stayed just weeks before he was killed. Very basic accommodation but clean and bright. Shown to my dorm room and decided to turn in for the night. The large man snoring below me and the window shut tight (25 degrees outside) made it impossible to sleep. The next day, I moved to a nearby hotel. Visited the Harry Ransom Center library at the University of Texas where Allan had researched George Bernard

Shaw. Met Kelly, the head librarian, who remembered Allan. Each day the elderly visitor travelled by public bus from the hostel to the library, she said, and then worked from 9 a.m. till 5 p.m. She handed me a file with Allan Chappelow's name printed on its edge. Inside I found a thick pile of pink request slips that Allan had submitted ten years before (all related to George Bernard Shaw). Also contained within was correspondence between the library and the Met Police, and an invoice to Allan addressed to 9 Downshire Hill for over 300 copies that were never sent because his credit card had been blocked.

Had dinner (BBQ spare ribs with corn, green beans and biscuits) with Allan's cousin Patty Ainsworth and her husband Steve. They remembered Allan fondly. He spoke angrily about the Iraq War, they said, and shared no love for President Bush or Tony Blair. Patty recalled that her cousin had a 'musty smell' about him, and that he always wore the same clothes whenever she saw him. He was clearly excited about his work at the Harry Ransom Center, telling them that he had found letters between himself and George Bernard Shaw from 1950. Like everyone else I spoke with in Austin, Patty said Allan was physically active, outgoing, sociable and engaged. A far cry from the 'frail old recluse' portrayed by the police and prosecutors.

Back in the UK, I visited the voice expert Dr Allen Hirson. In his small office in London's City University, Hirson explained the basics of forensic phonetics: his task is to identify each person's 'idiolect' (speech habit), including 'formants' (frequency bands), voice quality, pitch, fluency and accent. He then played me the audio files of the call to the Inland Revenue on 8 May 2006. Deeply moving to hear Allan Chappelow's voice. He sounded well-educated, funny, kind, self-deprecating. Hirson also said that it was clear to him that another man was in the room with Allan during the call. The other man could be entirely unconnected to the killing. But at the very least it goes against the police's theory that AC was a loner, a recluse. Who was this other man? A friend? Neighbour? Someone he met on the Heath?

I emailed Geoffrey Robertson about his statement as reported in The Times *that there were many possible suspects for the murder, including 'a young man that Mr Chappelow had befriended on Hampstead Heath'. Robertson responded: 'That is certainly the theory that I advanced as the most likely. I had gone through thousands of Chappelow photographs, knew something about a kind of fondness for young men and their availability at times on the Heath. You might call it a hunch, but it was a second sense that I had from years of experience.' When I mentioned Serpico's testimony, Robertson added, 'I had not heard that someone has come forward, do let me know the details and it might jog further memories.'*

Have been questioning the likelihood of a man in his eighties cruising for sex on West Heath. I emailed Serpico and he responded as follows: 'Regarding elderly guys who are into CP [Corporal Punishment], it is really not very hard to understand as many guys of their generation first encountered this activity at school and developed a taste for this kind of activity in later life.' [Note: Chappelow's early reports from the Hall School.] He said that he had regularly encountered two elderly males cruising on the Heath 'Looking for like-minded people'. He added 'a lot of the clients who visit a professional dominatrix for punishment are elderly men'. Serpico also responded to another email question I had sent him: did men who took part in corporal punishment sometimes engage with wax play? He said they did, and that it was exactly the kind of thing that 'Allan' would have enjoyed.

Trying to get basic information about the justice system so I can place Wang Yam's case in context. I have submitted eight Freedom of Information Act requests to the Ministry of Justice. Each one has been denied. My first request was, 'Can you please provide me with a list of all murder cases that were held "in camera" since 1990 and 1945, 1945 and 1980, and 1980 to the present time?' To this they replied that it is too expensive to research the information – 'The law allows us to decline to answer requests under FOIA when we estimate that it would cost us more than £600.' When I narrowed the search down to 'since 1990', their answer was, 'Our Crown Court case management system does not record whether a hearing was held in camera or whether a request was made for it to be held in camera.' Then when I asked them to tell me how many inmates married inside Belmarsh Prison in 2008, they responded that 'though the department holds the information that you have asked for', they said that they could not release the figures because the 'figure amounts to five people or fewer' and 'the release of this figure would risk identification of the individuals concerned'. I am really frustrated. How can I tell this story if I can't even get basic data out of the government?

I spoke again with Wang Yam. This was the fifteenth time we had talked. Each time on the phone for about an hour. I told him I was finding it hard to believe his story because I'd been unable to verify his Chinese background. He suggested I speak to his first cousin, Zhu Xiaoping. He didn't have any contact information for her, nor did he know where she worked (she might be a software engineer). 'We were close friends in Beijing,' he said. 'She is about my age. I think she lives in Seattle.' Need to find her contact details.

17

PRISON

Immediately after the judge's sentence, Wang Yam was escorted to a holding cell in the courthouse basement. A few minutes later, Kirsty Brimelow came down to see him, assuring her client that she would do everything she could to get his conviction quashed.

Once Brimelow left, Wang Yam was left alone in the holding cell. At the end of the day he was handcuffed and loaded into a large black van, and driven to a police station in central London. A few days later, he was transferred to the facility scheduled to be his home for the next eighteen years: Her Majesty's Prison Whitemoor.

Opened in September 1991 by the prime minister's wife Norma Major, HMP Whitemoor was situated near the village of March in Cambridgeshire, 100 miles north of London. As one of Britain's eight maximum-security prisons, three-quarters of its 440 inmates were serving jail time for murder. Around 40 per cent were Muslim, and foreign nationals made up almost a quarter. Whitemoor was also home to some of the country's most dangerous radical Islamic terrorists. A few weeks before Wang Yam's arrival, for instance, the *Sun* had reported with outrage that: 'An Al Qaeda terrorist involved in a plot to bomb London was enrolled on an eight-day "comedy workshop" at Whitemoor jail, alongside murderers and rapists.' Soon after the article's publication, the comedy course was scrapped by the Ministry of Justice.

There were three regular wings at Whitemoor – A, B and C – each containing three 'spurs' (red, blue and green) housing around forty inmates. The fourth, D or 'Fens' wing, was managed in conjunction with the National Health Service and comprised around seventy men diagnosed with personality disorders. A recent report found twenty-four instances of self-harm had taken place in Whitemoor in a single year, ranging from minor scratches to attempted hangings. The prison had a Suicide Awareness Management Team, made up of prison officers, members of the chaplaincy and healthcare providers, who met monthly and shared information on at-risk prisoners. The suicide-prevention charity Samaritans also trained and supported a network of prisoners who acted as 'listeners' for other inmates.

All Whitemoor prisoners slept in single cells measuring 2 by 4.5 metres, each with its own bed, stainless steel desk and toilet. There was a small window cut into one wall, overlooking the assembly area, and a television set hung from another. Showers were communal. And it was noisy. When the inmates themselves were not making a racket, any birdsong or other nature sounds were drowned out by the constant groan of the facility's laundry and heating systems.

Arriving at Whitemoor, Wang Yam was given a uniform and his six-digit prison number, A5928AL. He would be allowed to wear his own clothes after the first two weeks. A prison officer then outlined the routine. Wang Yam's cell door would be unlocked every day at 7.50 a.m.; he would then have breakfast with the other men in the canteen and report for whatever duties he had been assigned. He would be allowed to speak with other prisoners during 'association', which started at 5 p.m. and lasted just over two hours. During weekday evenings, he had to be back in his cell by 7.20 p.m., and on the weekends the cell door was locked at 4.50 p.m. He would start in C Wing, which contained an 'induction spur' for newly arrived inmates.

While in prison, Wang Yam was expected to busy himself with various activities. He was shown modern gym facilities that offered an array of fitness options, including badminton and basketball, circuit training and weight lifting, ping pong and volleyball. He could also use the library for up to thirty minutes each week. At any one time, he could borrow one of its 8,000 volumes, but he would not be allowed access to the internet. The library also had Turkish, Arabic and Irish newspapers available, but nothing from China. He was offered access to a fridge and a cooker and would be able to make his own food, if that was what he wanted. A dentist and an optician visited weekly and a counsellor to help you stop smoking were also available. Once he was settled in, he could sign up for a variety of educational courses.

Wang Yam was allowed up to three visitors at any one time. His family and friends could even email him and the message would be delivered to him the following day. All external communications, however, were reviewed by the administration, and anything deemed inappropriate was either redacted or confiscated. One of the prison's newest offerings was called 'Story Book Dads/Mums'. This free programme would enable Wang Yam to record a story for his young daughter and even younger son, which could then be enhanced by editors using digital audio software and sound effects. The completed story would be recorded onto a CD with a personalised cover and sent to the child.

On his second day in C Wing, one of the prisoners told Wang Yam that he was needed upstairs. A few minutes later, Wang Yam diligently walked up to the appointed place but found nobody waiting. He turned around just in time to see two men, before he was knocked unconscious. As he was recovering in the hospital wing, he was told two of his teeth had been knocked out.

Having lost the second trial, it was time for the defendant's legal team to regroup. The lead counsel Geoffrey Cox was fired – Wang Yam blamed him for the guilty verdicts – and, now that he was available, Geoffrey Robertson was once again back on the case.

In mid-February 2009, a conference call took place between Robertson, Brimelow and the lawyers from Janes Solicitors to discuss strategy. With their client serving a life sentence, they agreed that the next step was to ask the Court of Appeal of England and Wales to review the verdict. They knew that the appellate justices would only examine a lower court's decision if they felt that there had been an error in the law. They would not relitigate the entire fifteen-week trial. It was the defence team's task, therefore, to present specific grounds for overturning the lower court's decision.

By the meeting's end, the lawyers had narrowed the strategy to three issues: the unfairness of holding a trial in secret, the judge's biased summing up for the jury and what they believed to be the judge's mistaken instruction to the jury. Over the next few weeks they drafted and redrafted their application, striving to perfect their legal arguments. When they felt it could be improved no more, they submitted the paperwork and waited to hear from the clerk of the appeals court.

It took a year for the case to come before the Court of Appeal. On 5 May 2010, the hearing opened at the Royal Courts of Justice, a large gothic stone building on the Strand in central London. The proceedings were overseen by justices Hughes, Saunders and Thirlwall. Once again the Crown was represented by Mark Ellison and Bobbie Cheema-Grubb, while Geoffrey Robertson and Kirsty Brimelow appeared on behalf of Wang Yam.

As the defence had brought the case, Robertson spoke first. He began by arguing that Mr Justice Ouseley had incorrectly instructed the jury at the end of the first trial. Before they had left the court for their deliberations, the judge had told the jury not to find Wang Yam guilty of murder unless they also found him guilty of breaking into the victim's house. Since the jury in the first trial had been unable to find the defendant guilty of breaking into 9 Downshire Hill, Robertson said, this should have precluded a charge of murder at the second trial.

The judge's second mistake, Robertson continued, was that he had failed to adequately sum up their voice experts' evidence for the jury and, as a result, had put his thumb on the scales. The voice expert Dr Hirson, for instance, had heard an unidentified male voice during Allan Chappelow's call to the Inland Revenue which, in Robertson's view, 'destroyed the Crown case'. Yet, in his summing up, the judge had unfairly suggested that the deceased may have been talking to himself and therefore there might not have been a second person in the house. Furthermore, Robertson argued, the judge had undermined the evidence provided by the defence's other voice expert Professor Xu. In court, Xu had said that he was 'certain' that Wang Yam was not the man on the phone calling Allan Chappelow's banks, and yet the judge had not relayed this clearly to the jury.

Still questioning the judge's summing up, Robertson next argued that Mr Justice Ouseley had given too much credibility to the testimony of the postman Nicholas Sullman – the only witness who connected the defendant to the crime scene. Not only was Sullman lacking in confidence in his identification of Wang Yam, Robertson said, but the VIPER interview was improperly managed. Of the nine pictures shown to Sullman, only one had an unshaven man wearing a beige jacket, features that Sullman had previously described to the police, and this picture was of Wang Yam. Robertson also wondered why Sullman had been allowed to sit with the other witnesses prior to his interview, offering an opportunity for them to compare notes.

Finally, Robertson argued that the trials had been unfair because much of the defence had been held *in camera*. Repeating many of the same arguments he had made in the pre-trial hearing held in January 2008, Robertson questioned the validity of the verdict given the closed nature of the proceedings.

Having heard from the prosecution lawyers, who vehemently rejected each of the defence's claims, the hearing was concluded at the end of the third day. The judges then retired to consider their response. Five months later, on the morning of 5 October 2010, their opinion was published on the court's website.

First, the justices agreed that Mr Justice Ouseley should not have instructed the jury not to convict Wang Yam of murder if they did not find him guilty of stealing mail from Chappelow's house. They therefore quashed Count Four: theft from a house. This was a disappointment for the defence. They of course would have preferred that the murder charge be overturned rather than the burglary, which carried a much lower sentence.

The justices next addressed the judge's summing up. They concluded that the pictures shown to Nicholas Sullman showed a 'good mix of broadly similar men' and that Mr Justice Ouseley had made it clear that the postman's identification had been 'qualified'. They also agreed that Sullman and other witnesses should not have waited in the same room together, but concluded that 'there was no clear evidence of communication' between them, and that this was

Illustration of 9 Downshire Hill
from 'Old Homes in England'
1953 by Archibald Chappelow

9 Downshire Hill front hall,
1920s

Allan Chappelow in the Hall
School cricket team, 1930

Allan, his father Archibald and
aunt Lise, 9 Downshire Hill,
1952

'The Chucker-Out'
photograph of George
Bernard Shaw by Allan
Chappelow, July 1950

"THE CHUCKER-OUT"
(Shaw's Own Title)
G.B.S ~ July 1950 ~ Aetat 94

Downshire Hill with Allan Chappelow's
motorcycle parked in street, 1967

Allan Chappelow in leather
jacket, 1980s

Allan Chappelow and Patty
Ainsworth in Austin Texas,
April 2006

姓　名　任宏

性别　男
年龄　29
职务　教师
单位　[illegible]

注 意 事 项

一、此证必须随身携带。
二、不得转借他人，所填各项
　　不得涂改。
三、要妥善保管不得遗失，如
　　有遗失立即报告主管部门。
四、调离本校必须交回。
五、此证盖章有效。

京工证字　第　4024　号　　19 90 年 8 月 10 日签发

Wang Yam's student ID, 1980s

Ren Bishi, Wang Yam's
'grandfather', *circa* 1950

Ren Bishi's wife Chen
Zongying, son Ren Yuanyuan,
and daughter Ren Yuanzheng
(Wang Yam's 'father',
'grandmother' and 'aunt'), 1987

Wang Yam and Li Jia's
wedding, 1991

结婚人像片

发证机关

北京市西城区人民政府

一九九一年

Certificate of naturalisation

as a

BRITISH CITIZEN

The Secretary of State, in exercise of the powers conferred by the
itish Nationality Act 1981, hereby grants this certificate of naturalisation
to the person named below, who shall be a

BRITISH CITIZEN
from the date of this certificate

Full name	*YAM*WANG
Name at birth if different	*REN*HONG
Date of birth	27 APRIL 1961
Place and country of birth	XI'AN CITY, PEOPLE'S REPUBLIC OF CHINA

Wang Yam's certificate of naturalisation with
change of name, 1992

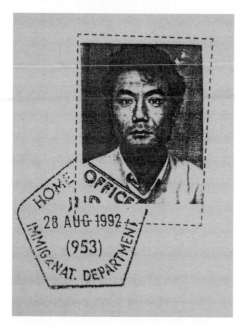

Wang Yam's UK
immigration photo, 1992

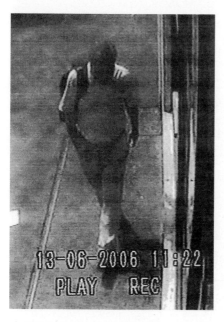

Wang Yam on CCTV at Tesco
Express, June 2006

Wang Yam's daughter
Angela's self-portrait, 2008

Wang Yam and Dong Hui cut wedding cake,
Belmarsh prison, 2008

Wang Yam's flat at 13c
Denning Road, 2017

Wang Yam's prison cell, 2017

Wang Yam's prison self-portrait, 2017

'Spanking bench' at West Heath, 2017

therefore insignificant. As such, they rejected the assertion that the witness's ID should be discounted.

Regarding the voice experts, the justices said that Mr Justice Ouseley had acted properly in what they described as complex evidence and that he had fairly contextualised the evidence presented. Going further, they criticised Dr Hirson for speculating that Allan Chappelow did not speak to himself, and Professor Xu for changing his opinion.

Finally, the justices addressed the issue of the *in camera* hearings. 'Most of the trial was conducted in public,' they said, and 'the defendant was able to name the three persons who he said were responsible for the supply of the cheques and to give a good deal of circumstantial identifying material'. Anyone who chose to be in court, they continued, could have heard this evidence. The Appeals Court judges were 'unable to accept' that there was 'a real possibility that other evidence would have emerged given further publicity and that such would have been exculpatory'. In reaching their conclusion they had taken into account 'the enormously strong evidence' that it 'was simply not true' that Wang Yam had only a limited involvement with the theft of Allan Chappelow's identity.

In concluding their fifteen-page decision, the justices unanimously dismissed Wang Yam's appeal. A coda was added beneath: 'Informative: Media organisations are reminded that purporting to reveal or speculating as to what was or may have been said *in camera* may be an attempted contempt of court, punishable as a contempt.'

Hearing news of the Court of Appeal decision, Wang Yam asked his lawyers what the next steps were. The best option, he was told, was they could appeal to the European Court of Human Rights. This could take many months, even years. For now, he would have to make the best of his situation in jail.

Most days Wang Yam was able to avoid contact with the other inmates in Whitemoor Prison. After the initial beating, the next challenge was the daily badgering by the Muslim Brothers. 'If you don't convert,' they told him, 'you will go to hell.' Their evangelical pleadings had extra weight given their size and the pummelling he had just experienced, but he resisted their efforts.

After two weeks in C Wing Wang Yam was moved to one of the permanent blocks and he quickly established a routine. He enjoyed the art and music lessons he sampled and he began guitar and singing lessons. He also played chess with some of the other prisoners and soon established a reputation as the prison's best table tennis player.

It was around this time that a new inmate moved into the cell next door. This was Yasin Omar, who had been found guilty in 2006 of attempting to plant a bomb on a London Underground train in what became known as the '21/7' attack. Most evenings, after the lights were out, they talked. Wang Yam spoke about domain names, table tennis and his young son. Omar talked about the corrupt West, the evils of capitalism and the benefits of Islam. Wang Yam felt that he was trying to brainwash him. One night, Wang Yam recalled Omar telling him that 'any Jewish people should be killed' and that 'people should follow God's instructions and bomb infidels'. When news of the latest radical Islam terrorist attack reached the prison, Wang Yam said that Omar and the other inmates would celebrate, cheering and banging their cell doors.

Now that Wang Yam was housed in Whitemoor he had less contact with his family. He had not heard from Li Jia or their daughter Angela since the murder sentence was announced. Meanwhile, Dong Hui and their son Brian rarely came to visit. It was too far from her flat in north London, and it was hard to arrange for a friend to look after Brian while she was away. Most weeks she would call and sometimes she would put Brian on the phone. His son spoke with an English accent, which amused Wang Yam.

There was one other Chinese man in the prison, who had been found guilty of a kidnap, and, while Wang Yam enjoyed playing table tennis with this man and occasionally talking about their lives back in the old country, he avoided getting into emotional conversations. He had no need of a friendship. After all, his lawyers would soon succeed in their appeals and he would shortly be out.

On May 2011, Wang Yam's legal team asked the European Court of Human Rights to review the case, complaining that his conviction was unfair because part of his trial had been held in closed session, and therefore violated article 6.1 of the European Convention on Human Rights (ECHR). Lawyers working on behalf of the UK government submitted that the 'application should be declared manifestly ill-founded and inadmissible', or alternatively dismissed on the merits'.

It took another year for the European Court to review the case. While they expressed willingness to examine Wang Yam's verdict, the court said that they could not properly examine it unless they could see the secret material. They therefore referred the matter back to the UK Supreme Court to determine if the sensitive material could be released to them.

During the spring and summer of 2012, Kirsty Brimelow QC (she had been appointed Queen's Counsel the previous year) and her counterparts in the CPS went back and forth arguing over whether it was appropriate according to the European convention, let alone on grounds of national security, to release intelligence documents to a court that was presided over by foreign judges.

During this period, Wang Yam heard less and less from his defence team. Where there was communication, it was by phone or letter. They no longer came to visit him in prison. As the legal process ground on, the gaps between correspondences appeared to lengthen. Wang Yam felt increasingly isolated and abandoned.

Wang Yam's time in Whitemoor was marked by annual reviews compiled by the prison authorities. At 2 p.m. on 13 November 2012, for instance, the Sentence Planning Board met to review Wang Yam's case. Having summed up the prisoner's background, the four board members reported that during their interview with him 'Mr Yam demonstrated interpersonal skills', and that 'he maintained appropriate eye contact throughout'. They continued that he 'did not demonstrate any pro-criminal attitudes' and noted, with some approval, that though he denied that he played any part in the murder, 'he is willing to complete offending behaviour programmes' at the prison.

The panel also recorded that Wang Yam did not smoke, take drugs or drink alcohol; indeed he 'enjoys playing table tennis on the wing' which he finds 'keeps him very fit and active' and 'feels that he is much healthier than he was a few years ago'. Teaching computer skills to other inmates he earned £14.02 per week, they observed, and 'copes on his wages'.

Allyson Beckford, who ran art classes for the prisoners, reported that Wang Yam had attended her lessons for approximately one year and that he had gained a distinction in portrait and drawing. She also said that he had received a commendation in the 2012 Koestler competition, an award handed out by the Koestler Trust, an offender art charity. 'Mr Yam is very interested in art,' she wrote, 'and gets along well with other members of the group.' Her one negative comment was that he did not always submit his work in a timely manner.

Having affirmed that Wang Yam was a Christian and that he now 'attends the chapel regularly', the report concluded with a statement from his supervising officer. 'Mr Yam has been on B Wing for some time now and is always polite to myself and presents himself in a good fashion,' wrote officer Ansell. 'His general demeanour is very good.' In their summary, the board recommended that the prisoner's targets should be to consolidate his 'positive custodial behaviour', to take part in a restorative justice course that would enhance his capacity for victim empathy, and to remain 'adjudication free' – or in plainer language, to keep out of trouble.

As to his family, the board reported that while Wang Yam stayed in touch with his second wife, Dong Hui, things were less cordial with Li Jia, his first wife. The inmate, they reported, stated that 'he was extremely worried about his daughter from his first marriage as he doesn't know where she is and does not know how to trace her'.

In fact, by the end of 2012, relations were also breaking down with Dong Hui. By this point, Wang Yam had been in prison for six years and all his appeals seemed to be going nowhere. It was time for Dong Hui to move on. Ever since the Court of Appeal announced that they would not reverse her husband's guilty verdict in 2010, she had decided that they must break up. She was seventeen years younger than him, after all, and soon would be out of childbearing age. But Wang Yam had told her that if she ever wanted to 'start a new life' then she should 'cut the ties slowly'. Out of kindness to him, or perhaps out of respect for the relationship she once thought they had shared, she did exactly that. After he moved to Whitemoor

Prison, she had only come to visit twice. She had said it was because the journey took her the whole day, but Wang Yam understood that she was pulling away. When she did visit, she no longer took Brian to see his father – it wasn't good for him to be around all those murderers and terrorists. Soon, they stopped speaking by phone altogether.

While the legal machinations bounced back and forth between the courts and the lawyers, a smaller, but perhaps more significant event – as far as Wang Yam's liberty was concerned – was playing out in a newsroom in King's Cross, London.

Late in 2013, a letter arrived at the *Guardian*'s mailroom. Addressed to Duncan Campbell, it was sorted and forwarded to his home office. Scottish by upbringing and married to the Oscar award-winning actress Julie Christie, the 69-year-old Campbell was one of Britain's most well-regarded investigative journalists. The letter that arrived on Campbell's desk that day in 2013 was written by Wang Yam. He had sent similar correspondence to scores of journalists and politicians across the UK but had received no response. Reading Wang Yam's story, Campbell was surprised that he had heard so little about the case. It involved murder, a reclusive writer, a fashionable address, as well as the alleged involvement of Chinese gangsters. When he saw that much of the trial had been held *in camera*, he was hooked. 'It was a fascinating story,' recalled Duncan Campbell. 'What puzzled me was why other journalists were not covering this story.'

In truth, though, he wasn't that surprised. Twenty years earlier, in the 1980s, there had been a flowering of investigative journalism. This followed a number of high-profile miscarriage of justice cases – such as the Birmingham 6 and Guildford 4 trials. Television broadcasters had launched programmes dedicated to uncovering police and prosecution errors, newsrooms had bolstered their crime reporters. Such efforts take time and money, however, and in the new millennium with the emergence of online media, broadcasters and newspapers were forced to tighten their belts. Since 2000, there had been little appetite for researching complex claims that might lead nowhere. Court cases were now barely covered by the press – long gone were the days when every local paper covered the courts. The press boxes at the Old Bailey were typically empty.

Over the next few months however, Campbell and his erstwhile colleague, Richard Norton-Taylor, chased down the story. They went to the house at 9 Downshire Hill and spoke to the neighbours. The police wouldn't tell them anything but they were able to find Philip Baker QC, who had helped Wang Yam when he had first arrived in the UK. Baker confirmed Wang Yam's backstory in China and they viewed him as credible given that he had received an OBE for his work with Chinese political refugees. While they acknowledged that Wang Yam had a 'rackety past' – his failed property speculations, for instance, and his bankruptcy – that didn't mean that he didn't deserve a fair trial.

Before long, Campbell and Norton-Taylor had 'lots of question marks' about the guilty verdict: if there was no forensic evidence tying Wang Yam to the crime scene, how could the jury be certain beyond a reasonable doubt of his guilt? Did the eight cigarette butts, the footmarks on the manuscripts covering the victim, and the mystery voice on the phone to the Inland Revenue suggest that there was more than one person involved in the murder? Most of all, was it fair to hold a trial in secret?

Campbell had attended plenty of hearings in which anonymous testimony had been given, including victims who sat behind a screen fearing that their identity might be revealed and children whose faces were digitally blacked out via video link. 'The reason that the case was held in secret', he said, 'was to avoid government embarrassment'. Campbell believed that the government 'hoped that the whole thing would blow over, and that Wang Yam would be sentenced to twenty years and that everyone would forget about him'.

It took them a while to convince the newspaper's lawyers that they could run the story. After all, there were rumours that *The Times* and the BBC had both been chastised for their reporting of Wang Yam's trial. Finally, on 23 January 2014, the *Guardian* ran the story under the headline MURDER IN HAMPSTEAD: THE AUTHOR, THE DISSIDENT AND A TRIAL HELD IN SECRET. They quoted Wang Yam via a letter from prison. 'I believe the only way to my freedom is [to] let public . . . to know what is my defence and what I had done in full picture. No cover-up.'

It was around this time that the Foreign Secretary William Hague was asked to approve a new PII that would prevent the sensitive material being sent to the European Court of Human Rights.

In his cover note to the PII, Hague wrote that 'I have concluded that there would be a real risk of serious harm to an important public interest' if Mr Justice Ouseley's order was 'discharged in its entirety, or in part, permitting disclosure of the *in camera* information, or were disclosure to be made to the Strasbourg court'.

On 27 February 2014, Hague's PII arrived before Mr Justice Ouseley, who agreed that the *in camera* material should not be disclosed to the European Court. Kirsty Brimelow then applied for and was granted judicial review of that decision, but the application was dismissed on its merits. Unhappy with this result, she then applied directly to the UK's Supreme Court.

In April 2014, Lord Phillips, who had recently retired as president of the UK Supreme Court, and was considered to be one of the most respected lawyers in the land, wrote an article in the *London Review of Books* on secret trials including the case of Wang Yam. For a senior judge, albeit retired, to insert himself into an ongoing case was highly rare; to do so publicly and before the case was heard by the court suggested a deep disquiet.

It is my habit every morning to cycle to Hampstead Heath and to swim in a bathing pond there. My return route takes me up Downshire Hill, a broad street lined with the homes of the very rich. One house always used to puzzle me. It was very poorly maintained and swathed in invasive ivy. Then, one day in 2006, there was something about it in my local newspaper. The owner was an 86-year-old man called Allan Chappelow, a recluse who had rarely left the house in his later years. He had been found dead under a metre-high pile of papers in a room filled with rotting furniture. A suspect was apprehended: a Chinese exile called Wang Yam. He was charged with murder. Very unusually, a large part of his trial was held *in camera*.

It was remarkable that a prominent judge appeared to be stepping close to the restrictive line established by Mr Justice Ouseley. Perhaps even more interesting was his general conclusion about the use of secret courts. Having reviewed the history of secret hearings, along with a recent parliamentary bill that examined this issue, Lord Phillips said that closed courts 'could be used only as a last resort'.

As part of her pre-trial efforts, Brimelow asked the government to reduce its restrictions regarding the secret material. At first the government's Treasury Solicitor's department refused her request. After further prodding from Brimelow, a government lawyer finally wrote back on 1 August 2014 laying out the conditions for her seeing the sensitive material, including a brief search prior to entry to the room; surrender of any personal electronic devices; signature of the Official Secrets Act (OSA); and surrender of any notes made during the viewing.

When Wang Yam's lawyers pointed out that these requirements were overreaching, the government lawyers responded:

> Irrespective of what has happened in the past, Counsel are required to sign the OSA in order to have sight of the material because the material, including the transcripts, notebooks and legally privileged material which makes reference to this, is all subject to the OSA. This is particularly so as this is the first time in these particular proceedings and context that access to the material is being given.

In response, Brimelow wrote back that she believed these restrictions to be unnecessary given that she and her team were already bound by Mr Justice Ouseley's contempt of court order. She also pointed out that some of the material that they were being denied access to were their own notebooks, which they had previously handed over for safe storage. 'We are extremely concerned', she wrote, 'that you appear to be treating these notebooks as your property.' She also asked why the government's lawyers were now referring to the *Regina v Wang Yam* litigation as 'Case A'. To this latter question she never received a satisfactory response, nor did she ever receive the notebooks. Instead, she set about preparing for the next hearing that would review the justice of holding a murder trial in secret: the UK's Supreme Court.

On 25 November 2014, the Whitemoor Prison Sentence Planning Board met again. Wang Yam no longer had family visits, they observed;

his last was almost two years earlier on 24 January 2013. He wrote to Dong Hui regularly, they said; however, he had been unable to call her as her phone had been disconnected. Most significantly, they reported that he hadn't heard anything from Dong Hui for roughly five months.

Once again the board summarised his offence and sentencing details, and noted that in addition to his art classes, which he attended weekly, Wang Yam also helped repair computers that were later sent to Africa. He continued to play table tennis with both staff and peers and described himself as a 'mentally strong man'.

In August 2015, Wang Yam finally received a letter from Dong Hui. The way things stood, their eight-year-old son would live his entire teenage years without his father. She therefore needed to move on with her life and, to do that, she needed a clean break. It looked like her parents had been right all along: marrying Wang Yam had been a mistake. She now wanted a divorce.

Wang Yam was devastated by this news. The agreement, however, had always been that he would let her go if she found someone else or just wanted distance, so he signed the divorce papers. He was now cut off from his son. 'It had the same impact on me', he said, 'as when I heard that I was sentenced to twenty years in prison.'

A few weeks after the article about Wang Yam was published in the *Guardian*, another letter arrived in the mailroom for Duncan Campbell. This time the writer was Jonathan Bean, a former resident of 14a Downshire Hill who said that he had a story that might interest the journalists. Campbell and Norton-Taylor interviewed the new witness, and his account was included in their next article published on 28 February 2014. 'I lived a few doors down from [Chappelow's house] back in 2006,' Bean told them. 'The following February [when Wang Yam was already in custody], I was in our house and heard a rustling on our porch. I opened the door to find a man with a knife going through our post. He pointed the knife at me and I shut the door . . . He said if I called the police he would kill me.'

Despite the threat, Bean recalled that he did tell the local police, who took a statement and created a crime incident report. This was then entered into the central police database, but it was not shared with Pete Lansdown's homicide investigation team, who never interviewed the new witness. 'It is clear to me that there was a violent person or gang operating in the street,' said Bean, 'and the lack of police interest was very bizarre.'

To Campbell, this burglary suggested that at the very least other gangsters might be involved with mail fraud at the time of Allan Chappelow's murder. When he learned that this incident report had never been shared with the homicide investigation team, Crown Prosecution Service or Wang Yam's defence team, he was incredulous.

So were Wang Yam's lawyers. They met with Jonathan Bean, took his statement, and then made a submission to the Criminal Cases Review Commission (CCRC). Set up following a wave of miscarriage of justice cases in the 1990s, the CCRC provided the final chance to prisoners wanting to have their guilty verdicts re-examined. It reviewed around 1,500 cases each year, of which fewer than twenty were referred on to the Court of Appeal.

First, Wang Yam's lawyers had to convince the CCRC that the case had merit and was worthy of review. Then they had to persuade the Court of Appeal that the police's failure to disclose evidence might have influenced the original jury. Only then could they hope that their client's conviction might be overturned.

Wang Yam's chances of success were slim.

CASE NOTE

Met Lord Phillips, the recently retired president of the UK Supreme Court, at his home on the south coast. He said he was a proponent of open justice, but conceded that there might be a highly unusual circumstance where open justice has to take a back seat to the needs of the state. For example to prevent the disclosure of security secrets during a murder trial. He then added, however, that it was 'specious' to argue that an 'in camera' trial would lead to fewer witnesses coming forward. How could this be so if, as was the case with Wang Yam's trial, the media provided extensive coverage precisely because the trial was held in secret? I also asked how the justice system is not impacted by 'confirmation bias' (tendency to only consider evidence that supports an existing theory). He said a key part of the judge's summing up at the trial's end was to protect a jury against confirmation bias. Ultimately, he cautioned, 'You can't safeguard against human bias.'

I went back to the criminal profiler Bill Fleischer and told him about Serpico's recollections. 'Perhaps there were two different crimes that took place,' he said, 'mail fraud and murder.' He then provided an alternative narrative: the victim brought someone home, they had a liaison, which may have involved 'corporal punishment' or wax play. Things 'exploded' from there. The *perpetrator became enraged and brutally killed the victim. And then, having covered the body with papers and the front door with branches, 'the criminal faded back into the woodwork'.*

I also spoke with Keri Nixon, a forensic psychologist who works with Merseyside and other police forces. She said that profiling in the UK has a bad reputation, particularly following a judge's ruling in the 1990s that dismissed it as dodgy science. Since then, profilers have been rebranded as Behavioural Investigative Advisors, or BIAs, but despite their cautious and more data-driven approach, they essentially do the same as their American counterparts. Like the ex-FBI profiler Bill Fleischer, Keri was quick to say that the murder of Allan Chappelow did not appear to be a bungled burglary; it was too interpersonal, she agreed, involving too much explosive rage, and too high a level of violence. She added that she was surprised that the Met Police had not made use of a profiler, or BIA, in their investigation, particularly given that it was, as Pete Lansdown put it, one of the most interesting whodunit cases of his career.

I asked Kirsty Brimelow about the possibility of there being two separate crimes. She said that she and her colleagues had also wondered about this. It would explain one of the mysteries of the case. Why would the thief repeatedly return to 9 Downshire Hill after Allan Chappelow had been killed (to collect newly ordered credit cards and passwords) and not search the house, where he would find lying on a bed Allan's passport, address book (with PIN numbers) and more credit cards? Answer: because the thief did not know Allan Chappelow was dead — he believed the house to be vacant, but didn't risk going beyond the front hallway. Quite neat, but who then was using Allan's mobile phone handset and SIM in the West End of London on 20 May 2006, presumably after Allan had been killed? The thief or the murderer?

18

THE COURT OF LAST RESORT

On 2 November 2015, while Wang Yam's submission was still being considered by the CCRC, his case came before the Supreme Court of the United Kingdom.

Only six years old, the UK Supreme Court was immature compared to its counterparts in France and the USA. Before its creation, the highest court in the land had been the House of Lords, which also voted on legislation. The UK Supreme Court had been formed to establish a separation of powers between the judiciary and government.

The proceedings were held at the Middlesex Guildhall in Parliament Square, opposite the Houses of Parliament. Reviewing Wang Yam's case were seven judges including the president, Lord Neuberger. Unlike other UK trials, hearings held before the Supreme Court were streamed live on the internet, and archived for future viewing by lawyers, scholars and researchers. Wang Yam was not present in court to hear these proceedings but would be notified of the result when it came in.

The media, who for so long had been fighting for the right to report on the material heard in the closed court sessions, now widely covered the case. From the *Camden New Journal* to *Russia Today*, the story spread. The *Telegraph*, for instance, reported that 'Jacqui Smith, the then Home Secretary, agreed to a Public Interest Immunity (PII) certificate, making it the first murder trial covered by a secrecy order on national security grounds.' The story concluded by stating that Wang Yam planned to argue his case before the European Court of Human Rights, as 'very significant parts' of his trial were held *in camera*. Wang Yam was delighted with the media exposure, hoping that it might lead to a new examination of previously unseen evidence.

Arguing on behalf of Wang Yam was Lord David Pannick, who with thirty-six years of experience as a barrister had been picked by *The Times Law 100* as one of the country's top ten QCs. With rectangular glasses perched on his nose and wearing a dark tailored suit, dark blue tie, and with a red poppy in his buttonhole, Pannick said that his client's original trial had been unfair because it was in breach of Article 6 of the European Court of Human Rights, particularly that part of his case had not been heard in public. 'We say that the trial judge had no legal power prohibiting the disclosure of this sensitive material to the European Court.' The distinguished lawyer then went on to say that the matter was of considerable public interest because the only reasons for not disclosing the material to the European court were either that they didn't have 'efficient procedures' to protect the sensitive material or the 'people could not be trusted'. By 'people' he was likely referring to the foreign-born judges who would have access to the files.

On behalf of the Crown, James Eadie and Jonathan Hall argued that the matter had been adequately dealt with by the lower courts and that it should not be left to a European court to dictate UK national security policy. During the hearing, one of the judges asked if the defence lawyers had requested a Special Advocate with high-security clearance who could have reviewed the sensitive material attached to the PII. This was the procedure that takes place before a PII is placed before a judge and was established to ensure that the government was not pulling the wool over a defendant's eyes. Wang Yam's lawyers said that they had not, to which the judge looked surprised.

In their decision, released a few weeks later, the Supreme Court justices declared that Mr Justice Ouseley had the power to prevent the *in camera* material from being shared with the European Court of Human Rights. Without access to this sensitive material, the European judges wouldn't know what national security issues were at stake and therefore would find it harder to determine if Wang Yam had been denied his rights. Given the judges' deference to each country's security issues, the defence lawyers' submission to the European court was now unlikely to succeed.

There was really only one last opportunity for the defence team: the appeal that they had lodged with the Criminal Cases Review Commission (CCRC).

On 30 November 2015, the Sentence Planning Board met once again to review Wang Yam's file. Only two people were in attendance this time – long-term prisoners rarely attracted a full panel: the offender supervisor and the board secretary.

In his board submission, Wang Yam wrote that he had been attending music classes – 'I enjoy it,' he wrote – and that he practised guitar in his spare time. 'I obey the rules and directions,' he added, 'and keep out of trouble.' Commending the prisoner for his continuing positive attitude and for keeping his head down (including zero incidents of violence), the board said that when a place became available he should be moved to a lower-security Category B facility.

The board, however, placed a note of caution in their report. They registered that nobody had visited Wang Yam for more than two years, and that there had been no recent contact with either of his former wives or children. When asked where he might live following release, Wang Yam stated that he would not be returning to Dong Hui and that he was 'unsure where he will reside, but does not want to return to China'. Concerned for the public's wellbeing, the board said that they were troubled by such uncertainty.

Towards the report's end, the board also observed that the prisoner was becoming less social. 'Mr Yam mixes with few other prisoners', they said, 'and is usually one of the first to be locked away.' According to his lawyer, Kirsty Brimelow, the many years of incarceration and the stress of continual appeals had finally worn down her client. 'He spends less time at the gym than he did before,' she said. 'He is losing hope, he is depressed.'

On 28 April 2016, the CCRC announced their ruling. It had been four years since Wang Yam's lawyers' first application to the panel.

In a press release provided to the media, the CCRC said that key to their decision had been 'the failure' by the police to reveal 'new evidence' which 'might have assisted the defence and/or undermined the prosecution case'. They also graciously credited the journalists Duncan Campbell and Richard Norton-Taylor for their efforts. 'The existence of the incident came to light as a result of an article that appeared in the *Guardian* newspaper in January 2014. The Commission subsequently found that police records of the incident were not made available to the defence during the disclosure process.' The official press release concluded that they had 'conducted a comprehensive investigation of the case' and had 'decided to refer Mr Yam's murder conviction to the Court of Appeal'.

Considering that 70 per cent of CCRC referrals resulted in a positive outcome for the defendant at the Court of Appeal, this was a major result for Wang Yam's defence team.

'Wow,' said Peter Devlin, upon hearing the CCRC's ruling. He was surprised that he hadn't been told about the violent robbery that had taken place in Hampstead around the time of Allan Chappelow's murder. If he'd known, he said, he would have followed up. It was up to the local police force to inform the homicide investigators about relevant crimes, he continued, but apparently they hadn't. 'I would have expected someone to have reported it.' A telephone call or email should have come through to the homicide investigation incident room in Colindale, he said, telling them to look up the crime number and suggesting that there was a possibility that it might have something to do with the murder inquiry. 'At the very least a statement would then have been taken from the witness and disclosed to the defence.' Devlin said that he found the CCRC ruling 'frustrating' as he still believed '100 per cent' that Wang Yam was guilty. 'I personally can't see how [the other robbery] impacts on the case,' he said. 'There is no evidence of a linkage' to Chappelow's murder.

'Oh my God' was Pete Lansdown's response to the CCRC decision. Adjusting quickly to the news, he added, 'It's another hurdle to get over, we will see where it goes.' He received word by phone the day after retiring from the Metropolitan Police and just as he was preparing to fly to the Cayman Islands to begin his new job as head of that country's homicide division. He said he wasn't aware of the other burglary, but perhaps it had been triggered by the media attention surrounding Chappelow's death, making people realise that there were 'easy pickings' to be had in Hampstead. Before hanging up he added that he might have to come back from the Caribbean to help if a third trial was prosecuted.

Learning of the decision, James Mullion and Kirsty Brimelow QC excitedly made arrangements to call their client in Whitemoor Prison. Yet, when he heard the news, Wang Yam had 'mixed feelings'. While he was of course pleased that his case would now be reviewed by the Court of Appeal, that they had given him 'a chance', he was disappointed that 'the CCRC did not touch upon the core issues' which would have revealed why he should not have been prosecuted in the first place.

Mullion and Brimelow did not have long to revel in their victory. A week after the CCRC's announcement they learned that they had been sacked by Wang Yam. Though grateful for the lawyers' efforts over the years, he wanted a team willing to deploy all of his arguments. His new lawyers would be Peter Wilcock QC and Edward Preston. Marketing himself as an expert in appeals, Wilcock had represented more than ten high-profile CCRC cases, advised various miscarriage of justice charities and was a featured speaker at various human rights conferences.

The Court of Appeal decision could go one of three ways. The judges might deny Wang Yam's appeal and, given that he had no further right to have his verdict reviewed, return him to prison to serve out the final ten years of his sentence. Alternatively, the original verdict could be declared 'unsafe', but the CPS might decide to re-prosecute (there is no double indemnity rule in English courts), in which case Wang Yam would be held in prison or released on license pending a third trial. Or, as Wang Yam hoped, the original sentence might be declared 'unsafe', and the CPS might decide not to re-prosecute. Wang Yam would be free.

Whatever the outcome, the Court of Appeal would be Wang Yam's very last chance at overturning his conviction. While eager for resolution, and hopefully a successful outcome, there would be only one bite at this cherry. The new legal team's task was to make it count. Before his case reached the Court of Appeal, however, there would be a series of pre-trial sessions, starting with a 'directions hearing' to determine the scope and date of the appeal.

CASE NOTE

_____

*Finally, news on Jill Dando. Tracked down the English policeman who sent
Wang Yam's inmate friend to prison in 2001. The policeman said that this man
was 'capable of doing something like [killing Dando], that he was a weapons
expert and would have no problem doing that'. The question remains, was the
inmate in the UK or Bolivia at the time of Dando's death? Spoke to the Met
officer monitoring Dando's cold case. He said the police's current position was
that 'Barry George was the killer' and that the file was 'not being actively worked
on, but still exists.' He had never heard of this new potential suspect but added
that the information I had was the most solid lead they'd had in years. 'There's
too much there not to check', he said. Following our conversation, he sent a request
via Interpol to the Bolivian authorities. After some time, the cold case officer sent
me an email: 'Bolivia can state that [the inmate] was definitely in prison there
in 1997 and again in 2000,' he wrote, but 'That is the extent of their official
records it seems.' He added that 'It would be conjecture for me to say at this time
that it was possible that he was in the UK in April purely based on Bolivia's
poor record keeping.' He said he would continue looking into the matter, that he
wanted to 'bottom it out to my satisfaction.' It seems that it is at least possible
that Wang Yam is telling the truth.*

Spoke to Luke David who used to work as journalist for local newspaper Ham & High. *In 2004, he wrote a story that helped police arrest a man who carried out a series of attacks against gay men on West Heath. Known by the press as 'Gold Tooth', the criminal was jailed for six years on multiple charges of robbery, blackmail and assault. David won a press award for his undercover investigative journalism. He said that his report followed a large increase in violent robberies amongst gay men on the Heath around the time of Chappelow's murder.*

Called Nigel Harris at Camden Forum. Back in 2005 and 2006 he had provided AIDS education and safety outreach to men cruising on the Heath. He remembered elderly men in black calling others to take part in sexual acts. Also said that it was not uncommon for hundreds of men to gather on West Heath on a hot summer's night. Confirms many of Serpico's details.

Spoke to a highly placed member of the Metropolitan Police's LGBT Advisory Group. Set up in the late 1990s, it helped solve lesbian, gay, bisexual and transgender serious crimes. He said that they had never been contacted about Allan Chappelow's murder. Added that though he highly rated Pete Lansdown as a police detective, in 2006 Lansdown 'wouldn't have known a gay crime if it had hit him in the face'. He showed me a list of unsolved LGBT-related murder cases from the time of Allan Chappelow's killing. Amongst these was the name of Hallam Tennyson.

Back home I read the online news articles. On 21 December 2005, Beryl Hallam Augustine Tennyson was found with serious head injuries and stab wounds in his flat in Highgate, North London. Tennyson was eighty-five years old, a writer and radio producer, and the great-grandson of the poet Alfred Tennyson. There were many similarities to Allan Chappelow. Tennyson had been a conscientious objector in the Second World War and a committed socialist. In 1953, after visiting communist Yugoslavia, he wrote a book entitled Tito Lifts the Curtain. *According to his diaries, Tennyson was gay, highly promiscuous and frequented West Heath. Family members told police that Tennyson invited men back to his apartment up to three times per week. The police had made no connection between the murders of Hallam Tennyson and Allan Chappelow.*

Visited Dan Carrier at his office in Camden. He told me of another elderly gay man who was murdered in Hampstead. In June 2005, retired school teacher Roger Hendra was attacked with a claw hammer and a knife at his flat on Pond Street opposite Royal Free Hospital. The man sentenced for the murder, Mark Papazian, met Hendra whilst cruising on West Heath. According to an article in the Camden New Journal, *entries in the victim's diary 'indicated the dangers faced by gay men involved in causal pick-ups on the Heath.' The BBC reported that the murderer had 'scoured nearby Hampstead Heath for gay men to kill in his quest to be a serial killer, the court heard.' Papazian could not have killed Chappelow, however, as he was in prison at the time. What are the chances that three elderly men who cruised for gay sex on West Heath were brutally murdered within the space of a year?*

I called Pete Lansdown at his office in the Cayman Islands. He said that he was working harder than ever. Asked him what he made of the theory that Allan Chappelow had brought the killer home from the Heath. Lansdown said that it sounded 'speculative' and that there was no evidence of a 'sexualised' crime scene. In his experience, if a murder had a sexual element – whether gay or straight – it was overt. I also told him that the two profilers thought it unlikely that a bungled burglary would result in the victim being bludgeoned to death. Lansdown admitted that he could not recall a bungled burglary resulting in a similar level of violence, but he was still 'absolutely confident' that they had the right man.

Visited Peter Wilcock QC and Eddie Preston, the appeals specialists now working on Wang Yam's Court of Appeal application. Very hot day; we met in a small airless office in Lincoln's Inn Fields, London. Wilcock poured himself a glass of water and said that the UK's justice system was overturning fewer cases than it had in the 1990s and that far less CCRC-referred cases were being quashed by the Court of Appeal. When I mentioned the profilers' certainty that the murder must have involved retaliatory rage, Wilcock said that English courts looked sceptically on profilers. He was more interested in the gay companion counter-narrative (they had never heard of the LGBT police advisor or the Hallam Tennyson murder), and would follow up with Nigel Steward, the head of the Hampstead Safer Neighbourhood scheme. He also asked me to put him in touch with Chappelow's family who might verify that the elderly victim was energetic and outgoing (i.e. the kind of person who might invite a sex-companion home and not a recluse as imagined by the police). They promised to let me know when the Appeals Court hearing date was set.

Following the CCRC's decision, I once again contacted the Ministry of Justice saying that in the light of a possible miscarriage of justice there was now a legitimate public interest in my meeting Wang Yam. I said that it would be easier to communicate with him if we were in the same room given his poor English skills, and that a face-to-face meeting would allow me to observe his body language. After numerous phones calls I finally received a response from the ministry's press department: 'It has been decided that there are no exceptional circumstances which would warrant the granting of an interview when Wang Yam's case is due to be considered by the Court of Appeal. The threshold is very high and we do not consider that it has been met in this instance.' I don't understand. What could the government be worried about?

After a long search on the internet, I found a Zhu Xiaoping (the same name as Wang Yam's cousin) living near Seattle. She was born in 1963, it could be the right person. Finally, at 4 p.m. GMT, I made the call. It was 8 a.m. West Coast time and the woman answering sounded a little surprised. Within a minute 'Betsy' – the name she uses in the USA – confirmed that she knew Wang Yam (Ren Hong), that she'd heard that he'd been found guilty in London of murder (she had read the stories online) and that she and her husband had been friends in Beijing before they had all left China. I asked if he was a member of the family. 'Is he still telling those lies?' she laughed. 'I can't believe it, after all these years.' In the late 1980s, she said, her mother (Ren Yuanyuan's sister) received a phone call from Wang Yam saying that he was in Beijing, that he was a long-lost member of the Ren family and would she like to meet? That afternoon he went round for tea and shortly after, she introduced him to her daughter, Betsy, who was also studying at Beijing University at the time. When they met, Betsy said, she challenged Wang Yam to tell her the truth. He admitted that his grandfather was a landlord in a rural province, and not Ren Bishi. From that point forward, she said, whenever she was asked if Wang Yam was really related to her she would explain that he wasn't, but she never brought it up with Wang Yam again. 'He was a victim of Chinese education,' she continued. 'He was taught how to lie.' Despite the fact that he wanted to take advantage of her family by lying, she said, they became friends. Her husband-to-be had shared a dorm with Wang Yam; they played table tennis together. What she couldn't believe was that he was still telling the lies (though she accepted that perhaps he used his fake connections to her family to hoodwink the British government into flying him from Hong Kong to the UK in 1992 and then providing him and his two wives and children with visas). 'Do you believe that he killed Allan Chappelow?' I finally asked. 'Yes,' she said firmly. 'Because he is a liar?' I asked. 'Because he is a bad man,' Betsy said. 'Because he was desperate for money.' And then she added, 'But what is so odd is that he gave you my name, why would he do that?'

A letter arrived at my home from the Ministry of Justice's litigation department. 'We write on behalf of the Attorney General,' it said. Noting that they understood that I planned to 'write a book about the murder of Allan Chappelow,' they wished to 'draw my attention' to Mr Justice Ouseley's order (a copy was enclosed). 'The effect of this Order is to prevent publication of the grounds or reasons for the making of the order excluding the press and public from part of Wang Yam's criminal trial, as well as to prevent publication of any evidence, submissions, judicial decision or other material heard or dealt with in camera.' They pointed out that breach of this order was contempt of court (punishable by imprisonment), and recommended that I seek independent legal advice.

19

ALONE

Throughout the summer and into the winter of 2016, I continued to speak to Wang Yam. He called almost every week. We talked about his health ('I'm doing fine,' he said, 'I am sleeping much better in a single cell'), and swapped news on the progress of his case (I had recently met his new legal team), and also discussed the stories circulating in the news: Brexit, the terrorist attacks in Europe, the refugee crisis. As the new year began, and with his Court of Appeal hearing likely to be heard in the spring, I wanted to push him on a few points I was struggling to understand.

I told him that I had spoken to Xiaoping, his 'cousin' in Seattle: 'She said that if you don't admit that you've been lying about being related to Ren Bishi,' I relayed, 'she will never speak to you again.' 'She would say that,' he replied calmly. 'I told my family that they should deny knowing me, it's better for them.' I told him that Xiaoping believed that he had committed the murder. There was silence on the line.

'That is not right,' he finally said, sadly. 'In China society, when you have a family member convicted for murder you go to hell, you can't get a job, you can't face the friend, you can't do anything about it.' He then reminded me that he had stayed with Xiaoping's mother during the protests in June 1989. 'If I am not a family member,' he continued, 'do you really think she would take me in?'

Next we spoke about Wang Yam's 'half-brother' Ren Jining, who also said that they were not related. 'I expected this,' he said. When I challenged him again, Wang Yam grew animated. 'You joking,' he proclaimed. 'You think I'm lying?' He said that he had often brought Ren Jining with him to play computer games at his university office in Beijing. His supervisor Professor Chen was unhappy that the computers were being used like this, and told Wang Yam to stop bringing in his half-brother. Wang Yam said he continued anyway. I didn't respond. It was up to my judgment, Wang Yam said. I could write it whichever way I wanted. Perhaps when it came to his family I should write it both ways. 'What I suggest you do', he added, 'is just say that I "claim" to be related. If you believe, it's up to you.'

Wang Yam then said I needed to focus on his meeting with the landlord, Deborah Sheppard, on 7 June 2006. 'Look at the telephone logs put together by the prosecution,' he said. While he was still on the phone, I searched through my archive and found the relevant page. He told me to find the calls made around 2pm. There were four calls made using the Royal Free Hospital cell-tower in Hampstead: a 1.20 minute call at 2.01 p.m. to directory inquiries, a 7 second call to voicemail at 2.03 p.m., a 1.22 minute call immediately after to Allan Chappelow's credit card company Sainsbury's, and then a six minute call to Camden Council ending at 2.12 p.m.

'So?' I asked him, 'what's the significance?' The prosecution, he replied, said that all these calls were made with Allan Chappelow's handset but at that very time he, Wang Yam, was with Deborah Sheppard. He then directed me to her statement at trial, in which she said that she met Wang Yam 'shortly after two o'clock' on 7 June 2006 and for 'about an hour'. At trial, Sheppard produced her diary confirming this appointment. The prosecution argued that 'shortly after' could mean fifteen minutes after the hour and that Wang Yam could have made the calls before seeing the flat (I later called Mrs Sheppard and she said that 'shortly after' could be five past or possibly even ten past the hour, but definitely not quarter past, which she would have considered late). This was all highly significant, for if someone other than Wang Yam was using Allan Chappelow's phone, and pretending to be the victim during calls to the bank, then at the very least this undermined the prosecution's fundamental argument that Wang Yam was acting alone and supported his story that he had been working with a gang.

I then asked Wang Yam why he had left London the day after Allan Chappelow's body was found. This timing had been one of the key factors that had made the police suspicious of him. He said it was an unfortunate coincidence. He had set up a company called First Front Holding in Zug, Switzerland, and had planned to meet various lawyers and accountants to help file a patent application for smartphone software. He said that he had visited Zug at least three times before 2006; he even had a bank account in Zurich from the 1990s. He said he would send me the name of a lawyer he worked with who could confirm that he had business interests in Switzerland in the years before his arrest.

We also discussed why he hadn't simply admitted that he had stolen Allan Chappelow's credit cards and cheque books. I said that it might have encouraged the jury to find him guilty of burglary instead of murder. 'It would make no difference,' he said. 'But anyway it's not true, so I cannot admit it.' He then gave an example of what he saw as the prosecution's failings. 'I wear glasses reading the newspapers. In the normal environment I not wear glasses.' He then added that the CCTV footage that captured him at the bank and taking money from an ATM didn't have him wearing glasses. This point was of course important as the prosecution relied heavily on the postman Nick Sullman's evidence: that he had met a Chinese man wearing thick dark spectacles close to Downshire Hill.

I also asked him about his first wife, Li Jia. He said that she was 'traumatised' by what happened to him. 'I destroyed her. I am very sorry about that. Her colleagues all became very senior Chinese leaders. Her position was very privileged. I destroyed her future. I destroyed her career. I destroyed her life. I don't know what I can do. In my life there are things that make me very sad: that I was not with my father when he died. [What I did to] Li Jia. And of course that I am not with my son and daughter. These are my life's regrets. I wrote three letters [to Li Jia] saying I feel deeply sorry, I didn't murder anyone. I spoke about secret trial, and asked her to protect herself. If she had not married me, her life would be totally different.'

At the end of one talk, I asked Wang Yam why he was speaking with me. 'I would rather die in prison or be assassinated,' he said, 'than the public not know what happened.' When I asked what would happen if he lost at the Court of Appeal, Wang Yam said, 'I am ready for that.' He would disclose 'everything', he said. Though he had been tempted to go to the press many years earlier, he had held back because he was a 'loyal British citizen'. I asked a few tentative questions, but he refused to discuss it any further.

We talked again about life after his release. What about this claim about a new combustion engine? Surely, I said, he didn't expect me to believe that. 'I am a trained engineer,' he responded coolly, 'I have been thinking about it for many years, long before I came to prison. You don't expect that I haven't been busy, do you?'

Through the spring of 2017, Wang Yam prepared for his final day in court, rereading the witness statements, forensic reports and legal submissions that he kept in cardboard boxes in his prison cell. He wrote detailed memoranda exploring potential new lines of arguments to pursue and sent long letters to politicians, judges and journalists outlining his case. He spoke to fellow inmates to see if there was any new legal strategy that he might be able to deploy and he met with his lawyers, helping them to formulate his appeal.

Finally, on 15 March 2017, a directions hearing was held and the parameters for the Court of Appeal were agreed. Most notably the defence team were given permission to call new witnesses. A court date was listed for mid-July. This would be Wang Yam's last chance.

CASE NOTE

The appeal is only a week away and things are heating up. The police's crime scene manager Francesca Spennewyn has written a statement saying that she found nothing of a 'sexual nature' at 9 Downshire Hill. Gerry Pickering, the former family liaison officer, has also issued a new statement: 'At no time did I mention to Torben Permin that a gay pride video or condoms were found at 9 Downshire Hill. I do not know where this information came from, it certainly was not me.'

I call Torben. Apparently, the police account is wrong. PC Pickering sent him an email, which mentioned that the investigators <u>had</u> found condoms and a gay pride video in 9 Downshire Hill. I ask Torben to send me a copy of the email. If verified, it will add weight to the theory that Allan used to bring people home. With Serpico's testimony that a man called 'Allan' was a regular at the gay cruising spots on the Heath, it might be enough to convince the judges that there may be another suspect. It will also look very bad for the police.

A few days pass and still no word from Torben, so I call again to ask how the search is going. He says that he can't find the email. I write again suggesting he at least provide a statement to WY's lawyers, this time copying in his wife.

I receive the following reply: 'If the police can't help you more, so we can't do more.'

It's two days before the trial and time is running out. I call Allan's American cousin Patty Ainsworth and her husband Steve and update them on the case. I tell them that Torben doesn't want to speak with Wang Yam's lawyers and that I am uncomfortable pressing him any further. Patty agrees to contact him. 'While we do believe that Wang Yam is guilty of mail fraud and theft, we are not convinced that he actually murdered Allan,' she writes to Torben. 'Our main concern is that the truth comes out, whatever that is, and that the person who committed the crime is punished. We just want justice for Allan.' This is the first time I've heard Patty say that she believes Wang Yam may be innocent of murder. She hears nothing back.

After weeks of searching I finally find Jonathan Bean, the former Downshire Hill resident who had been a victim of a violent robbery. Bean says that like all his neighbours, he was well aware of the brutal murder of Allan Chappelow. 'We were only five doors down,' he tells me. We discuss the fact that there is no mention of the assailant carrying a knife in the crime report. When I ask if he told anyone at the time about the weapon, he forwards me an email he'd written to a friend two days after the crime which mentioned the knife. I pass this information to Wang Yam's lawyers in case they need it for the trial.

I find myself constantly thinking about what might happen at the appeal. Replaying the possible scenarios over and over in my mind. I've been reaching out (obsessively) to those involved, asking for their expectations. I first try the barrister who will be representing the Crown Prosecution Service, but unsurprisingly, there's no reply. I do manage to speak with the official at the CCRC in charge of Wang Yam's file; he says that he's never seen a weaker prosecution case. Kirsty Brimelow is also optimistic, believing the police's failure to disclose evidence is enough to make the verdict unsafe. Wang Yam's former barrister, Geoffrey Robertson, is more ambivalent; he worries that the new evidence *might not be sufficient to persuade the court. Meanwhile, Wang Yam's new lawyers Eddie Preston and Peter Wilcock are talking their chances down. Duncan Campbell says that Wang Yam should be freed based on the new evidence, but won't be, because in recent years the Court of Appeal has been less willing to overturn lower court decisions. I don't know what will happen. My heart says Wang Yam will walk free. My head says he will spend the next ten years in prison.*

20

THE DECISION

At 10.30 a.m. on 18 July 2017, three judges walked into Number 4 Court at the Royal Courts of Justice in central London. To the left and right stood Justices Nigel Sweeney and Juliet May, in the centre was the country's most senior judge, Lord Chief Justice, Roger Thomas. Each of the judges sported a long black gown and white collar, their heads covered by an off-white horsehair 'bench wig'. Of the three, Justice Thomas's wig appeared the oldest and most tatty, a matter of pride amongst his peers. After bowing to the court, the judges sat down in one of the red leather swivel chairs arranged on the raised platform at the front of the room.

Beneath the judges sat Wang Yam's lawyers, Peter Wilcock QC and the solicitor Eddie Preston. In the row behind sat Geoffrey Robertson QC who had represented Wang Yam in the first trials and was here to provide support. On the other side of the court, was Duncan Atkinson QC, who would be presenting the case for the Crown Prosecution Service.

On the press bench were perched the three journalists who had followed the case for so many years, Dan Carrier from the *Camden*

New Journal, and Duncan Campbell and Richard Norton Taylor for the *Guardian*. Also present was an experienced reporter from the Press Association. In the public section were gathered a number of observers, including Mrs Xing, the wife of Chairman Mao's bodyguard's son (who I had met in a Richmond restaurant), a case manager from the CCRC, along with a small group of tourists eager to see British justice at work. There was nobody from Allan Chappelow's family.

The three large flat screen monitors suspended on the ancient court's wood-pannelled walls flickered, revealing an empty room with the words 'HMP Nottingham Court 1' affixed to a blue-green wall. 'Mr Wang Yam', the moustached clerk said into the microphone, 'are you there?' A moment's silence, and then a man wearing a crisp white shirt sat down in front of the camera. His face was clean shaven, his head almost bald, and on his puffy face were a pair of silver reading glasses. He looked like he'd had little sleep. 'He has really, really aged,' said Dan Carrier.

Justice Thomas turned to the prisoner. 'Can you hear us Mr Yam?'

'Yes', said the prisoner.

'Mr Yam if you want something raise your hand.'

'Okay, thanks' said Wang Yam softly.

The Lord Chief Justice now asked the appellant to proceed with his case. Peter Wilcock stood and formally announced that he represented Wang Yam and that Duncan Atkinson appeared on behalf of the Crown. He then turned and with a sweep of his hand introduced Geoffrey Robertson as his colleague 'sitting behind me', making the justices chortle. They all knew Robertson was far senior to Wilcock, and would normally be the barrister standing in front. Having secured the goodwill of the court, Wilcock quickly moved on and explained the background to the case: that following the police's possible failure to disclose evidence, the CCRC had referred the matter to the Court of Appeal for review. Then, with the court's permission, the barrister called his first witness, Jonathan Bean.

At the back of the court a door opened and in walked a middle-aged man with short curly dark hair, wearing brown corduroy trousers, a striped brown t-shirt with bright orange collar and trainers. Jonathan Bean followed the clerk along the side of the room, up a couple of narrow stairs, and onto a platform on the same level as the judges. He declined to swear on the bible and instead affirmed that he would tell the whole truth.

'Mr Bean,' said Lord Chief Justice Thomas, 'you will need to speak loudly. This is quite a big room, and there is no amplification.' From the screen, Wang Yam was waiving his hand. 'Lord,' he said, 'I can't hear what you say.' The Lord Chief Justice began to respond but was interrupted by the prisoner, who repeated twice more, 'Lord, I can't hear what you say.' Justice Thomas smiled wryly, then moving closer to the microphone asked 'Can you hear me now?' Wang Yam said he could, and Wilcock was invited to continue.

Having asked the witness to confirm his name and that he lived at 14a Downshire Hill, Wilcock asked Bean to describe in his own words the events of 14 February 2007.

Bean: I was at home that day, planning to move to New York, packing up things to ship. I heard a rustling by the front door. My wife and baby had left a little time before, and I thought that possibly my wife had left the outer door open. I opened the inner door briefly, I saw someone in the porch area, I saw a glint of a knife, it was only open for a fraction of a second. My immediate reaction was to pull away from the danger, so I slammed the door very quickly.

Wilcock: What happened next?

Bean: The man said through the door, 'Do not call the

police or we will kill your wife and your baby.'
After a few minutes, I could still hear him, I
wondered what I should do. I was looking around
to see what I could get to protect myself. Frankly
I was terrified. It was going through my mind that
my neighbour was killed in similar circumstances.

When asked about the mail thief's voice, Bean said that he was
unsure, he didn't remember an accent. He added that he reported the
crime to the police later that evening, when he, his wife and baby
were safely at a friend's house. Two officers came over and he told
them that he was concerned for his family's security, especially given
his neighbour's 'brutal murder', and that he believed that the two
crimes were somehow linked. He was told that his crime 'had nothing to do' with the murder of Allan Chappelow and 'not to worry
about it' because they already had the criminal in custody. Bean then
told the court that he was 'very surprised' when he later learned
that the knife had been omitted from the crime report. When the
barrister then asked the witness to 'check his state of mind' about
this recollection, Bean said that he was sure as he had told a few
people about the knife in the aftermath of the robbery, including
sending an email to a friend two days later. Wilcock then passed a
copy of this email to the justices and read the text to the court.

It was then Atkinson's turn to cross-examine. After checking some
points of chronology with Bean – the time of the crime (mid-
afternoon), when he had called the police (around 9 p.m), when he
had left the country (two weeks later) – Atkinson asked whether
anything had actually been stolen from the house. Bean said that
perhaps some mail had been removed but that no money had been
taken from his account. 'Are you sure?' asked Atkinson. 'Yes,' said
Bean. As soon as the thief had departed, he had called his bank's fraud
department. 'So no funds were withdrawn from your account?'

Atkinson pressed again. 'I didn't lose money,' the witness responded carefully, 'but I don't know if attempts were made.' Having determined that the witness was both cautious and credible, Atkinson knew that there was no advantage in proceeding. 'I have no more questions m'Lords and Lady.'

Wang Yam's barrister then called two further witnesses. First was Michael Dunn, a soft-spoken elderly gentleman who had lived in Hampstead since the 1960s. As Wilcock continued, he appeared relaxed, with his left hand in his pocket and left knee raised off the ground and resting against the wooden bench before him. 'Tell me', Wilcock asked gently, 'what happened outside of 9 Downshire Hill?' Dunn recalled that around the time of the murder, he came across a suspicious-looking man with a two-metre-long plank of wood near the gates of 9 Downshire Hill. He was 'carrying it in an awkward position', he told the court, and not 'in a workman-like manner'. The man with the plank had a strong northern-Irish accent and told him that Allan Chappelow had recently driven his motorcycle up to Liverpool. This was clearly nonsense, reported the witness, as the two motorcycles parked in Chappelow's garden were overgrown with bushes and had not been ridden for years. Dunn also recalled how he had attempted to tell his story to one of the police officers involved with the search of 9 Downshire Hill but she appeared uninterested in taking a statement from him and had just 'walked off'. Once Wilcock had finished, and with neither the prosecution nor the justices having any further questions, the Lord Chief Justice thanked the witness for his time and said that he was free to leave.

The final witness to appear was Serpico, or Peter Hall, as he now disclosed his name to be. Dressed in a puce-coloured shirt, black tie and suit, Hall appeared nervous and out of place. Having set his black briefcase on the ground, he took an oath on the bible and swore to tell the truth. Leaning hard into the wooden railing that rimmed the witness box, Hall recalled that he had visited Hampstead's West Heath three or four times a week for more than a decade and that 'there was hardly a time' when an elderly man dressed all in black was not present. Peter Wilcock asked where on the Heath he met this man in black?

> Hall: A place called the 'spanking bench'.
> Wilcock: An area that is well-known for gay men?
> Hall: Yes.
> Wilcock: Did the man tell you his name?
> Hall: We didn't talk for two years, then we just exchanged names. I just knew him as 'Allan'.
> Wilcock: Does anything stand out about him?
> Hall: He slapped the spanking bench with a paddle or belt to attract like-minded people to that location.
> Wilcock: Apart from the paddle and belt, was he in the habit of carrying anything else?
> Hall: Yes, an improvised cat o'-nine-tails. It was homemade, tied at one end with lengths of 10 to 12 pieces of cord.

Throughout this question and answer session, the voice and pitch of Wilcock's voice never wavered. Similarly, neither the justices, the prosecutor nor the appellant showed any sign of surprise or response of any kind. The same could not be said for the journalists, who were making feverish scribbles in their notebooks.

> Wilcock: Did you ever form a view as to the accent of the man by the spanking bench?
> Hall: He certainly did not have a regional accent. It was a very, how can I put it, educated accent. I would say 'it's a rough night', he would say 'it's somewhat inclement'. On another occasion, he said 'I have been less than ebullient'.

Wilcock: Did you have other sessions with him?

Hall: Occasionally, I took handcuffs up there. I would like to emphasise, it was not for pleasure.

Wilcock: Did he mention about you going back home with him?

Hall: Yes, on one occasion.

Wilcock: Did you?

Hall: No, I didn't go back. I thought it might be a possibility of a sexual advance and I am not into necrophilia.

Wilcock resumed the questioning. Did the witness know where the man at the spanking bench lived? Hall said that he believed that he must have been a local as he visited West Heath so frequently. At the end of the night he'd often seen 'Allan' walk home in the direction of Downshire Hill. Twice he had seen 'Allan' leave with a companion. Hall added, 'I am normally a private person, except, that is for today.' He then asked the court's permission to remove his jacket. Lord Chief Justice Thomas smiled reassuringly, and said that was fine.

When the witness was ready, Wilcock then asked when Hall had first learned about the killing on Downshire Hill. Hall said that he had first heard vague stories about a murder in Hampstead in the summer of 2006. It was not until later that year, however, when he read a story about the murder in the *Evening Standard*, which included a photo of the victim, that he realised that his 'Allan' was Allan Chappelow. By this time, he heard there had been an arrest, so he didn't think to contact the police. 'Why would I?' he asked. Feeling like he had obtained as much as he could from his witness, Wilcock said 'I have no further questions,' and sat down.

Now it was the turn of the prosecution. Atkinson started aggressively. 'In 2003,' he asked, 'did you tell the police you were a Borough

Intelligence Officer?' The question seemed to confuse Hall. 'What is a Borough Intelligence Officer?' he asked. 'Well that suggests you weren't,' scoffed the prosecutor, before moving swiftly to the next question. 'Were you ever an Officer in the Royal Parks police?' Hall said he wasn't. 'In 2007 didn't you tell a gentleman called Mr Hancock that you were?' Hall said he hadn't. As the rapid-fire interrogation progressed, Atkinson's voice took on a harder, disbelieving edge. With each retort, he jutted his left hand stiffly through the air, punctuating the point. 'Between 2006 and 2016,' pushed on the prosecutor, 'did you on numerous occasions pass information along to the police?' Hall said that he had. 'And did you report your contact with the man at the spanking bench?' Hall coolly said that there was no reason to, he thought the police had their man. It was only in 2014, after he saw an appeal in the local press for new witnesses, that he had offered his testimony to Wang Yam's lawyers.

Atkinson then asked the witness a series of unrelated questions. In which direction had the 'man at the spanking bench' walked towards at the evening's end? Was his black jacket knee-length or waist-length? Did he have facial hair? Can you describe the paddle he used? At times the prosecutor appeared to be trying to provoke the witness, at others to find holes or inconsistencies in his testimony. Then, rather abruptly, Atkinson declared he had no more questions. Peter Hall then asked if he might say something else. Perhaps out of kindness, Lord Chief Justice Thomas said that would not be possible, and dismissed the witness.

After a brief pause, the Lord Chief Justice looked at Wang Yam's lawyers and, while holding up a bundle of paper including more than fifty pages, he said, 'We have received a number of letters from the appellant, have you seen them?' Taken aback, Wilcock said that he had not. To receive correspondence directly from a defendant and without the supervision of counsel was 'extraordinarily unusual', huffed the justice. He suggested that both sides review the contents of the letters and report back to him after lunch. At 1 p.m., Justice Thomas adjourned the court.

Wang Yam had spent most of the morning's session with his hand cupped to his ear. It appeared that the courtroom technology had failed to provide the prisoner with a clear transmission of the proceedings. As he stepped away from the chair a sign was revealed on the wall behind: 'Everything you say they can hear.'

At 2.15 p.m. the three justices returned to court. When asked about his client's letters, Peter Wilcock said that he had frequently discussed the issues with Wang Yam and explained that the matters had been addressed in the previous trials. He did not feel that raising the issues once again in court would help Wang Yam. Putting the bundle to one side, Lord Chief Justice Thomas asked for the barristers' closing arguments.

Addressing the justices, Wilcock again stood first and said that there were multiple similarities between the postal theft suffered by Mr Bean and the mail fraud that had taken place at 9 Downshire Hill. Yet this information was never disclosed by the police and surely the jury would have wanted to know about this evidence when they made a verdict? Central to the prosecution's case against Wang Yam, he continued, was that he acted alone. The idea that nobody else was involved in the crime was now 'diminished'.

In response, Duncan Atkinson conceded that there had been an error, that the local police should have shared the information with the homicide team, that this should have been investigated, and disclosed to the defence. There had been an 'inadvertent failure to disclose', he said, but it was no more than that. There was nothing malicious involved, there had been no cover up. It was just a simple mistake.

Most importantly, even if this crime had been disclosed, it would have made no difference. The jury had been told about other burglaries in the area and this other incident would not have influenced their decision.

Wilcock jumped up to disagree. This was not just yet another burglary, he said, his voice raised for the first time that day. It involved a knife, a threat to kill, a mention of a gang and mail fraud. It happened just yards from Chappelow's house, also in a front porch, and within just a few months of Chappelow having letters stolen. As such it was remarkably similar to the mail theft that took place at 9 Downshire Hill and no matter the cause, should have been disclosed. Mr Bean's evidence would have had a 'dramatic impact' on the jury. Wilcock then took a breath and declared, 'On Mr Bean's evidence alone, the court should allow the appeal.'

Duncan Atkinson then briefly addressed Mr Dunn's testimony. He could not really see how the description of the 'strange man with the plank' would have influenced the jury. During the trial, he continued, more than one witness had reported that they'd seen numerous strangers walk in and out of Chappelow's garden. At one stage, Atkinson appeared to get lost. 'I have completely forgotten the point I was going to make,' he confessed. Lord Chief Justice Thomas came to his rescue, neatly summarising the prosecutor's argument, which he then delivered, though not quite as well as the presiding judge.

Finally, Atkinson said that Peter Hall's colourful recollections were of little value. If he had believed that his gay companion had been murdered, why had he not informed the police with whom he had frequent contact? How could he have seen his companion's face in the pitch black of the West Heath night? And furthermore, there was no evidence of Allan Chappelow being homosexual and that nothing of a sexual nature had been found at 9 Downshire Hill. To this last point, Peter Wilcock stood and rather sadly conceded, 'that appears to be the case'. If Torben Permin had shared Gerry Pickering's email which he said had detailed the gay pride video and condoms, this part of the discussion might have gone a different way.

Perhaps sensing that the momentum was slipping from them, Geoffrey Robertson passed a note to Peter Wilcock who, after a quick read, addressed the court. 'One further matter,' the barrister said. 'I have been provided a note from Mr Robertson. At trial the possibility of Mr Chappelow being murdered by someone from the Heath was floated.' Wilcock's point was to give credence to the witness Peter Hall.

Leaning in to the microphone, the Lord Chief Justice asked Atkinson if he believed that Peter Hall was a credible and relevant witness. The prosecutor tried to duck the question but the justice persisted, now interrogating the interrogator. 'Why not accept the witness's view?' the judge continued. 'It's only fair. He came to court of his own free will.' Realising he could not wiggle out of the answer, Atkinson responded, 'The court should proceed on that basis.'

He then moved on. The jury had clearly accepted the prosecution's central argument, Atkinson said: Wang Yam was solely responsible for the hijacking of Allan Chappelow's identity through mail fraud. The evidence against him was overwhelming. 'Fraud first,' he said with a flourish, 'therefore murder.'

Wilcock took this head on. There was no forensic evidence tying his client to the crime scene, and the very fact that the Crown once again was fixated on the fraud underscored they had nothing on the murder. He wasn't sure if the deceased had been killed by gangsters or a companion brought home from the Heath, really it was not up to him to prove either way. What he was sure about was that his client was not responsible for the murder of Allan Chappelow and the conviction should be now found to be unsafe.

By 3.15 p.m. the arguments were over. The justices disappeared to a back room for a quick conference and then returned two minutes later. Lord Chief Justice was brief. 'The court will take its time to consider this matter,' he declared. 'We will then hand down judgement as soon as possible.' A pause, and then the clerk called out, 'All rise,' and the justices disappeared for good.

Wang Yam remained in his seat while the clerk clarified what had just been said. 'The decision will not be made today. When the decision is delivered in court you will be notified.' The prisoner was led away. He would have to wait once more.

On 28 September 2017, a listing appeared on the Royal Courts of Justice appeal court website: the Court of Appeal Criminal Division would meet the following day at 12 noon before the Lord Chief Justice of England and Wales, Mr Justice Sweeney and Mrs Justice May DBE, for a 'hand down' judgement in the case of Wang Yam vs Regina. After two months of deliberation and work, a final decision was to be announced.

I arrived at the Royal Courts of Justice at 10.30 a.m. and made my way to Court 6. It was the final day of the summer recess and, save for the friendly security guards and a handful of petitioners waiting for legal advice, the hallways and corridors of this ancient gothic building were quiet. It was also the Lord Chief Justice's final day before retiring. This would be the last judgement handed down in his name.

By 11.45 a.m., the blue-cushioned benches of Court 6 were still almost entirely empty except for four journalists: Richard Norton Taylor from the *Guardian*, a home affairs correspondent from the BBC, a reporter from the Press Association, and myself. Surprisingly to me, there was a complete absence of lawyers. I had been told that the prosecution and defence teams would have been sent copies of the judgement to check earlier in the week, but after so much work, I thought they would have wanted to be here in person to hear it delivered. The TV monitors were also turned off – Wang Yam was back in his cell at Lowdham Grange, and would not witness the result. I wondered what he was doing, how he was feeling.

When the court's clock showed exactly noon, a bewigged clerk called out 'All rise', and in walked a bare-headed Justice May. The clerk quickly removed his wig as the judge sat down.

'This is the court's judgement,' said Justice May in a clear and dry tone. 'It has been supplied in draft to counsel last week, who have provided corrections. The final version I will sign and hand down.'

She then uncapped her pen, signed her name, and handed down the document to the clerk sitting below her. The clerk stood, called out 'All rise', and the justice walked out. The entire proceedings had taken less than two minutes.

I followed the lead of the other journalists and stepped quickly to the clerk who began passing around copies of the judgement. I scanned the first page, confused. 'Go to the end,' whispered the woman from the Press Association. I leafed to the last paragraph, and there it was: appeal dismissed.

The court quickly emptied. I walked to the café on the ground floor of the Royal Courts of Justice with my copy. I purchased a cup of tea and a surprisingly cheap sandwich, and sat down at a small table. The judgement was thirty-five pages long, and set out in 135 paragraphs. I began to read. It was clear the judges had attempted to be even-handed, summarising the position of both prosecution and defence, along with the testimonies from the witnesses from the appeal hearing and the conclusions of the previous Court of Appeal. They also went out of their way to say that the original judge, Justice Ouseley, had been 'fair' and 'crystal clear' in the summing up of the second trial, when the jury had delivered their guilty verdict. It was only in the final ten paragraphs, the 'discussion', that the justices set out their own views. They believed that whoever was involved with the fraud was responsible for the murder, that there could *not* have been two separate crimes, and that even the defence accepted the logic of this argument. The 'key connection', they wrote, was between the use of Chappelow's mobile SIM card and the murder itself. They added that the trial jury 'clearly concluded that the web of activity undertaken by [Wang Yam] in relation to the deceased's identity and accounts was so thoroughly interwoven with the murder itself that he, and only he, could have been responsible for the latter'.

Besides the lack of evidence to support the justices' assertion that the fraudster was the murderer, the other major problem was that it failed to explain or attempt to explain many of the case's mysteries, such as the front door being blocked by wood (which would help a murderer but impede a thief), the passport and PIN numbers not being removed from the victim's bed (surprising if a thief returned to the house knowing about the murder), the extent of the violence (not the *modus operandi* for a burglar), or the cigarette butts found at the crime scene with the unknown DNA. These facts were best explained by at least two sets of criminals, unknown to each other, carrying out separate crimes.

As to the new witnesses, the justices wrote that they could see no basis that 'the new evidence would or might reasonably have affected the jury's decision in this case' because it could not have 'disrupted or diluted the unique connection between the appellant [Wang Yam] and the murder established by that web of evidence'. They added that it was not their task to double-guess the thinking process of the jury; they were inherently reluctant to overturn a decision made in good faith at the end of a well-run trial.

In conclusion, although Mr Wilcock had made a 'powerful case', the justices wrote 'we are satisfied that the Appellant's conviction is safe; accordingly his appeal is dismissed.'

My phone started buzzing. The screen read 'Lowdham Grange HMP'. I picked up.

'Hello,' came a timid voice. 'It's Wang Yam.' I paused for a moment.

'Hello Wang Yam,' I said, 'this is Thomas.' Another pause. 'I am so sorry.'

'Was it dismissed?'

I held my breath – I realised that Wang Yam had not yet been told. 'Yes, I am afraid it is not good news.'

'I know, I know. I am not surprised.' His voice was quiet, slow. 'I had a feeling.' He sounded pensive, shaken. After a few moments, I asked him how he was doing. 'I will be okay,' he said. 'Don't worry about me. I am a strong man. I will find a way forward.' After a few moments, Wang Yam said that he needed to end the conversation.

Five minutes later, my phone rang again. It was Wang Yam, calling back. This time he was angry. He spoke quickly, describing how the UK government had betrayed him, how he was framed by the Mafia, how the Chinese police had evidence of his innocence, and how he intended to 'disclose material' to contacts in Hong Kong. He might even send it to Russia. 'I have no choice now,' he stated. I didn't respond. We agreed to talk later and then he was gone, submerged once again into the day-to-day of prison life.

My phone rang once more – it was Peter Wilcock, Wang Yam's QC. He said that he too was not surprised by the decision. 'I do feel sorry for the guy,' said Wilcock. I let him know that I had to break the news to Wang Yam. Wilcock asked me how he reacted. I told him. 'The system is imperfect,' he said and then added, 'it's one of the strangest cases I have ever done.'

Once I finished with the barrister, I began texting the news to everyone I had spoken to about the case. From the Cayman Islands, Pete Lansdown texted back: 'Justice prevails'. Peter Devlin replied 'It was the correct decision. I'm sure he did it and think his defence was all smoke and mirrors.' Duncan Campbell said that he was not surprised, but that the court had made a mistake. Based on the evidence, Wang Yam should not have been found guilty.

From Allan Chappelow's family, Patty Ainsworth expressed sympathy for Wang Yam, adding that the judges 'seem determined to cover their tracks at any cost'. Merete Karlsbourg, one of the Danish cousins, simply wrote: 'What a surprise.'

It was over.

EPILOGUE

As I walked away from the Royal Courts of Justice, many questions swirled around my head. But one thing had become clear to me: Wang Yam should not have been found guilty. His conviction should have been overturned.

What had gone wrong? Were the police to blame? They certainly appeared to have made a number of mistakes. From the very beginning, a narrative about the murder was established: Allan Chappelow had interrupted a burglary, a struggle had ensued, and he was killed. According to Lansdown's building blocks, it had to be Wang Yam: he had motive (he was in financial distress), he had opportunity (he lived around the corner), he was linked to the crime scene (he was in possession of the victim's credit cards and cheques) and he tried to evade arrest (he fled to Switzerland).

Yet, Lansdown and his team never seriously investigated alternative scenarios. The case manager Peter Devlin, for instance, didn't explore the victim's sexuality, nor did he consider the unsolved murder of Hallam Tennyson – a case that shared many similarities with Chappelow's murder. Equally, the family liaison manager missed a crucial aspect of the victim's personality, that rather than being a frail old recluse, Allan Chappelow was also energetic, sociable and adventurous. And as to the flight to Switzerland, Wang Yam had travelled there previously and made no effort to hide his whereabouts, he even gave his details to the British consulate in Zurich.

Worse, the police were unable to provide any physical evidence linking Wang Yam to 9 Downshire Hill. This was, the police explained, due in part to the building's dilapidated state, but also due to the fire that broke out on the first floor during the investigation. The Met and later the prosecution claimed however that all the relevant and pertinent evidence had been identified and removed prior to the conflagration. So if Wang Yam was the killer, why did he leave no trace? And what caused the fire in the first place? At the very least, the questions remaining over the evidence gathering damages the investigation's credibility.

Perhaps worst of all, the police failed to disclose evidence to the defence. The local police had recorded a number of burglaries and break-ins around the same time as the murder (including Mr Bean's), yet for some reason this information was not automatically forwarded to the homicide investigation team in Colindale. The problem seems to be that the Met's crime reporting system relies on individuals not algorithms to pick up connections between cases. Given the large number of crimes that take place every year in London, it is easy to see how things might fall through the cracks.

But Wang Yam's faulty conviction flows from wider problems in the justice system, above and beyond the failures of the Met. First of all, it appears that he suffered from multiple instances of 'confirmation bias'. Not only did the police stick with their operating theory of a bungled burglary despite mounting contradictory evidence, but some of Wang Yam's own lawyers doubted him from their first meeting and held onto this view even after many of his stories had been confirmed. Equally, the jury concluded that it was Wang Yam on the phone pretending to be Allan Chappelow despite the evidence of two voice experts.

It also appears that Wang Yam fell foul of society's need for results, its thirst for neat solutions, its aversion to 'I don't know'. The police like to claim a high rate for solving murders; the judiciary doesn't want to think that they are wasting their time (and taxpayer's money); the public doesn't want to be told that a killer is still on the loose. As Lansdown put it, 'if it walks like a murderer, and talks like a murderer, it is a murderer.' But life is sometimes more complicated.

It also must be said that Wang Yam was at times his own worst enemy. His history of dodgy financial dealings, his bankruptcy, his tendency to exaggeration and verbosity, his firing of his lawyers, his chaotic writing to judges, journalists and politicians, all built a picture of an unreliable, scheming, desperate character. Most damaging, was Wang Yam's refusal to admit to defrauding Allan Chappelow, despite being caught on CCTV as he deposited the elderly man's cheques and later as he withdrew money using Chappelow's bank card.

Beyond the tragic and brutal murder of Allan Chappelow, and the wrongful conviction of Wang Yam, this story contains a third injustice. In December 2007, Home Secretary Jacqui Smith decided that the media would not be allowed to see certain aspects of Wang Yam's defence. In the interim, her decision has been upheld by a series of ministers and judges and consequently significant parts of the judicial process – including parts of two murder trials, two court of appeals hearings and innumerable preliminary hearings – have been held *in camera*. As a result of this shadowy process, the press has been unable to fully interrogate the evidence put before the courts. Even more extraordinarily, journalists (myself included) are even barred from *speculating* about the reasons for the trial being held behind closed doors.

In effect, this means that not only am I not allowed to report material that might speak to what happened *in camera* but, according to the letter of the law, I cannot repeat articles, testimonies, emails or other reports already in the public domain for fear of triggering a contempt of court ruling from the judge. Indeed, the government is so anxious that I don't contravene the judge's order, that the Attorney General for England and Wales sent a letter to my home address with a warning: we know what you are doing, watch out.

So what can I say about the closed court sessions? Not much. All I can do is walk up to the wall set by the judge and try to describe it. I can't look over it, nor can I guess why the wall was built. What I can say, is that whatever is contained within the secret appendix attached to the Public Interest Immunity certificate, and disclosed during the *in camera* sessions, must be of such scope and scale, that it is important enough to override centuries-old tradition of open justice. After all, Wang Yam's was the first murder trial in modern British history to be held behind closed doors.

Wang Yam is now back in prison, where he will probably serve out the rest of his twenty-year sentence. But does he belong there? The courts of law say yes. I am not so sure. After two years of research I believe that Allan Chappelow was a victim of two separate crimes committed by two or more different people: a burglary and a murder. I believe that Wang Yam was involved in the fraud but given the evidence against him, however, I do not believe that Wang Yam should have been found guilty of murder. At the very least he deserves a retrial.

If it was not Wang Yam, then who killed Allan Chappelow? Was it the Triad gangsters? A friend or acquaintance that the elderly victim had invited home? Or some unknown stranger seeing an opportunity?

Of all the possibilities, I think that the murderer is most likely to be a person that Allan Chappelow brought back to his house. Maybe his was the voice that was caught on the phone call to the Inland

Revenue. According to the profilers, such a companion would fit the crime's intimate and violent nature. It would also explain why there was no signs of struggle between the front door and the room where Allan Chappelow's body was found – because there had been no struggle. Instead, the companion had been invited inside 9 Downshire Hill, and finally to Room Six where the bloodshed had taken place. This however, is speculation. A decade since the killing of Allan Chappelow, little is certain. It is a good example of how our highly illuminated world is still interspersed by areas of profound darkness. What we know is this: an elderly man was brutally murdered. A man was found guilty of the offence and imprisoned for more than a decade. The British government still refuses to release the full details of the crime – or its own involvement in the case. And a killer may still be walking the streets of London.

It would be nice to imagine the ghosts getting together at the end of this story as they did in George Bernard Shaw's Saint Joan: Chappelow, Wang Yam, the judges, the lawyers, the detectives, the witnesses, the journalists. They would review the crime with the benefit of hindsight. They might arrive at a new conclusion.

POSTSCRIPT

When writing about a murder case such as this it is easy to forget the most important figure: the victim. The murder of Allan Chappelow is this story's greatest injustice. An elderly man was beaten to death in his own home and buried under four feet of paper. What is also shocking is the fact that his body lay undiscovered for over a month.

It was widely believed in Hampstead that Allan Chappelow was an eccentric: a hoarder and a recluse. It was clear to anyone who passed his crumbling house that something was amiss. Yet, Allan made it known that he wanted to be left alone. At his funeral, relatives he had never met mingled with the police officers in charge of investigating his murder. So little was known about him that the priest was forced to resort to reading his biography from a book published half-a-century before.

Perhaps in earlier days, back when the house was built, Allan would have been better cared for, or missed sooner. Those on society's fringes were often looked after by one of the neighbours. Today, it seems the only thing that links one neighbour to another is location. It is the sheer fact of living physically close to each other that provides the connection. Without this, neighbours would be strangers, like any other person we pass in the street.

Yet, neighbours can have a profound impact on our lives. We share space with them, hear their music, smell their cooking, see their washing or the condition of their home's exterior decorations. The relationship, however, is not intimate. What takes place behind our neighbour's closed doors is a mystery. The bible tells us to 'love thy neighbour like thyself', but the truth is that despite our proximity, we rarely know our neighbours, let alone love them. They are typically alien, other, their lives private and hidden. Perhaps Allan Chappelow's death should serve as a warning.

In the autumn of 2017, I returned to Hampstead to take a walk around my old neighbourhood.

I started at Hampstead Underground station, with its familiar oxblood-red tiles. I turned right, walking up the hill past the small church and art gallery, until I reached Whitestone Pond, where Allan Chappelow had once exhibited his photographs. Crossing the road I skirted Jack Straw's Castle, and dropped onto a narrow sandy path that led me to the West Heath. Discarded tissues, condoms and beer cans littered the ground. It was twilight now, and amongst the trees and bushes I could see figures in the shadows. An elderly man with crutches stood next to a tree, watching. Nearby, another man walked slowly through the undergrowth. The world-famous cruising spot still appeared to be active.

A few hundred metres into the park, I emerged into a dusty clearing. The space was surrounded by large oaks and elms, with branches reaching out perpendicular to the sky. One long tree branch stood out, a thick curvy limb that hovered inches from the ground. At its centre was a patch rubbed shiny. Could this be the spanking bench?

I retraced my steps back through the woods until I found myself at Whitestone Pond. On my left dim streetlamps illuminated Spaniards Lane, once the haunt of highwaymen and thieves, and the spot on the corner where makeshift gallows once stood. I walked away from the Heath, back down towards the lights of Hampstead, past mobile phone shops, restaurant chains and coffee houses, but also some recognisable fronts: the arts cinema, the Hungarian tearoom, and, finally, the shuttered police station on the corner of Downshire Hill, rumoured to become a school to accommodate Hampstead's burgeoning population.

I passed the glass-cubed house on the right and the redbrick row of flats on the left, until I reached 9 Downshire Hill, the entrance marked by two neatly reconstructed columns and a 'For Sale' sign. Peering through the remote-controlled double wrought iron gate, I could see that the property had been completely rebuilt. The overgrown front garden had been cleared for a gravel driveway large enough for three cars to park, dotted by a handful of neatly trimmed trees. Beyond, stood the tall rectangular house, four stories entirely reconstructed, its smooth surface painted in rich ivory, with two perfectly symmetrical balconies protruding from its front façade. Now on the market for £14.5 million, with a swimming pool in the basement, marble floored kitchen, private cinema and freestanding bathtub, I wondered what Allan Chappelow would now have made of his father's much-prized Regency home.

I walked on to my childhood home, number 13a. I could see the front lawn, the winding flagstone path, the well-groomed flower beds. It was here that we buried our cat, Ivan. Here that my sister celebrated her twenty-first birthday. Here the local newspaper took a photograph of me aged seventeen, just before I left for a year's cycle ride across South and North America. The church of St John's stood opposite, and beyond, Keats House Library, where Allan Chappelow would sometimes be seen reading the day's newspapers.

Further on down the street and I came to the Freemasons Arms, a few solitary smokers outside enjoying the last warmth of the day. I walked across the road to the Heath, past the swimming pond, through a dark wooded path, until I came to the foot of Parliament Hill, whose familiar slope I climbed.

Reaching the crest, I sat down on one of the wooden benches and took in the view. Looking out across the rooftops, I saw rows upon rows of buildings: one neighbourhood flowing into the next. The city spread out before me, alive and anonymous.

For more information on this story, please visit
www.bloodonthepage.com

NOTES

Chapter 1

10 'Next came the poets and the artists, the novelists and the actors . . .' Like many streets in Hampstead, Downshire Hill has been home to numerous stars of the creative industries, including the creators of the Muppets (no. 1b), the writers Edward, Constance and David Garnett (no. 6), the poet Edwin Muir (no. 7), stage designer Gordon Craig and writer Elizabeth Jenkins (no. 8), author Theodora Benson (no. 10), poet Sylvia Lynd (no. 11), artist Elena Meo (no. 30), the Carline family, also known as hosts to the 'Hampstead Set' of artists (no. 47 – during the Second World War the house was the headquarters of the Artists' Refugee Committee; one of those given sanctuary there was the German inventor of the photomontage, John Heartfield), art expert Sir Roland Penrose (no. 21), the artist John Constable (nos. 25–26), actress Flora Robson (no. 37), artist Gaetano Meo (no. 41), author Amber Blanco White (no. 44), poet Anna Wickham (no. 49), and the architects Sir Michael and Lady Patty Hopkins (no. 49a), to name but a few.

10 'Moving up Downshire Hill towards Hampstead High Street . . .' According to *The Streets of Hampstead* by Christopher Wade, Downshire Hill was established around 1814. The name relates to the first Marquis of Downshire whose family name was Hill.

17 'A few years later . . . able to move into the large house at 9 Downshire Hill . . .' According to the *Metropolitan Borough of Hampstead Register of Electors* kept at Holborn Library in London, Archibald and Karen Chappelow were first registered as living at 26 Downshire Hill in 1925 and at number 9 in 1935. A similar account is provided by the *Borough of Hampstead General Rates* 1934–1935 book, which contains a note made in red ink that number 9 Downshire Hill was 'bought by A. C. Chappelow of number 26 Downshire Hill' and that he 'moved on 4 January 1935'. The rates book also notes that until 1935 a Herbert and Bertha Green lived at number 9 Downshire Hill (presumably as tenants), and that Archibald Chappelow purchased the property from a Mrs A. G. Spurling. Confusingly, however, The Hall School's records have the Chappelow family as living at number 9 Downshire Hill when Allan left in June 1933.

22 'They had come to view him as an eccentric and recluse . . .' Despite his local reputation, Allan Chappelow was not a recluse. According to the *Oxford English Dictionary*, a 'recluse' is a person 'shut up, secluded from society'. Equally, *Webster's* defines a recluse as someone 'retired from the world, or from public notice'. Yet, just days before his murder, Allan had returned from a month-long trip to the USA where various witnesses described him as social, engaging and outgoing. Furthermore, his neighbour Peter Tausig said he had recently visited Germany, while his cousin Torben Permin said he went to Denmark a number of times. According to a stamp in his passport, Allan Chappelow visited Cairo, Egypt in October 2002. Another stamp suggests he visited Hungary and Slovenia in the early 2000s. Equally, he remained engaged with his local community. He read the newspaper at the local library on Keats Grove and voted in the local elections, casting his last ballot just days before

his death. Similarly, on 20 March 2006, a few days prior to his trip to the USA, he set up a standing order with his bank whereby £10 would be donated each month to the Salvation Army.

Chapter 2

30 'Pete Lansdown considered himself a local boy . . .' An amateur geneal-ogist, Lansdown had determined that his family had lived near St Pancras in north London since 1795. His grandfather had been a Corporal of Horse in the Household Cavalry and his father had served as a gunner in the tank regiment. 'Dad always pushed me,' Pete recalled. 'He was always encouraging me to "be the best that you can be. Be proud of yourself and your family."'

30 'Three years later he became an accredited detective, and was sent to Harlesden in Brent . . .' Perhaps Lansdown's most famous case before Allan Chappelow's murder was the arrest of Mark Lambie, the so-called 'Prince of Darkness', who was suspected in the murder of PC Keith Blakelock and of various violent crimes associated with the Man Dem gang which he led. Lambie was imprisoned for twelve years for kidnap-ping two men and torturing them with a hammer, a hot iron and boiling water. Following intimidation of various key witnesses Lansdown said that the Lambie case confirmed his view that 'we should not have to rely on the evidence of victims, because they can be easily distracted in court. Much better is to use professional witnesses – police, bank evidence, mobile phone evidence and so on.' An account of Lansdown's role in this case can be found in *Guns and Gangs* by Graeme McLagan.

38 'on the roof of the Cumberland Hotel . . .' Coincidentally, this hotel was owned by my mother's family. My grandfather Samuel Salmon, who was also an air-raid warden at this time, may well have shared a rooftop with Allan.

41 'The more likely answer, he said, was a bungled burglary . . .' Coincidentally, Allan Chappelow's hero George Bernard Shaw was aware

of the possible outcomes of a bungled burglary. In the preface to his 1905 play *Major Barbara*, he wrote: 'It is exceedingly difficult to make people realise that an evil is an evil . . . In the case of a man breaking into my house and stealing my wife's diamonds I am expected as a matter of course to steal ten years of his life, torturing him all the time. If he tries to defeat that monstrous retaliation by shooting me, my survivors hang him. The net result suggested by the police statistics is that we inflict atrocious injuries on the burglars we catch in order to make the rest take effectual precautions against detection; so that instead of saving our wives' diamonds from burglary we only greatly decrease our chances of ever getting them back, and increase our chances of being shot by the robber if we are unlucky enough to disturb him at his work.'

42 'Leaving the hot meeting, Detective Sergeant Peter Devlin . . .' On 14 June, just after learning about the murder, Pete Lansdown asked Peter Devlin to contact the senior officer on duty for Hampstead police station. As they were at the station, Devlin thought this would be a simple task. Downstairs he found two junior officers working at the front desk who 'didn't have a clue what was going on' and were unable to provide a contact number. Frustrated, Devlin called the new centralised police communications switchboard, telling them that he was DS Devlin at Hampstead police station and asking to speak to a senior Hampstead officer. 'That's in Islington, isn't it?' came the reply. He told them that it was actually in Camden. The switchboard operator then suggested that he 'call Hampstead, someone there will know'. Without listening to his response – 'I am in the front office!' – she put him through to the Hampstead police station. By this time Peter Lansdown was standing next to Devlin, listening to the conversation. A moment later a phone rang in the front office and Lansdown picked it up and shouted, 'There's nobody fucking here, he's told you!' It would take them a while longer to track down the senior officer on duty for the Hampstead station.

43 'Peter Devlin was born in 1953 . . . grew up in a tenement building in Glasgow's Pollokshaws district . . .' According to Devlin, Pollokshaws

was an adventurous place for a boy to grow up. When open-sided lorries slowed down at the end of the road, he and his friends jumped on and held tight for as many streets as possible. They also climbed onto the railway track that ran behind the tenement block, daring each other to stay on the lines as the horn-blaring locomotives approached. In the early 1960s, the family moved to Drumchapel and his parents were pleased, for though this Glasgow district was known for its vandalism and drugs, at least they had an inside toilet.

43 'I was looking for adventure . . .' Arriving in London, Devlin recalled, was a bit of a shock. He didn't just have to learn the differences between English and Scottish law, but also had to adopt a new vocabulary: 'fire-raising', for instance, was known in London as 'arson', 'housebreaking' was called 'burglary', and a 'panel' was known as a 'defendant'. And where he had become accustomed to the intensity of working with drug and gang violence in downtown Glasgow, he found the small police station that he was assigned to in north London sleepy and tedious.

52 'his last few weeks of life . . .' George Bernard Shaw died in his sleep on 2 November 1950. Upon hearing the news, the Indian cabinet adjourned, a two-minute silence was held in Australian theatres and the lights were briefly blacked out on Broadway and in Times Square. The last picture of George Bernard Shaw was taken by Allan Chappelow, and it was this image that dominated the newspapers around the world.

Chapter 3

57 'Back at the *Camden New Journal* . . .' Another article on 22 June 2006, reported that the inquest for Allan Chappelow took place on 19 June 2006 at St Pancras Coroner's Court under coroner Dr Andrew Reid. Reid resigned in 2012 after hiring his wife as a deputy assistant coroner (for the inquest into the death of singer Amy Winehouse) who did not have the appropriate qualifications

62 'He added that he "never saw a single unhappy, miserable or wretched child" . . .' He made no mention that at this time there were over 3 million political prisoners held in the Soviet gulags and labour camps.

Case Note

64 'He added that Wang Yam's lawyers had played games with them . . .' In an email, Kirsty Brimelow said that Devlin's claim is 'nonsense, outrageous and wholly without any factual basis.' She said that they had to push for disclosures repeatedly. 'The only games being played' she added, 'were on the police/prosecution side.'

Chapter 4

69 'The following summer . . . Torben Permin . . .' Torben's grandfather Aage Permin was Karen Chappelow's brother. Allan and Torben were therefore first cousins once removed.

73 'McDonald's purchased a property . . .' The campaign to stop the burger chain in Hampstead was supported by more than 5,000 residents and store-owners. It attracted celebrity support including the actor Tom Conti, novelist Margaret Drabble, and Peggy Jay, the grande dame of the Labour movement. After a twelve-year campaign and a High Court hearing, however, McDonald's finally opened the doors of its Hampstead High Street branch in June 1993. As a compromise, the typically red and yellow storefront was painted black. On 16 November 2013 it served its final Happy Meal after the company announced that it had sold its lease to another chain.

Case Note

78 '*Lowdham Grange* . . .' Based near Nottingham in the north of England, Lowdham Grange is a privately run prison operated by a company called

Serco. According to its website, Serco operates six adult prisons under contract to the Ministry of Justice's National Offender Management Service (NOMS) and the Scottish Prison Service. They also run a Secure Training Centre for juveniles on behalf of the Youth Justice Board of England and Wales. Serco is listed on the London Stock Exchange.

Chapter 6

93 'He also found that the red sweater . . . bore burn marks . . .' Kirsty Brimelow points out that 'there was a red thread in the wax on the blue jumper which indicates that the damage to both happened at the same time (thread picked up whilst wax warm) – evidence of Robert Lewis.'

Chapter 7

100 'Devlin realised that the phone-owner's flat was just around the corner from Allan Chappelow's house . . .' Wang Yam admits that he walked along Downshire Hill on a number of occasions. He drank at the Freemasons pub at the bottom of the road next to the Heath (his favourite drink was Guinness; Dong Hui's was red wine). He frequently attended the Keats Practice at 1b Downshire Hill, located at the top of the road opposite the police station and next to Hampstead High Street. In 2003 he looked at a house on Downshire Hill with a view to buying it. On 4 May 2006, he voted in the local elections at Keats Grove library. He reported that this was between 4 p.m. and 5 p.m., as he remembered that a member of the Liberal Democrat party called him shortly afterwards to check that he had voted. It is worth noting that Allan Chappelow also voted at the same polling station that day, though the time of his visit is not recorded. Both Wang Yam and Allan Chappelow's names are recorded in the December 2005 Register of Electors for Hampstead residents.

Chapter 8

109 'Xian is considered one of China's four great cities . . .' Today it is also known as host to one of the world's cultural icons, the Terracotta Army of horse and soldier statues, discovered by farmers looking for water in 1974, a decade after Wang Yam's birth.

109 'Wang Yam was born in Xian's main hospital on 27 April 1961 . . .' Traces of Wang Yam, though widespread, are unreliable. In Britain, for instance, Wang Yam used a variety of names. According to his British naturalisation certificate, he was called Ren Hong. Yet this was not the only name he went by in London. On one of the computers left at Denning Road, the police found an email sent on 13 April 2006 to Wang Yam from his girlfriend 'Vivien' Dong Hui: 'Hi, there. This is Vivien at home from Hampstead, London. I want to tell you one news: I will marry to a man, his name is John Richard, also called John Wong, Wang Yam, Zhang Jia, Ren Hong, Wang Hong Yam . . . Anyway, I don't remember all the names he has got. But it doesn't matter for my love. I will tell you more story about him. Are you interested to share my feeling? – V'

109 'His birth name was Ren Hong . . .' This is according to Chinese police records. Note that in China family names are first, so 'Ren' is the family name.

109 'His 21-year-old father Ren Yuanyuan . . .' On his application for British citizenship, in other documents, and in conversation with the author, Wang Yam claims Ren Yuanyuan to be his father. During his trial, Philip Baker QC asserts the same. If true, this would make Wang Yam the grandson of one of China's most famous military figures, Ren Bishi. According to Ren Bishi's grandson, Ren Jining, and his granddaughter, Zhu Xiaoping, however, Wang Yam is not a member of their family.

118 'his mother's sister Zhang Xuying and husband Ren Li Yi . . .' According to Wang Yam, his uncle Ren Li Yi had been a private secretary to Peng Dehuai, one of the most senior military leaders of the Chinese revolution and, from 1954, the country's defence minister. In 1959,

however, Peng Dehaui published a poem that criticised the failures of the mass collectivisation programmes of the Great Leap Forward. 'Grain scattered on the ground, potato leaves withered', Peng Dehaui wrote, 'allow me to raise my voice for the people.' Over the next few months, he continued to vent his opposition to the government's policies and, most extraordinarily, openly criticised Chairman Mao. Shortly afterwards, Peng was forced to step down, and to take part in a series of public 'self-criticisms'. During the Cultural Revolution, Peng became one of the most high-profile targets of the Red Guard. In January 1967, wearing a dunce cap and a board around his neck with the word 'crimes', Peng was paraded in chains before several thousand Red Guards. Later, he was repeatedly tortured and sentenced to life in prison. Meanwhile, with his former boss now considered an enemy of the state, Wang Yam's uncle Ren Li Yi returned to his home province in Shanxi.

Case Note

121 *'I'm certain that the police activity triggered his flight . . .'* Wang Yam maintains that they had packed up their flat in February or March, in anticipation of having to leave pending the eviction. 'We had always intended to go to Switzerland,' he said. 'It had nothing to do with the murder of Allan Chappelow.'

Chapter 9

131 'The scientist suggested that the murder had therefore likely taken place sometime between 9 and 16 May . . .' On 4 May, three days after his return from the USA, Allan paid a £50 top-up for his mobile phone bill using his Sainsbury's card. The police believed this to be Allan Chappelow's last financial transaction.

131 'On 17 September 1991, they were granted a marriage licence . . .' Zhu Xiaoping (Wang Yam's friend and perhaps first cousin) said that

she did not know that Wang Yam had married in Beijing, despite their being close at this time. She admitted that this may have been because she emmigrated to the USA in May 1991, four months before the wedding, yet she was surprised that Wang Yam had not mentioned anything to her in their subsequent telephone conversations.

133 'British-controlled Hong Kong . . .' In 1997, the governance of Hong Kong would be transferred from Britain to China. Many of the territory's residents worried about the future. Would Hong Kong retain its pro-business culture and its reputation as a centre for capitalism or would the press be curtailed and the mainland's one-party system be imposed? Equally, Britain was concerned that by giving up control over Hong Kong they would be losing their ability to keep an eye on developments in China. In the previous year, over 1 per cent of the population had fled Hong Kong, the very people who looked most favourably on the West.

136 'The 43-year-old He Jia Jin controlled a number of London businesses . . .' According to a BBC report released on 26 November 2013, He Jia Jin, also known as 'Anthony Ho', was fined £1.9 million in 2013 in Bristol Crown Court for failure to pay taxes. In 2012, he served eight months in jail after pleading guilty to fraudulent trading. He paid just £1,000 in income tax on an empire worth some £370 million, a court heard. If he did not pay this fine by May 2014, he would be imprisoned for five months. It is not currently clear what happened.

137 'Wang Yam grabbed a pen and wrote his email . . . johnwongmbox@ hotmail.com . . .' To secure copies of Wang Yam and Dong Hui's various Hotmail and Yahoo email accounts, PC Rob Burrows contacted the US Embassy in London on 19 July 2006. He was referred to the Deputy Legal Attaché, agent Scott Gickering, who reminded him of the Mutual Legal Assistance Treaty (MLAT) between their two countries and suggested that Burrows submit a written request. On 31 July, Gickering confirmed that the email accounts had been preserved.

Chapter 10

148 'Jenny said that she had first met John Wong . . . in 1993 . . .' Wang Yam
has a slightly different story. He believed he first met Jenny at a 1992
pro-democracy protest in Chinatown. This was when Li Jia was still in
China. 'She [Jenny] is a pretty and well-educated woman,' Wang Yam
recalled, 'she always remembered to send us gifts on our birthdays.'

149 'Would she mind, he asked, helping Dong Hui pack? . . .' According
to Wang Yam, he had originally arranged that their belongings be stored
at 18 Melrose Avenue in Wimbledon, which he still owned with Li Jia.
When Dong Hui said she didn't want to see his ex-wife or visit her
house, they agreed to find an alternative place.

Chapter 11

153 'In 1997, Wang Yam . . . set up a number of business ventures . . .' It is
possible to confirm from records held at Companies House that, during the
1990s, Wang Yam set up more than fifteen companies. Six were under the
name Wang Yam, including Sun Life PLC, Kingston Networks PLC, First
Direct Trust and Investment International Ltd. Others, like City Computer
and Network Service Ltd, First Direct Financial Service Ltd and Rainbow
Publishing Ltd, were registered under the name Wong Yam, but with the
same date of birth. His fellow directors typically included his first wife Li
Jia (who was sometimes listed as 'Alison Lee') and his cousin, Lijun Wang.
None of these companies are currently operating. Yam's activities in Britain
are almost as hard to pin down as those in China.

154 'In traditional identity parades . . .' The first recorded mention of police
identity parades can be traced to a Metropolitan Police Order dated
24 March 1860, after some remarks – presumably encouraging – by an
assistant judge in Middlesex. Over the next few decades the procedures
were improved and standardised, so that in 1905 the Home Secretary
encouraged all forces to make use of them.

154 'Even worse, these lineups gave police numerous opportunities . . .' Indeed, there had been so many wrongful convictions based on mistaken identifications in ID parades that in 1976, the Devlin Committee [no relation] on Evidence of Identification in Criminal Cases recommended that identity parades should only be taken into account if corroborated by other evidence.

155 'Known as the Virtual Identity Parade Electronic Recording system . . .' To see a demo of how VIPER works go to www.viper.police.uk/pages/demo_video.html

156 'Anna Toma the landlady had been clear . . .' On 13 July 2006, nine days after the VIPER parade and nearly a month after Wang Yam and Dong Hui had left the country, Peter Devlin received a phone call from Anna Toma regarding the flat on Denning Road. She said that both flat C and D had been burgled. The doors had been forced. There was an untidy search of flat D and a laptop computer was stolen. Nothing was taken from flat C (which was largely empty). Finger marks were retrieved from the front door of flat D and from a jewellery box taken from inside. Footprints were retrieved from the front door of flat C but the police were unable to match them to any on file. After a few hours' inquiry, they concluded that the burglary had nothing to do with the Chappelow murder.

158 'Credit General Group Plc . . .' While in prison Wang Yam wrote to various politicians to raise interest in his case. According to a letter Wang Yam wrote to former secretary of state for business Vince Cable on 5 July 2012, 'I used to worked as Director of Credit General Group plc, which regulated by MCCB (the Power of MCCB later transferred to FSA). I also been trained as Independent Financial Advisor and know the money laundering regulations from FSA, which updated after "September 11".' On 10 May 2005, the Financial Conduct Authority lists Credit General Group plc with a 'warning', saying, 'We believe this firm has been providing financial services or products in the UK without our authorisation. Find out why to be especially wary of dealing with this unauthorised firm and how to protect yourself from scammers.' On

January 2013, Wang Yam also wrote to then Home Secretary Theresa May, to share details of his case and to alert her as to 'what kind of injustice has done to me, this defendant.'

160 'Any opportunity to settle out of court . . . had been missed . . .' One of the few exceptions to this occurred in early 2006 when Wang Yam sold some domains to a young food journalist called Richard Ross, who worked for the publishing company William Reed. Ross was looking for a domain name to match his wine and spirit blog. Using the 'Whois' tool on the internet, he tracked down the owner of 'wine-spirit.com'. It was Wang Yam. After a series of 'stilted' email exchanges, Ross became 'mildly unsure' of the seller. He couldn't quite put his finger on it, but 'there was something about his manner' that worried him. For a while he considered going over to Denning Road to check Wang Yam out, but then decided that given the small size of the deal it wasn't worth it, and bought the name. 'I was used to dealing with the lonerish people who inhabited this world,' he said. On 24 February, he sent a letter to Wang Yam along with a cheque for £450. A few days later he received control of the domain.

168 'worked for Credit Suisse bank in Mayfair . . .' According to the police statement provided by Daniel Epstein of T K International estate agents, Wang Yam said he worked at 'Credit Zurich offices in Mayfair'; presumably this is Credit Suisse in Mayfair, whose headquarters are in Zurich.

Chapter 12

176 'It had been uncomfortable . . . "a little sad" . . .' Later, Michael Chappelow wrote an email to Patty in which he shared his thoughts on the funeral. 'Dear Patty, Since the funeral I have felt very flat and keep thinking how much more we could have done to make it more fitting for Allan – even if we were the ones who didn't get the inheritance. That was the most grim experience – imagine a service in the little church in Downshire Hill, where there was a chance for all his friends and neighbours to include their reminiscences, even if one of us had put

them together in a eulogy. I blame the police really, they should have continued to involve us as a family, rather than leaving us in the cold when they found that we were not the next of kin. The Danes, however, should have worked with us to give Allen [sic] a better send-off . . . The one good thing was having a chance to meet you! I only wish we had more time . . . I'm going to have a word with Det. Pickering about how I felt we were not given a chance to help plan the funeral and include the reflections of his friends and neighbours as well as our own. With Love, Michael.' Patty replied by email: 'Even though this was a very sad way to meet,' she wrote, 'I feel very lucky to have gotten to know both you and James as well as the Danes. I am also very happy that I got to know and spend a little time with Allan.' She added, 'I agree that the service might have been better handled, but what's done is done.' That same day Michael responded, saying that Gerry Pickering had spoken to a woman in Hastings on the south coast of England who had known Allan for sixty years. She had spoken to him about making a will and he had said that if anything happened to him then 'his relatives in Denmark would get everything'. Apparently mollified by this, Michael wrote that this 'is the clearest expression of Allan's wishes anyone has. I think it would have helped to know that from the beginning, but I am now satisfied that the right thing has been done.' He added that he had spoken to his mother about Allan's murder, and she had said that any Chappelow would 'have a go' at an intruder, and that 'according to detective Pickering this was most probably the case'. He finished his email promising to 'keep in touch', that he hoped she would soon get over her visit to London, adding 'these things take their toll on us older ones!!'

Chapter 13

180 'registered more than twenty new names . . . beijingwatch.org . . .'
Later, Wang Yam would claim that he had managed beijingwatch.org

as a blog for Chinese dissidents starting in the early 1990s, which is surprising as he only registered the name in 2006.

181 'A week later, on the evening of 27 September . . .' Eleven days later, on 8 October, Patty Ainsworth received an email from her cousin Michael Chappelow in England saying that he had heard from detective Gerry Pickering. 'The main suspect has now been arrested,' he said, 'and is in custody in Switzerland awaiting extradition.' Though it had taken four months, Allan Chappelow's family were pleased that the police now had their main suspect in custody. They only hoped that the trial would not be long delayed and that there was sufficient evidence to obtain a guilty conviction.

183 'It would likely take between one and two months . . .' A few days later, news of Wang Yam's arrest was leaked to the British media. Under the headline 'MURDER ARREST', the Camden New Journal covered the news. 'Detectives hunting the killer of Hampstead recluse Allan Chappelow arrested a man in Switzerland' ran the story. 'Swiss police swooped in on Friday to arrest a 45-year-old man. Now police are preparing extradition papers to bring the suspect back to Britain, where he is facing a murder charge.'

186 'It was nice to have him back in England . . .' Wang Yam had a similar memory of the event. After he had confirmed his identity and been given the standard police warning, he said that Peter Devlin nodded his head as if to say, 'I've got my man.'

186 'Amongst other items inside the box . . .' Later, these were examined by the Metropolitan Police's Forensic Science Service, who found Dong Hui's number listed on one of the phone's contact directories as 'lover'.

188 'and was then driven to HMP Pentonville . . .' Just as Wang Yam was settling into his new accommodation at HMP Pentonville, Detective Sergeant Gerry Pickering wrote to Patty Ainsworth in the USA. 'Today 14th November the main suspect Wang YAM was extradited from Switzerland, he was taken to Heathrow Police Station and was charged with Murder, Burglary Deception x2, Theft, Handling Stolen Goods

and will appear at Highbury Corner Magistrate Court on 15 November at 10.00. He will be kept in custody until his trial which will be in several months early to mid 2007. I will let you know dates and times.' When Michael Chappelow saw this email – which had been forwarded to him by his American cousin – he wrote, 'I'm not sure I want to go to the trial. I once went to one at the Old Bailey in London and it was very unpleasant.'

Chapter 14

194 'Over the next few weeks, Wang Yam met his legal team . . .' Kirsty Brimelow is now one of Britain's most accomplished barristers. In 2012, she was elected head of the Bar Human Rights Committee of England and Wales, becoming the first female chairman. When she was appointed Queen's Counsel in 2011, women comprised only 13 per cent of all QCs. The ratio today remains stubbornly close to this level. Brimelow is the only lawyer who has stuck with Wang Yam's case from the beginning. When asked why she keeps going, after more than a decade, she says, 'It's my responsibility, I have worked like a dog on this case, and I will continue until Wang Yam is out of jail or we have tried every last opportunity.'

198 'Home Secretary Jacqui Smith . . .' If the sensitive material impacted foreign relations, the secret intelligence service or international trade, then the PII would have to go before the Foreign Secretary.

199 'in the interests of national security and to protect the identity of a witness or other person . . .' As quoted in press release provided by the UK Supreme Court 16 December 2015.

199 'On 13 December . . .' On 16 December, James Chappelow emailed his American cousin Patty. 'The trial was mentioned in *The Times* last week,' he wrote. 'The government has stepped in to insist that it is held *in camera*, i.e. with no reporting and no public present. He added that Allan's house on Downshire Hill had been sold for £4.5 million,

'so if you are still in touch with the Danes ask for some money!!' Patty replied a few hours later. 'Steve, my husband, had a Google alert set up with Allan's name,' she wrote, 'so we have been reading all of the recent articles. The whole situation with the trial is very interesting.' A few days later on 30 December, Patty emailed her cousin Michael Chappelow. 'Apparently everyone over there is really baffled over the attempt to hold the trial in secret.' A journalist from *The Times* had been in touch with her, she said — James had given him her contact details — and asked her about the reasons for the secret trial and information about Allan's trip to Austin. 'The reporter wants some background on Allan to see if that explains anything,' she wrote to Michael, 'although I'm sure it doesn't.' The following day Michael replied. 'I'm not too sure about Allan's background,' he wrote. 'It's possible there was some connection with his time at Cambridge, when the Russians were recruiting people, but I don't see him in any way as a Russian spy!! Most unlikely in such a family.'

201 'A graduate from University of Wales, Ellison . . .' One of Ellison's most famous cases was the 1980s Guinness share trading scandal. In 2006, he was appointed as head of a group of seventeen Treasury barristers who prosecuted the most serious criminal cases in the country at the Old Bailey. Having conducted numerous terrorist, murder and Official Secrets Act cases, he was known as an intelligent, hard-working lawyer and a straight dealer. Ellison had been involved with the Wang Yam prosecution ever since the case was taken up by the CPS.

201 'He was assisted by the 41-year-old Bobbie Cheema-Grubb . . .' Dame Bobbie Cheema-Grubb is the first Asian woman to serve as a High Court judge in the United Kingdom.

204 'In a separate order . . .' Two days later on 17 January, family liaison officer Gerry Pickering provided an email update to Patty Ainsworth. 'You may be wondering why part of the trial has been requested to be heard in private,' he wrote. 'Unfortunately I'm not allowed to explain, but it has nothing to do with Allan, but all to do with Wang Yam's defence.

Hopefully I will be allowed to explain after the trial.' He added, 'I know that you may not be satisfied with my answer, but my hands are tied.'

Case Note

206 'and then covering him with 560kg of paper . . .' To determine the exact weight of the paper, Gerald Pickering loaded a van with the manuscripts and then drove them to a weighing station where he had the vehicle weighed with and without the papers.

Chapter 15

210 'The following day in court, the BBC . . .' It was Pete Devlin who told me that the BBC had been reprimanded in court about the Newsnight coverage of the trial. However, the show's editor, Simon Enright, told me that 'I don't remember getting into trouble for what we broadcast. I do remember we took great care in what we said', adding that there was some 'corporate memory' that they had been warned about in their report, 'we have not found any note of a contempt of court rulling against Newsnight.'

217 'Later in his evidence . . . Wang Yam described how he tried to "get alongside" the Chinese gangsters . . .' From the judge's summing up of the trial.

217 'He named them as Gaz, Zhao Dong and Ah Ming . . .' This from Supreme Court judgment 16 December 2015. Also, Peter Devlin said that he made strenuous efforts to find these associates and was unable to obtain statements from them.

219 'four witnesses provided their evidence in closed sessions on Wednesday 20 and Friday 22 February . . .' Mentioned in Supreme Court judgment, originally quoted in the 5 October 2010 appeals court judgment. See also UK Supreme Court judgment given on 16 December 2015 which states, 'He [Mr Robertson] contends that if the evidence which was

taken in private, which consisted of four witnesses plus that of the defendant, had been heard in public, there would have been likely to be significantly greater media coverage of the trial, and that there is a real possibility that additional witnesses supporting the defendant in his case would have come forward on seeing it.'

219 'The jury then left the courtroom . . .' On 2 April 2008, Gerry Pickering sent Patty Ainsworth an email about the trial's outcome. 'Sorry it's taken so long to contact you. The trial only finished yesterday evening (10 weeks). As you are aware there were 6 charges against Wang Yam. The jury took several days to reach there [sic] verdicts. They found him guilty of 3 of the charges, 1) Money transfer of £20,000 2) Theft of cash from a cash machine 3) Handling and receiving stolen goods. The other charges of Murder, Burglary and Theft of Mail from the House, the jury could not all agree on his guilt so the judge discharged the jury and there will be a retrial later this year. Yam will stay in custody till the retrial.'

219 'on 2 April, after four days of deliberations . . .' Robertson left after his closing speech as his father was unwell (in Australia).

Case Note

222 '*Called Allan Chappelow's Danish cousin Torben Permin* . . .' In the introduction to his book *Shaw the Villager*, Chappelow refers to a certain Kathleen who joined him on a boat ride down the River Cam in Cambridge. It was during this trip, he remembered, that he had first conceived of the idea of interviewing George Bernard Shaw. He called her a 'girl friend' rather than a 'girlfriend'. In the police interviews with the neighbours, there had been mention of a friend named 'Eric', but there was no implication that this was a sexual liaison. Allan's romantic life was a subject of media interest. The *Independent* quoted his friend Peggy Sparrow saying, 'He was naive. He used to say to me how terribly clever I was to have had four children. To Allan, it was like a miracle.' She added that Allan 'did occasionally have his eye on people. He once tried to get

my sister to go on a holiday to Albania on his motorbike. She politely declined.' I have not been able to find anyone who had ever known or seen Allan with a girlfriend. According to Cynthia Reavell, Allan may have had more than platonic relationships with women. 'Chappelow was a boyfriend/admirer of my glamorous divorced mother, "Johny" Dunbar-Marshall,' she wrote 'and I remember him visiting us occasionally in Cambridge from the late 1940s, when I'd have been about seven, and he in his late twenties and studying at Trinity College. He'd arrive at our semi-detached house in Belgrave Road by motorbike, and would always take me for a ride around the quiet side streets, off the then unfashionable Mill Road, where we were unlikely to encounter a policeman ... As for the nature of their relationship, I think it likely that he was one of her succession of "boyfriends", who were almost always younger than she was. I have no idea whether she had sex with him or with any of the others; neither would there be kissing in front of me, let alone overnight stays. But I don't think she went in for platonic friendships – men were very attracted to her, and she enjoyed this.'

Chapter 16

225 'Geoffrey Cox was also the Conservative member of parliament ...' According to a *Telegraph* article published on 4 February 2016, 'Tory MP Geoffrey Cox will only have to apologise after failing to declare hundreds of thousands of pounds. The Standards Committee found that Geoffrey Cox QC had committed a "serious" breach of rules, [but] decided not to formally punish him.' Earlier in 2015 it emerged that Cox declared earnings of £820,000 from outside work and second jobs – twelve times the annual income for an MP. According to the latest register of members' financial interests, 'Mr Cox received £325,000 on June 15 and 16 this year for 500 hours of work carried out between June 2014 and March 2015.'

231 'The judge had ordered that . . . this time his entire testimony would be heard *in camera* . . .' Taken from Supreme Court judgment 16 December 2016. The full quote is as follows: 'During the [retrial], because of the appellant's difficulty in keeping distinct the sensitive and non-sensitive aspects of his evidence, the entire defence case was heard *in camera* in the presence of the appellant and those representing him, who were Mr Robertson QC leading Ms Brimelow instructed by Janes Solicitors. At the end of the retrial, Ouseley J made a further order that nothing be published revealing any evidence or other matter heard or dealt with *in camera*, other than that which had been said in public during the proceedings.'

233 'Hearing the news, Wang Yam did not move . . .' Instead, he said he felt deep anger that the jury hadn't understood the complexities of his case, that his lawyers had failed to communicate his side of the story, that the British government had abandoned him. 'The jury was stupid,' Wang Yam later recalled.

235 'On 29 January . . .' According to Wang Yam, the date of his sentencing was not a coincidence. Two days later, he pointed out, the Chinese premier Wen Jiabao landed at London's Heathrow Airport for a three-day state visit. According to a BBC report, the premier was expected to promote China's economic prospects and push for more investment from the UK. It followed an announcement earlier that month by the UK's Foreign Secretary David Miliband that improving relations with China was to be a 'major priority' for the UK in the years ahead. During his tour, Wen Jiabao planned to visit Cambridge University and London's Chinatown to celebrate the Spring Festival, also known as the 'Chinese New Year'.

236 'With the defendant now standing . . .' Later that day, Gerry Pickering informed Allan Chappelow's family members of the verdict. 'As you know in England a life sentence does not always mean life, [but] he will serve a long period of time in prison. I know the above result will be a relief to you all.' When she received this email, Patty Ainsworth forwarded it to her cousin Michael along with the words, 'Here's some good news.' He replied the following day: 'Hello Patty, thank you for that! Let us hope

he will be out of circulation for as long as possible. He must be a danger-ous man. It's all so sad and I regret not having spent some time with Allan.'

Case Note

238 'for over 300 copies that were never sent because his credit card had been blocked . . .' This was another transaction that puzzled the detectives. On 14 June, an attempt was made to pull £81.67 from his credit card. The vendor was the University of Texas. Two weeks later, on 22 June, Peter Devlin received an explanation from Richard Workman, the head librar-ian, at the Harry Ransom Center. This amount was equivalent to $146.50, the amount that the library had charged for making 360 pho-tocopies. In the end, the transaction had not gone through as the card was blocked and the copies were never sent to London. 'We are all quite shocked by the news of his murder,' wrote Workman. 'He was a some-what eccentric fellow who didn't exactly endear himself to the staff, but we are sorry to hear of such a terrible thing.' The following day, Devlin received an additional email in which Richard Workman wrote, 'I speak for everyone at the Center when I say that we sincerely hope that you find and punish the person who did this.'

238 'Had dinner . . . with Allan's cousin Patty . . .' The next day we drove two hours to Patty's family's country house south-west of Austin. There she showed me family correspondence, family trees and photographs going back a hundred years. The Chappelows had a multi-generational trad-ition of writing letters to each other across the Atlantic. Patty said that she had shared the same archive with Allan during his visit. Patty also shared emails she had exchanged with her English cousins Michael and James Chappelow.

Chapter 17

247 'In concluding their fifteen-page decision . . .' In addition, the justices argued, Wang Yam had been able to advance in open court a number of allegations against the Chinese businessman He Jia Jin, 'and to put before the jury material which suggested, perhaps without much in the way of proof but advantageously so to the defendant, that that man similarly participated in nefarious activities'.

249 'Lawyers working on behalf of the UK government . . . ill-founded and inadmissible . . .' From press release UK Supreme Court 16 December 2015.

252 'Addressed to Duncan Campbell . . .' Between 1987 and 1999, Campbell had served as the paper's crime correspondent. During this time he had reported on the Guildford Four and Birmingham Six trials, which had revealed deep-rooted corruption within the police force and had triggered reform of the judicial system. One of the main results was the establishment of the Criminal Case Review Commission, or CCRC, an independent court of last resort for those prisoners still maintaining their innocence. After a brief tour in Los Angeles, between 1999 and 2005, Campbell had returned to the *Guardian*'s London offices, and it was then that he noticed a change in the ability to cover crime stories. Whereas in the 1990s it had been fairly easy to arrange a journalist prison visit, now it was virtually impossible. A journalist had to jump through a series of bureaucratic hoops to obtain access, including the approval of the Justice Minister who had to be convinced that a face-to-face meeting was in the public interest. Even if granted, which was rare and typically took almost a year to arrange, the prisoner had to select a single journalist from one news organisation with whom to speak and he or she was limited to a single one-hour interview, which was sat in on by two government minders and was recorded by the authorities. As a result, one of the only ways for a prisoner to communicate with a member of the press was by mail.

258 'then made a submission . . .' The solicitor Edward Preston was also involved with the CCRC application. After the CCRC decision, another court decided that Preston would represent Wang Yam at the court of appeal, not Brimelow and Mullion.

258 'the CCRC . . . reviewed around 1,500 cases each year . . .' According to their annual report, in 2016/17 the Criminal Cases Review Commission referred 12 cases to the appeal courts. This means that they referred 0.77 per cent of the 1,563 cases concluded that year. In the previous year the referral rate was 1.84 per cent, in 2014/15 it was 2.2 per cent, in 2013/14 it was 2.7 per cent, in 2012/13 1.6 per cent and in 2011/12 it was 2.5 per cent. In 2009/10 when they also referred 31 cases, the number represented a referral rate of 3.5 per cent. The Commission's long-term referral rate stands at approximately 3 per cent.

Chapter 18

265 'He received word by phone . . .' After retiring as a senior investigating officer in 2012, Pete Lansdown spent a year working for free as a special constable and then started working sixty hours a week training homicide inspectors for the Metropolitan Police. Like the professor character in *Indiana Jones*, he spends his time teaching those eager to tread in his footsteps, whilst itching to once again pick up the bullwhip. In May 2016, Lansdown started a five-year contract working for the police in the Cayman Islands. Pete Lansdown was stunned when fifty people threw him a surprise goodbye party on his last day of work at the Met. Amongst the presents he received was a pair of brown shoes. Throughout his years as an instructor and supervising officer he had insisted that homicide investigators must always wear black shoes. Lansdown had worked for the Met for thirty-six and a half years.

266 'A week after the CCRC's announcement they learned that they had been sacked . . .' Brimelow and Mullion were invited to continue the European Court of Human Rights case, Mullion declined this offer.

Chapter 19

275 'At the end of one talk . . .' When I asked if perhaps Wang Yam had forgotten or suppressed what had happened, he said 'no, I never lost memory, I didn't do it.' He also added that 'I know I made mistakes', for example inviting his gangster associates to his flat on Denning Road 'three or four times', but he insisted that he had never walked with them along Downshire Hill or pointed out Allan Chappelow's house.

Chapter 20

293 'Besides the lack of evidence to support the justices . . .' To bolster their point, the justices said that even the defense QC Peter Wilcock had conceded that 'the jury was entitled to conclude that the theft, identity takeover and murder were connected.' This surprised me as I did not remember Wilcock making this point during the appeal back in July. When I texted him about this he replied, 'We had to accept what had previously been accepted in the previous appeal!' To double check, I asked Kirsty Brimelow who had run the earlier appeals. She responded as follows: 'Mmm. Not when it's a fresh appeal – plus there wasn't acceptance that there couldn't be two separate crimes.'

Epilogue

299 'If it was not Wang Yam . . .' Wang Yam is sticking to his story: 'I am innocent.' When I asked Wang Yam who he thought killed Allan Chappelow, he said he did not know. But he had some ideas. At first, he said, he thought it had something to do with the gangsters he was working with; perhaps they had attempted to steal his mail and, like the prosecution argued, the recluse had interrupted them, a struggle had ensued and they had killed him. Now, he believed, it had something to do with his ownership of Rank PLC shares, a British gambling and

entertainments company. Wang Yam noted that the victim called Rank a few times just before his death (Allan Chappelow did not have a significant shareholding in Rank). He also said that he had heard from his contacts in China that Chinese gangsters or gamblers were somehow involved, perhaps even the Chinese or Taiwanese intelligence services were trying to 'frame me up'. He noted that there have been other instances in the UK of violent death involving Chinese gangsters. In August 2008, for instance, a Chinese couple were found brutally murdered in Newcastle; their heads had been smashed in and their cat killed and stuffed in a bowl under the kitchen sink. One of the victims was involved in making money out of a fraudulent internet betting operation.

300 'It would be nice to imagine the ghosts getting together . . .' While Allan Chappelow's photograph of George Bernard Shaw is held by the National Portrait Gallery in London, the playwright is no longer the revered figure he once was. He is still praised for his more famous works such as *Pygmalion*, *Major Barbara* and *Man and Superman*, but many question his support for Hitler's regime, eugenics and Stalin.

ACKNOWLEDGEMENTS

I would like to thank the various librarians, archivists and researchers who have helped me with this project, including: Jacqueline Cox (Cambridge University Library), Mark Curteis (Chelmsford Museum), Sue Donnelly (LSE), Christian Dupont (Boston College), Mike Fitzmaurice (Hall School), Catherine Harpham (Imperial College), Elspeth Langsdale (Oundles School), Rhodri Lewis (Oxford University), Rebecca Lodge (Burgh House), Imogen Lyons (National Portrait Gallery), Melanie Richardson (Trinity College, Cambridge University), Rose Wild (*The Times*), Pat Swire (Anglo-Albanian Association), Andrew Young (*Daily Mail*). Also those at the Harry Ransom Center in Austin, Texas, including Stephen Enniss, Cheryl McGrath, Kelly Kerbow Hudson and Richard Watson. And to my indefatigable researchers in China, Yadan Ouyang and Kevin Jia.

As someone who is fascinated by the law, but untrained in it, I am particularly grateful to those experts and public servants who kindly provided their views and insights. In addition, some of those who have assisted in my attempt to nail down this story include Carolina Aguire, Rosie Blau, Paul Crook, Alex Drake, James Kynge, Simon Enright, Luke Harding, Frances Gibb, Patrick Gibbs QC, Harold Olmas, Helen Praeger

Young, Diane Stokes, Louise Shorter, Sarah Casey, Deborah Gold, Jennifer Steil, Sarah Chapman, Michael Capuzzo, and Sir Ken Macdonald.

This story bears the words and recollections of the characters that it features. For their generosity, openness and patience, I would like to thank Patty Ainsworth, Philip Baker QC, Tom Best, Kirsty Brimelow QC, Mrs Tom Carr, Dan Carrier, James Chappelow, Duncan Campbell, Steve Cook, Steve Derrick, Peter Devlin, Mark Ellison QC, Martin Hall, Tony Hillier, Allen Hirson, Merete Karlsborg, Pete Lansdown, Gavin Millar QC, James Mullion, John Newall, Richard Norton-Taylor, Torben Permin, Edward Preston, Geoffrey Robertson QC, Richard Ross, Serpico, Nigel Steward, John Sparrow, Peter Tausig, Peter Wilcock QC, and of course Wang Yam.

Thanks also to Allan Chappelow's family for giving permission to use his writing and photographs. I would also like to thank my readers, including Lucy and Zam Baring, Nigel Barton, Trevor Cornwell, Amanda Harding, Angela Harding, Frank Harding, James Harding, Michael Harding, Jane Hill, Rupert Levy, Charlie McCormick, Cait Morrison, Taylor Robinson, Philip Selway, Charles Sweeney, Nick Viner, Kate Weinberg, and Amelia Wooldridge.

I am grateful to Patrick Walsh who encouraged me to take on this project and reviewed early drafts. Thanks especially to my agents Sarah Chalfant and James Pullen and everyone at the Wylie Agency.

Once again, I am grateful for the insights, hard work and support provided by my extraordinary editor, the one and only Tom Avery. Also to Glenn O'Neill for his brilliant cover and Darren Bennett for his terrific maps, along with everyone at Penguin Random House who helped deliver this book so efficiently to the readers.

Finally to Deb and Sam, who have tolerated far too much talk of crime scenes, forensic evidence and alternative suspects, who have, as ever, given incredibly useful feedback on the manuscript, and who put a smile on my face every day.

BIBLIOGRAPHY

Capote, Truman Capote, *In Cold Blood* (Random House, 1965). An investigation into the murder of four members of the Cutter family in Holcomb, Texas. This 'non-fiction novel' is considered a classic example of the True Crime genre.

Capuzzo, Michael, *The Murder Room: The Heirs of Sherlock Holmes Gather to Solve the World's Most Perplexing Cold Cases* (Penguin, 2011). Brilliant exploration of the world of profilers and forensic psychologists.

Chappelow, Allan, *Russian Holiday* (Harrap, 1955). Chappelow's description of his trip behind the Iron Curtain in the early 1950s.

Chappelow, Allan, *Shaw the Villager and Human Being: Symposium* (Skilton, 1961). Chappelow's first book on George Bernard Shaw, includes recollections from the local residents and acquaintances, his famous photograph of the writer, and a foreword by Vera Brittain.

Chappelow, Allan, *The Chucker-out* (George Allen & Unwin, 1969). Chappelow's second book on George Bernard Shaw, including extracts of Shaw's writings.

Chappelow, Archibald, *The Old Home in England* (1953). Allan's father's investigation of buildings that he loved, including his much-prized house at 9 Downshire Hill. Features beautiful drawings by Chappelow senior.

Conan Doyle, Arthur, *The Case of Oscar Slater* (Hodder & Stoughton, 1912). There are many striking similarities between this investigation of the murder of Marion Gilchrist in 1908 and the killing of Allan Chappelow in 2006: the victims were both in their eighties, both brutally bludgeoned to death and both bodies were covered up (hers by a rug). In both cases the police quickly blamed a foreigner (the Chinese-born Wang Yam and the German Jew Oscar Slater), and believed them both to have fled to the country following a bungled burglary. Slater was released from prison after serving 18 years following a public campaign. His is known as one of Scotland's most egregious miscarriages of justice.

Hollinghurst, Alan, *The Swimming-Pool Library* (Vintage, 2015). Bestselling novel that depicts gay life in London, including the cruising scene.

Holroyd, Michael, *Bernard Shaw* (Pimlico, 2011). One of the best biographies of GBS.

Holroyd, Michael (editor), *The Genius of Shaw* (Henry Holt, reissued 1988). Leading experts discuss key aspects of GBS's life, full of helpful photographs.

Jenkins, Elizabeth, *The View From Downshire Hill* (Michael Russell Publishing, 2004). The author Elizabeth Jenkins lived next to Allan Chappelow from 1939 till 1984. She describes her home at number 8 Downshire Hill ('a beautiful but shabby six-room house'), life on the street and her friends who live at number 7 and number 10, though poignantly fails to discuss her next-door neighbours, the Chappelows.

Keeble, Harry, *Crack House: The Incredible True Story of the Man Who Took on London's Crack Gangs and Won* (Simon & Schuster, 2009).

Useful description of police fight against London gangsters in 1990s.

MacLaughlin, Duncan, *The Filth: The Explosive Inside Story of Scotland Yard's Top Undercover Cop* (Mainstream, 2002). A former police detective spills the beans on Scotland Yard.

McLagan, Graeme, *Guns and Gangs: Inside Black Gun Crime* (Allison & Busby, 2005). One of the best summaries of police efforts to combat gang violence. Contains interviews with Pete Lansdown and description of his previous cases, including the arrest of Mark Lambie.

Phillips, Marie, *Gods Behaving Badly* (Vintage, 2008). Humorous novel about ancient gods adapting to life in today's London. According to the author, the house in which they lived is based on 9 Downshire Hill.

Shaw, George Bernard, *The Quintessence of Ibsenism* (Walter Schott, 1891). Written about the Norwegian playwright Henrik Ibsen, Shaw's exposition follows a request for essays by the Fabian Society about 'Socialism in Contemporary Literature'.

Shaw, George Bernard, *Major Barbara* (1907, revised 1930, 1945). Meditation on the arms trade.

Shaw, George Bernard, *Pygmalion* (1916, revised 1941). Poignant account of a poor girl who is bullied into learning to speak like the higher classes. Famously, the film *My Fair Lady*, upon which it is based, had a different ending.

Shaw, George Bernard, *Saint Joan* (1924). Play featuring Joan of Arc, with ghosts returning at end to discuss the truth of the matter.

Young, Helen Praeger, '*Choosing Revolution: Chinese Women Soldiers on the Long March*' (Illinois University Press, 2001). Best English language introduction to Ren Bishi's family including interviews with Wang Yam's 'grandmother', 'father' and 'aunt'.

Susskind, Richard, *The End of Lawyers?: Rethinking the Nature of Legal Services* (Oxford University Press, revised edition 2010). One of the UK's leading lawyers offers his thoughts on the future of the British legal profession.

Tennyson, Hallam, *The Haunted Mind* (HarperCollins, 1984). The great-grandson of Lord Tennyson provides a candid account of his life.

Wade, Christopher, *The Streets of Hampstead* (Camden History Society, 1984). An examination of the history, architecture, culture and residents of Hampstead.